MW00577928

THE THREE MARYS

Alexander Moody Stuart

1809–1898

Alexander Moody was born in Paisley in the west of Scotland on 15 June 1809, the sixth son of Andrew Moody and Margaret Fulton McBrair. After entering Glasgow University aged twelve, he proceeded to train for ministry in the Church of Scotland, first at Glasgow, and then at Edinburgh under Thomas Chalmers. During this time he came under conviction, and during a communion season in 1829, the words of Ephesians 5:14, 'Awake thou that sleepest, and arise from the dead, and Christ shall give thee light', spoke to him with fresh power. From that moment he experienced a new assurance of salvation by faith in Christ.

After spending a year as a missionary on Holy Island off the Northumbrian coast, he returned to Edinburgh and was charged with planting a church in the New Town (St Luke's). In 1839 he married Jessie Stuart, and in order to retain her association with the family estate, appended the name of Stuart to his own. At the Disruption in 1843 the congregation of St Luke's left the Establishment, and Moody Stuart continued an active ministry there until 1887, when old age and ill-health compelled him to cease preaching.

His was a deeply spiritual ministry, and many found a home at Free St Luke's under his pastoral oversight. His fervent commitment to the Free Church's mission to the Jews was a prominent part of his ministry, as was his defence of the authority of the Bible in days when this was being called into question.

Alexander Moody Stuart

THE THREE MARYS

MARY OF MAGDALA

MARY OF BETHANY

MARY OF NAZARETH

THE BANNER OF TRUTH TRUST

THE BANNER OF TRUTH TRUST

Head Office
3 Murrayfield Road
Edinburgh
EH12 6EL
UK

North America Office
610 Alexander Spring Road
Carlisle
PA 17013
USA

banneroftruth.org

First published 1862 (Second Edition 1863)
First Banner of Truth edition 1984
Reprinted (retypeset) 2023
© The Banner of Truth Trust 2023

*

ISBN
Print: 978 1 80040 233 1
EPUB: 978 1 80040 234 8
Kindle: 978 1 80040 235 5

*

Typeset in 10/13 Minion Pro at
The Banner of Truth Trust, Edinburgh

Printed in the USA by
Versa Press Inc.,
East Peoria, IL.

Contents

Publisher's Introduction   xi

Author's Preface   xv

MARY OF MAGDALA

I   Mary of Magdala

    1. Magdala the birthplace of Mary; a place of light
and darkness; probably a happy home in childhood.
2. Magdalene not the sinful woman of the city: The
penitent harlot could not have wealth; was sent away
by Christ; and had been no demoniac   3

II   Mary the Demoniac

    1. Mary's heart in the power of Satan; not a new
creature while possessed; and previously in Satan's
power. 2. Satan dwelling in her with a sevenfold possession: Magdalene specially exposed to his assaults;
may have laid herself open to them; her soul entered
by seven devils; yet not like the entrance into Judas   14

III   Mary Not Seeking But Resisting Jesus

    1. Mary not seeking Jesus; no demoniac sought him;
the damsel in the Acts no exception. 2. Mary resisting Jesus; the ejection of devils violent in the mildest
cases; much more in the most malignant like hers   24

IV Mary Redeemed by the Lord's Right Arm

1. Jesus vanquishes Satan for her; first in the wilderness; finally on Calvary. 2. He casts Satan out of her; by his own act; by his word; the devils leaving her, she is filled with the Holy Spirit; the tumult of hell followed by the calm of heaven. 3. Hers is a lasting cure   35

V Mary as Christ's Devoted Servant

1. Mary gave the Lord her whole heart; the goods may be given without the heart, but she gave herself. 2. She gave her whole substance; we are called to give all in heart surrender; and to hold ourselves ready for actual surrender. 3. She gave her whole time: sanctioned by usage; by relief from home duties; by Christ's warrant   47

VI Mary as Christ's Constant Follower

1. Mary follows Christ's steps. 2. She hears Christ's words, in the synagogue; by the way; at the table; in the secret conclave. 3. She sees Christ's work in others; is a living witness in their sight; meets cases resembling her own. 4. She shares Christ's cross   55

VII Mary the Patient Seeker of Her Absent Lord

1. Mary's earnest seeking of an absent Christ. 2. Her mistake of gain for loss in seeking, through unbelief; a mistake often made; unbelief erases Christ's words from the memory. 3. She waits patiently, alone, fearlessly   69

VIII Mary Finding Christ

1. Mary finds Jesus; in answer to faithful promise; in sovereign mercy. 2. She does not recognize Christ found; like many inquirers still. 3. She is asked by Jesus the object of her search; he ever asks our desire; and teaches us to make petitions special. 4. Christ reveals himself; calls Mary to her own remembrance; grants her fellowship with himself; speaks to us as to her   83

IX Mary Saluting Christ as Rabboni

1. Rabboni, my teacher; Mary's teacher and ours.
2. Rabboni, my leader; in the old covenant, Adam; in
the new, Christ. 3. Rabboni, my Lord; Master implies
in us humility of heart, and singleness of eye   98

X Mary Forbidden to Touch Jesus

1. Jesus will be reverenced by Mary; a warning
against unholy familiarity; a check to holy boldness.
2. Mary has no need to touch Jesus; like Thomas
who is commanded; like the other women who are
permitted to touch. 3. Mary has no occasion to touch
him now; not because of other opportunities on
earth; but because of perfect nearness in heaven   109

XI Mary as Christ's Messenger to the Apostles

1. Mary must not tarry with Jesus, but run as his messenger; a woman must go to the apostles; the finder of
the King must carry his word; to go from Christ with
his message is better than to tarry beside him; this
message the crowning transaction of Mary's life.
2. Mary's message: Christ's assurance of brotherhood
to the disciples, and ascension to the Father   120

MARY OF BETHANY

I Mary of Bethany

1. The earthly friendship of Jesus with the family at
Bethany: his personal friendship; their hospitality;
their individual characters; characteristic habits of
Jesus. 2. The everlasting friendship of Christ with
every believer   135

II Mary the Soul with a Single Need

1. The one great need of man is God; of lost man,
peace with God; therefore Christ is man's great need.
2. Jesus Christ is near to the soul that needs him   147

III Mary the Wise Chooser

Mary needs Christ; Martha thinks that Christ needs
her. Mary's portion: 1. in her choice; 2. in its oneness;
3. in its goodness; 4. in its eternity   157

IV Mary the Quiet Listener

1. Martha charge-taking and restless. 2. Mary listening to Christ's words; in lowliness; in hunger; in faith   168

V Mary the Noble Worker

1. Mary is prepared by the Lord for a great work; and
in due time accomplishes it. 2. Mary defended and
honoured by Christ in her work; her work is good; it
is well done; and is better than almsgiving to the poor   179

MARY OF NAZARETH

I Mary of Nazareth

1. Nazareth gives Jesus the title of Nazarene. 2. Noted
for its faith, and for its unbelief. The boyhood of
Jesus without marvels; he has no believing friends
of youth; faith disappears where it once flourished.
3. Nazareth loses grace, yet escapes desolating
judgment; the Lord's work brings responsibility;
familiarity with holy things tempts to despise them;
God's holy sovereignty   195

II Mary the Thoughtful Child of the Covenant

1. Mary's mind stored with the word of God; interesting as regards herself, and the childhood of Jesus.
W2. Nurtured with the love to Israel; as her own
people; as the Lord's people; a love strengthened by
solemn feasts. 3. The promise of the covenant the
hope of Mary's soul   209

III   Mary the Earnest Inquirer

> 1. Mary's fear of God; peculiarly fit for her high calling; a rich portion for all. 2. Her humiliation of heart; like every child of God; the subject of special humiliation. 3. Her hunger for righteousness; her heart cannot feed on itself; longs after the Lord   220

IV   Mary the Simple Believer

> 1. Faith Abraham's great distinction. 2. Mary's great distinction. 3. The distinction of all the redeemed; faith in the power, goodness, truth of God revealed in Christ   232

V   Mary the Magnifier of the Lord

> 1. She rejoices in the Lord's goodness, with no mingling of pride. 2. She is filled with joy in the Holy Ghost; has the seal of the Spirit to her faith; rejoices in the Lord himself. 3. She praises the Lord; with thanksgiving; and in an inspired song   244

VI   Mary the Patient Endurer

> 1. Is exposed to reproach for Christ; has a good conscience, God's favour, friends; but is threatened with divorce as an adulteress, hypocrite, blasphemer. 2. Leaves her cause quietly with God. 3. Is delivered by divine interposition   255

VII   Mary the Quiet Ponderer

> 1. She remembers the great things of the Lord; all his words; all his works. 2. She ponders the great things of the Lord; they are equally to be pondered by us   267

VIII   Mary the Corrected Disciple

> 1. Chastened for losing sight of Jesus. 2. Admonished for hastening his delay. 3. Associated with the brethren of Jesus in chiding his zeal; reproved for her presumption; her error recorded for our warning   280

IX Mary the Witness of the Death and Resurrection of Her Hopes

1. The quiet witness of the death of all her hopes in the cross of Christ; is graciously prepared for that death; meets it with noble submission. 2. The joyful witness of the end of the Lord in Christ's resurrection. 3. The willing subject of the new dispensation of the Spirit   293

Publisher's Introduction

ALEXANDER Moody Stuart was possessed of a weak voice, and yet his preaching was widely appreciated by many who gathered each Sunday at Free St Luke's Church in Edinburgh. A clue to his attractiveness as a preacher is perhaps found in an address he gave to fellow ministers in 1865, in which he identified 'freshness of spirit' in the preacher as that which told more on people than any other frame of mind:

> The greatest of all effects has sometimes been produced by a preacher awakened and enquiring, and *carrying his people along with him* step by step; directing his people toward a Saviour still only sought for by himself, and at length finding him along with them.

The necessity for the minister, and indeed all Christians, to speak out of their own experience, was likewise expressed by Moody Stuart in his chapter entitled 'Mary Finding Christ', contained in this book. There he observes,

> It is not what we seek for others, that usually profits them most. Commonly God makes us seek and find for ourselves, and then testify to others what we have seen, and *speak what we know*. It is the lack

of this element that makes much of our preaching so powerless; *for it is the God-taught man, who is the God-sent messenger.*

In these devotional chapters looking at the life and faith of Mary Magdalene, Mary of Bethany, and Mary the mother of Jesus, there is a strong sense that Moody Stuart was himself speaking not only from scholarly study, but from his own lived spiritual experience. Addressing his fellow ministers in the Free Church of Scotland in 1875, he confessed,

> To myself, Fathers and Brethren, it is always new every time that I see that Jesus Christ came into the world to save sinners. It does not appear to me as if I had never seen it before, but each successive sight of it is new and bright—sometimes newer and brighter—as fresh as if it were now for the first time; and it always seems as if I had forgotten it daily, and daily recovered it again.

It is striking when reading these chapters that Moody Stuart habitually ends on the theme of Jesus Christ. Just as for Mary Magdalene, so for his present readers: 'Jesus comes to save us, and to destroy sin and Satan, our deadly foes.' And in another chapter, 'Only let us be sure of this, that if Mary's Christ be ours, he expects the same from us as from her. There is but one heaven for Magdalene and for us… There is only one Jesus Christ, the way to the Father…' This returning to Christ is a repeating pattern in both his preaching and his writing, and his customary concluding exhortation and invitation to the unconverted reflected his strong belief that it was a minister's duty not only to pastor the converted, but to preach the Saviour to the lost.

These chapters possess an enduring clarity and depth which will continue to move Christian believers to greater meditation on, and faith in, the Lord Jesus Christ. His character and work, as manifested in his interactions with these women of the New Testament, is here vividly expounded by one of whom it was said by Dr John 'Rabbi' Duncan, that he 'knew not a greater master in spiritual analysis.'

THE PUBLISHER
Edinburgh, January 2023

Author's Preface

THE title of *The Three Marys* has sometimes brought up the question of the other Marys of the New Testament, to whom I have made no reference because none of them can be mistaken for any of the subjects of this volume. Of Marys they constitute a second three, but we cannot assign them so high a place in the collective list of the pious matrons of their day; while the mother of Jesus, the sister of Lazarus, and Mary Magdalene form the first three in all the holy women of the New Testament.

Of those other Marys, the first and most distinguished is the wife of Cleophas, mother of James and Joses, called also distinctively 'the other Mary.' She is commonly believed to have been sister to our Lord's mother, from John 19:25; yet this is not quite certain, because there may be four women, and not three, named in that verse. Mary, the wife of Cleophas, was one of the company of noble Galilean matrons who ministered to Jesus in their own country and followed him on his last journey to Jerusalem, where she was his honoured witness upon the cross, in the tomb, and after the resurrection. The second is Mary the mother of John, surnamed Mark, and accredited as the writer of the Gospel. She was the sister of Barnabas, Paul's companion, for Mark is called his nephew or sister's son; or perhaps rather, the original term may more commonly signify cousin, which would make Mary aunt to Barnabas. The most interesting circumstance in her history is that she owned the house in Jerusalem where so many were assembled to pray for Peter; and that at her well-known door the apostle stood knocking so long, because the damsel Rhoda could not open it for joy at the unexpected sound of his voice. The third Mary lived at Rome, when Paul addressed his Epistle to its Christian people. Nothing is known of her, except that she is highly commended by the apostle for having shown much kindness to himself or his friends; but where, or in what manner, we are not informed. Luke 24:10; Acts 12:12; Rom. 16:6.

As this volume does not claim any originality, so its title is not a new one. In the works of Calmet there is a treatise entitled 'Dissertation sur les Trois Maries,' replete with information on the theological opinions and speculations upon the subject; only his *Three Marys* include the woman that anointed Christ's feet in the Pharisee's house, and not Mary the mother of Jesus. There is also, under the same title, a little volume published some years ago in Ireland; which, however, I had not the pleasure of seeing till after the publication of my own. It is by the Rev. Dr Bryson, and entitled *The Three Marys of the Four Gospels*.

The author has only to add his request for the reader's prayer for a blessing on these pages; for the gracious covering of all in them that may be of man; for the breathing of the Spirit on whatever is of God; and for the sprinkling of the whole with that blood of the Lamb, which alone cleanses every work, and renders any effort of ours either acceptable to God or profitable to men.

ALEXANDER MOODY STUART
Edinburgh, 9 March 1863

MARY OF MAGDALA

I

MARY OF MAGDALA

'Mary called Magdalene.'—Luke 8:2

IN the sisterhood of holy women who ministered to Jesus on earth, Mary Magdalene is usually named first, as if denoting some excellence of grace in her above the others; and Jesus rising from the dead reveals himself to her first, first not only of all the women, but of all the disciples. In all that sisterhood her own place had been the last, and she still retains within the kingdom the distinctive title of 'Mary Magdalene, out of whom went seven devils.' But the same grace that makes one to differ from another often ennobles the vilest, and enriches most those who had been sunk in lowest poverty; 'for many that are first shall be last, and the last shall be first.'

The apostle Paul, after characterizing himself as the 'chief of sinners,' adds, 'Howbeit for this cause I obtained mercy, that in me first Jesus Christ might show forth all long-suffering, for a pattern to them who should hereafter believe on him to life everlasting.' Mary Magdalene presents to us a similar pattern; an encouragement for the greatest sinner to believe in Jesus Christ unto everlasting life; an example of 'sin abounding, but grace much more abounding.'

In considering her character and history, let us look first at Magdala as Mary's birthplace, and then on Mary the Magdalene as bearing no brand of infamy in the eye of man.

1. Magdala the birthplace of Mary

Magdala was a place of mingled light and darkness in Mary's womanhood; probably a home of happiness to her in childhood.

1. In Mary's womanhood Magdala was a place of *mingled light and darkness.* By universal consent, Mary is allowed to have received the designation of Magdalene from the town of Magdala, which is therefore regarded as the undoubted place of her birth, and of her dwelling. Magdala is situated on the shore of that Sea of Galilee from whose bosom Jesus preached to the wondering multitudes, within whose depths he guided the finny shoals by his mysterious power, and whose waves he quieted with his word, or used as the pathway for his feet. From around this Galilean lake Jesus gathered most of his immediate followers, its waters were honoured to bear the ships that were abandoned for the 'one pearl of great price,' and on its shores were spread the nets forsaken by the fishermen who were now to be 'fishers of men.' Thence he called all his true apostles; for, with the single exception of the traitor Judas Iscariot, all the twelve are believed to have been Galileans. Magdala was formerly supposed by some men of great learning to be situated on the farther side of the sea, and only a Sabbath-day's journey from Gadara, and the haunts of the fierce demoniac with the legion of devils. But it is now regarded as ascertained to be

the same as Mejdel, on the western shore of the lake, immediately to the south of the plain of Gennesaret, and not far from those well-known cities toward the north of the lake, Capernaum, Chorazin, and Bethsaida, the scenes of so many of the mighty works of the Lord. 'Mejdel is a wretched hamlet of a dozen low huts huddled into one, and the whole ready to tumble into a dismal heap of black basaltic rubbish. It is the city of Mary Magdalene, out of whom went seven devils; and it seems to be in very significant keeping with the only incident that has given it a history. Evil spirits of some sort must possess the inhabitants, for they are about the worst specimen in the country; and yet they dwell on the shore of this silvery lake, and cultivate this plain of Gennesaret, which Josephus calls the "ambition of nature."'[1]

2. Magdala stood, then, on the border of visited waters, and in the midst of a privileged land. Yet that was emphatically the land of darkness, and its people dwelt in the shadow of death. 'The land of Zabulon, and the land of Nephthalim, by the way of the sea, Galilee of the Gentiles,' was the chosen battle-field between the powers of good and evil. There the people 'which sat in darkness saw great light; to them which dwelt in the region and shadow of death light is sprung up.' Magdala lay in the heart of this region of conflict between the light of heaven and the darkness of the abyss; and Mary lived in Magdala in the heat of the great contention. From the waters of the sea that washed the shore of her native town, Jesus was drawing the fish to the hook and the net of Peter and his comrades; and into those same waters the ejected devils were driving the maddened swine to destruction.

[1] *The Land and the Book,* by Dr W. M. Thomson.

Magdala was probably a *happy home of childhood* to Mary. A daughter of Abraham, a child of the ancient covenant, Mary was called by a name famous in Israel from the days of Miriam the prophetess, the sister of Moses, for Miriam is the same as Mary. Her childhood we can only imagine, for it has left no record. But we conclude that she was not a demoniac in her earliest years; both because in that case she could not well have attained the domestic and social requirements that fitted her afterwards to minister to Jesus, and because maladies of so long duration are usually noted as such in the Gospels. We gather also from her subsequent life, that in her childhood and youth she probably enjoyed the advantages that attend circumstances of comfort, if not of affluence. After her deliverance from the power of Satan, she was possessed of means not only for living independently of labour, or of obligation to others, but sufficient to enable her to minister to Jesus of her substance during his life, and to purchase costly spices to anoint him after death. Luke 8:2-3: Mark 16:1. This substance, if by inheritance, implies a childhood and youth of outward comfort, along with the nurture and education suitable for a daughter of Israel. The local scene of her childhood was one of great beauty. Magdala stood on the very border of the lake, near its centre between north and south, and at its point of greatest breadth between east and west. 'The lake itself, seen from any point of the surrounding heights, is a fine sheet of water; a burnished mirror set in a framework of rounded hills and rugged mountains, which rise and roll backward and upward to where Hermon hangs the picture against the blue vault of Heaven.'[1]

[1] *The Land and the Book.*

Thus may Mary have spent her youthful years on the lovely margin of the blue Sea of Galilee; attending to household duties, hearing the law in the synagogue, listening to the marvels wrought by the Lord in Egypt, in the desert, and in the covenanted land, going up to Zion and joining with the daughters of Jerusalem in Israel's solemn feasts. Then also, as afterward, her natural character was, doubtless, more deeply marked than in any other of the devout and honourable women of the New Testament. Mary, the mother of Jesus, excelled her and all the others in simplicity and strength of faith, and this invests her whole history with a matchless nobleness, a loftiness that soars above all around her. But this simple greatness leaves her character less deeply traced than that of her sister in the kingdom. Intense ardour of affection, indomitable energy of will, and heroic courage, mark the Christian character of Magdalene in her riper age; and these features could scarcely fail to disclose themselves as natural characteristics in childhood and youth. Womanly she ever was, a weeping woman more than any of her sisters in Christ; but a woman with the lines of personal feature so deeply cut, that we can scarce conceive her other than a marked child, and growing into womanhood an ardent, affectionate, energetic, and resolute Hebrew maiden.

Nor are we called on to darken this picture, by supposing that the natural innocence of youth was blighted for ever by the foulest of all earthly stains. Mary of Magdala was certainly no Magdalene in the figurative sense of the modern word, which leads us to consider:

2. *Mary bearing no brand of infamy in the eye of man*

Mary Magdalene has been popularly and very generally taken for the 'woman in the city that was a sinner;' who washed the feet of Jesus with tears of penitential gratitude, loving much because forgiven much. Luke 7:36-50. This loving penitent is indeed a reproving pattern for us all; for most of us love Jesus little. And why? It can only be because we have been forgiven little; for infallibly, and therefore invariably, 'to whom little is forgiven, the same loveth little.' Have we sinned little? We answer, No, we have sinned much. But much sin never creates much love; much forgiveness always does. The great debt may only awaken enmity; the great remission draws forth love. We must believe, then, that we have been forgiven little, and therefore do we love little. Yet, if forgiven at all, we have been forgiven much; and if we believe that much has been forgiven us, we cannot but cleave with much love to him 'who frankly forgave us all that debt.'

But although the name of Magdalene has been univer-sally and irrevocably applied to sinners now penitent, but once openly abandoned, there is no evidence whatever that such had ever been the character of Mary of Magdala, and no probability in identifying her with the weeping penitent who anointed the feet of Jesus.

Magdalene had wealth, which she could scarcely possess; Magdalene ministered to Jesus, while she was sent away; Magdalene was a demoniac, which she was not; yet Magdalene's name is given to her and her fallen sisters, and let them ever retain it.

The women, who ministered of *their substance* to Christ, appear to have been matrons of established reputation, mostly possessing means of their own, and one of them, Joanna the wife of Herod's steward, occupying a position of influence. Amongst these Mary Magdalene takes the first place; and there is every reason to believe that her character and standing were similar to theirs. She is introduced as ministering to Christ immediately after the narrative of the anointing, without a hint of any connexion with that narrative. The simple fact of those holy women supplying the wants of Jesus with their substance, may be held as excluding the 'woman of the city' from their number. In her abandoned life she owned the ointment that she poured on the feet of Jesus; but this was probably nearly all her wealth, and she can scarcely be thought to have possessed independent riches, enough not only to maintain herself, but to share with others.

Christ was the friend of sinners; he received them, and he ate with them; but there is no reason to suppose, that he either invited or suffered one that had been so branded with infamy to accompany him as a ministering attendant. The narrative itself seems plainly to contradict the supposition. Christ freely grants to the penitent pardon, peace, and blessing. Nay more, on being called by his murmuring host to vindicate his own reception of her, he does not justify himself at all, but simply justifies her before the face of accusing men on earth, even as he justifies her now in the presence of the Father in Heaven. 'Simon, seest thou this woman? I entered into thine house, thou gavest me no water for my feet, but she hath washed my feet with tears, and wiped them with the hairs of her head. Thou gavest me no kiss, but this woman from the time I came in hath not ceased to kiss my feet; my head with oil thou didst not anoint, but she hath anointed my feet with ointment. Wherefore I say unto thee, Her sins which are many are forgiven, for she loved much; but to whom little is forgiven the same loveth little.' But having justified this woman that was a sinner, he dismisses her. He gives her indeed his bless-ing, yet he couples with it no invitation to follow him, but expressly sends her away. His last words to her are words of authority, as well as love, 'Go in peace;'—words doubtless obeyed, by her immediate departure to her own house.

As in all things else, so in dealing with 'the fallen', Jesus has left us an example; an example of the wisdom of the serpent in union with the harmlessness of the dove, of tenderest love along with most vigilant prudence. That which is recorded of him elsewhere is applicable here; that though many believed on his name, he did not commit himself unto them, for he knew what was in man. John 2:24-25. On the 'woman that was a sinner,' he freely bestowed the largeness of his grace, and from her in return he joyfully accepted all tokens of gratitude and penitential love. But he never committed to her the honour of his kingdom, by calling her to share in ministering to himself and his apos-tles.

There is a further important element to be added, in evidence that Mary Magdalene was not the sinner in the city. Mary was *a demoniac*; and under the effects of satanic possession the demoniacs of the Gospel narratives were virtually lunatics. The penitent had newly abandoned her course of sin; and mad though such a course had been in the worst sense of the word, hers was not the life of a wretched lunatic, but of one 'living in pleasure, and dead while she lived.' Her own name has not been recorded in the sacred page; for such honour had been needless; and probably unfitting. Her origin is altogether uncertain. She may have been either Jew or Gentile, and some suppose her to have been a heathen; which is very possible, yet also an open sinner. It is enough for the consolation of others to be assured that her great sins were blotted quite from the Book of God, and that her great love gives her a high place amongst the redeemed of the Lamb. Her salvation through grace is preserved in everlasting memorial, her name is buried in oblivion.

But while there is therefore no reason to imagine that Mary of Magdala was either the same that anointed the feet of Jesus, or like her in character; and while there is now the nearly unanimous consent both of critics and of careful readers of the Bible, in holding them to be different; it is too late to recall the *name* of Magdalene from the penitent that had formerly fallen, not only in the sight of God, but before the sterner eye of man. By the usage of ages and the consent of Christendom 'Magdalene' is, and will be while the world lasts, an honoured name, held as a sacred shield over the weeping penitent. And let it be. Such a healed one needs all the hope and consolation for herself that can be set before her from among the ranks of the redeemed, and all the honour in the eyes of men that the church can safely bestow.

The example is real, though it lacked a name. A sinner nameless, but her sin notorious, is called by grace, and numbered with the chief of saints, yet still unnamed. A saint most noted, and often named in the Book of God, but stained by no sensual sin, has her fair name transferred to her nameless sister. They were both one in Christ, and are now singing together 'to him that loved them, and washed them in his own blood.' Mary Magdalene in heaven does not grudge the earthly transference of her name to her redeemed sister, and does not shrink from the yet more humbling element of having it made even a certain byword in the earth, if the dishonouring of her own name may bring any honour or relief to her fallen but restored sisters in Christ.

This indeed is nothing, is not worthy to be mentioned in connexion with the Lord Jesus Christ 'enduring the cross and despising the shame' for her and for us; taking the name of 'transgressor,' and made 'sin for us,' that in him we might be called 'The Lord our righteousness.' Jer. 33:16. Far more than the vilest sinner on earth can be supposed to need any sainted name for a shield in the sight of man, reminding the world that even such sinners have by grace become most holy saints; far more do we all need in the sight of God the name of Jesus to cover our vile iniquities; and ample for all our need is the broad shield of that name stretched over us, so that 'the iniquity of Israel is sought for, and there is none; and the sins of Judah, and they are not found.' Jer 50:20.

It is not the church that has given us a better name than our own; but the Father himself who has given Jesus a name above every name in heaven or in earth, and has held out that name to every sinner that will accept it. Oh for grace to sink our name and let it go for ever; to sink it as bearing any character or recommendation to please the Father; to sink it also, as bearing any stain to exclude us from his favour; and to take boldly the name of Jesus freely given us, given to open the door of entrance to the Most High, to clothe us with acceptance in his sight, to obtain for us all that is stored within the promises! 'Whatsoever ye shall ask the Father in my name, He will give it you; hitherto ye have asked nothing in my name: ask, and ye shall receive, that your joy may be full.' John 16:23, 24.

II

MARY THE DEMONIAC

*'Mary, called Magdalene, out of whom went
seven devils.'*—Luke 8:2

OUR attention must now be turned to a dark period
in Mary's history, the record of which is contained in
few words; but these are words of tremendous significance,
and that intensified by repetition. The commencement of
her history by Luke is 'Mary Magdalene, out of whom went
seven devils;' and the close of her history by Mark, 'Mary
Magdalene, out of whom he had cast seven devils.' Her
whole state previous to her calling by Jesus Christ is char-
acterized by the one great fact, that those seven devils dwelt
within her. This is the one outstanding mark of her condition, sinking all else into obscurity; it is that by which she
was noted amongst others at the time, and that which in all
her early history must have been ever most memorable to
herself. When those spirits entered, and how they wrought
within her, is not narrated; yet we may gather much from
the record of other similar cases.

In the light of these, we shall consider Mary's heart as in

the power of Satan previous to the entrance of the demons; and then Satan occupying her soul with a sevenfold possession.

1. Mary's heart in the power of Satan before the entrance of the devils

These two things are to be noticed here; that Magdalene was not a new creature while indwelt by the unclean spirits; and that, therefore, she had not previously been a child of God, but of Satan.

1. She was not a new creature *when the evil spirits dwelt in her.* It may be, that in the nature of things demoniac possession is possible within the soul of a child of God in a state of declension. As the old man remains where the new creature has been formed, and as Satan tempts and even prevails where he no longer reigns, so possibly his evil angels might obtain a temporary lodging in the soul where his throne and seat have been cast down. But there is no such case recorded in Scripture, and we need not imagine it here; yet may safely conclude that her soul's deliverance from the seven devils was simultaneous with her heart's conversion to God.

The cure of bodily ailment by Christ was often accompanied by the healing of the soul, and the outward health became the symbol of the new life within. The healed paralytic, taking up his bed and walking, carried in the sight of all both the earthly token of heaven's healing, and the outward proof of unseen pardon. 'That ye may know that the Son of man hath power on earth to forgive sins, I say unto thee, Arise, and take up thy bed, and go thy way into thine house.' Mark 2. 10-11. This double healing, so frequent in the removal of bodily disease, must have been still more marked in casting devils out of body and soul at once. But many a cleansed leper lived on with a thankless heart, and a conscience all unclean; the impotent man made strong may often have gone and sinned more, till a worse thing happened unto him; and the unclean spirit going out of a man may have returned to the empty heart with seven spirits more unclean than himself.

Such, however, was not the case with Mary Magdalene. When the seven devils were cast out of her, her soul was saved, and was thenceforth and for ever a temple of the Holy Ghost. That temple it had doubtless never been before. The demoniac sitting at the feet of Jesus, clothed and in his right mind, is also the sinner accepted in that same hour; lost before, saved for ever now. So likewise with Mary Magdalene: the expulsion of the evil spirits by Christ must be held as simultaneous with her spiritual entrance into the kingdom of heaven.

2. But if Mary the demoniac was no heir of grace, then also *before that possession* she was held fast in bondage by Satan. She was 'a child of wrath even as others, a child of disobedience, a stranger from the covenants of promise, having no hope, and without God in the world; walking according to the course of this world, according to the prince of the power of the air, the spirit that now worketh in the children of disobedience.' Eph. 2:2-3, 12. In her own imagined freedom, she was led captive by Satan at his will: her will and his so agreeing in one, that the bondage was not discovered; in willing union with the world, and unconscious thraldom to the god of the world.

How many of you are in the same condition now; bound

with an invisible chain, a silken cord whose strength you will never know till you try to break it! Jesus, the friend of sinners, addresses you: 'Ye are of your father the devil, and the lusts of your father ye will do.' John 8:44. There is no contest between his will and yours, for the one is the parent of the other; his desires and yours the same; he the god of this world, and you the children of this world; he the father of lies, and you, even the truest of unrenewed men, the children of lies.

The case of Magdalene, so far as we have traced it, is common to all the unconverted; but we have now to turn to a darker picture, and consider:

2. *Satan occupying the soul of Mary with a sevenfold possession*

Magdalene was specially exposed to satanic assault; she may have laid herself open to his inroads; her soul was entered and occupied by seven of his evil angels, yet with an inworking quite distinct from that in Judas the traitor.

1. Magdalene is *specially exposed* to Satan's assault. It is an attempt of satanic malice, at a season when he is coming with great wrath because he knows that he has but a short time; it is an effort of satanic strength, in a land where nocturnal darkness gives the evening wolf free opportunity to devour; it is a licence of divine sovereignty, permitting the roaring lion to break the habitual fetters that chain him within his own place. As heaven was opened at Pentecost, and the Holy Ghost came down upon Jerusalem, and made it for the time a centre of heavenly influence, so now the shores of the Lake of Gennesaret seem for a season to have been the main pathway into earth for the unclean spirits

from the deep. It may have been that the dark border-land between Israel and the Gentiles, more than the heart either of Judea or of heathendom, yielded opportunity to the hosts beneath for claiming a neutral territory between earth and hell. At all events, the country of the Gadarenes appears to have now become the great central haunt of unchained demons; and in the towns of the Gospel narrative Magdala lay among the nearest to that haunted land. Mary was, therefore, so far peculiarly exposed to satanic inroad; yet only in common with hundreds around her, who were not equally Satan's victims.

2. There may, however, have existed *predisposing causes* leaving her more open to the Wicked One to take her for his prey. Mental derangement, more or less, seems invariably to have accompanied satanic possession; probably first preparing the way for his entrance, and then greatly aggravated by his presence. Extreme moral and spiritual degradation appear to have been the fruits of the possession, both from the account of its working in other cases, and from the emphasis laid on the casting of the devils out of Magdalene. Among the healed followers of Jesus, none others are marked in the same manner. It is not the blind man seeing, or the cleansed leper, or the woman that touched the hem of the garment, that is afterwards distinguished as following Jesus; for such are merely named in general as 'healed of infirmities.' Luke 8:2. But the casting out of the seven devils is particularized, as if a singular work of the Lord in one plunged into the lowest depths both of sin and misery.

Yet the sinner, afterwards so sunk by Satan, may have first been self-prepared to become his victim. In some, it may have been so fulfilling the lusts of the flesh as to become an open wreck of body, mind, and spirit, inviting his entrance into the miserable man. In others, it may have been fulfilling the desires of the mind, and so resisting the Holy Spirit as to open the soul to the Evil One. The unhappy Saul, the king after Israel's heart, by no means hardens himself in sensual indulgence; but ever halting between two opinions, divided between two masters, fearing God and quailing before man, lured by ambition and goaded by conscience, he lays his own distracted spirit open to the yet more terrible distraction of 'an evil spirit from the Lord troubling him.' 1 Sam. 16:14. In Magdalene there may have been kindred contentions with the Lord, proud resistings of the Holy Ghost striving to convert her into a little child, a stubborn refusal to yield herself as a living sacrifice to the God of Israel; and the Holy Ghost being grieved, it may have been with her as with Saul, that 'the Spirit of the Lord departed, and an evil spirit troubled her.'

3. But however conjectural the process, the fact is certain that *evil spirits enter Mary's soul,* and intensify all moral and spiritual evil within her. Satan desires to have her wholly for his own, and is permitted to take to himself seven other spirits to lodge within her, to occupy body, soul, and spirit. It is not temptation, but possession; it is no longer Satan gently leading the willing captive, but overmastering the whole man, and tormenting his helpless victim. The possessed are described in Acts 10:38, as 'oppressed of the devil;' that is, overpowered and borne down by Satan through the evil angels that are subject to him.

The child of God, when not so much tempted as assaulted by Satan, can comprehend this condition. With him it is widely different, indeed, both because the devil has not the mastery over him, and because there is within him the new man in which the Holy Spirit dwells. But the believer knows some assaults of the Wicked One, distinct from the workings of the old nature within; and taking the form not of seducing and alluring the heart, but of attacking and harassing the mind and soul. Though this yields but a faint shadow of the violence and power of satanic working in the possessed, it brings out distinctly enough the possibility of a conflict between Satan and the mind and conscience of an unrenewed man. In that conflict with the possessed, the devils had so the mastery in power, that the man had not the command of himself and his acts; and the mastery in deceit and deep indwelling, so that he mistook the thoughts of the fiends for his own. Yet the man remained; with his conscience beclouded and his will fettered, but neither of them destroyed; and hence an afflicting conflict. The constant description of all these demoniacs is that they are vexed, or troubled with unclean spirits. It is a daughter 'grievously vexed with a devil;' a son 'lunatic and sore vexed;' king Saul 'troubled' with an evil spirit; and all 'those that were vexed with unclean spirits.' Matt. 15; Matt. 17; 1 Sam. 16; Luke 6; Acts 5.

This satanic vexing literally signifies 'crowded,' or harassed by a tumult, and expresses the tossing, tearing, and distracting of the soul, as by a multitude of conflicting forces. The complaint of the Psalmist, 'My soul is sore vexed,' is answered by the song, 'In the multitude of my thoughts within me, thy comforts delight my soul.' But if the multitude of our own thoughts can distract us fearfully, how much more those thoughts when aggravated by the indwelling of an unclean spirit, and the multitude of his thoughts also in the soul! Terrible, indeed, to Mary must this vexation have been, a grievous tormenting; when by satanic hate and divine permission not one, but seven devils entered and made their unblessed abode within her; each of them a spirit evil, wicked, and unclean, each of them accursed of God, held in chains of darkness, reserved unto judgment. What a horror of great darkness had then invaded Mary's soul! what a tumultuous battle-field had that soul become of fallen angels, unholy and wretched, conflicting within her night and day!

4. The inworking of the devil in Magdalene is entirely distinct from his work *in Judas Iscariot,* though parallel in some respects. There is the entrance of Satan in both instances; in both it is by divine sufferance; and in both into a heart that has no other occupant. But the one is temptation, and the other possession. The most marked feature of the one is sin; Satan the father of it entering along with the sop, aggravating the heart's besetting sin by his occupation of the whole soul, and impelling the traitor into mad-like malignity and greed. It is the lusts of earth set furiously on fire by the unfettered flames of hell. There is no vexing of his spirit, no troubling of his soul, no conflict of contending elements within. He has sold himself to work iniquity, yielded his heart to the tempter; and there is no contest between the two, but oneness of sinful desire. The entrance of Satan, far from working division within him, stops the last expiring protests of conscience, and effects an unholy unity such as never was before; an unmingled oneness of wicked desire, unwavering fixedness of purpose in evil, intense hasting of the soul to its accursed aim. Then

follows remorse, which the same indwelling drives forward into despair and self-destruction; Satan impelling the man, through his own heart's desires, to cast himself into the abyss.

But in the possessed, like Mary Magdalene, the most marked feature from the first is misery. It is the evil spirits from the deep seeking some relief from their own torments, by making a human heart their habitation, and turning it into a temporary hell. But it is sin as well as misery; not sensual sin, but spiritual. There may be lunacy and madness toward things human and earthly; but there is this great distinction from all ordinary aberration of mind, that in another direction there is intelligence acute, unfailing, and supernatural. Toward the great Spirit, the Father of all spirits, the intellect is wakeful and clear, and the perception far surpassing the ordinary human faculties. Combined with the quick discernment of his presence, are hatred and horror toward the person, character, and work of the living God. Man's own carnal mind is enmity against God, but this enmity becomes fearfully intense in such a soul. It does not sleep, as in most human hearts, by a brutish ignorance of the glorious divine presence; but is awake and earnest, and has only one utterance to Jesus, 'What have I to do with thee? I know thee who thou art, the Holy One of God.'

What a warning to all the unrenewed! Mary, living under the spiritual power of Satan, was delivered over to his tormenting power. It was only for a season, for Jesus came and ransomed her from the hand of the enemy. But Christ has been preached to you, and pressed upon you; and how shall you escape, if you neglect so great salvation, for there remaineth no more sacrifice for sin? Yours is not the fear of devils living with you on earth, but of yourselves living with them in hell; not of their invading your dwelling for a time, but of your being driven into their dwelling for ever, the place prepared for the devil and his angels; not of earth being turned into a transient hell, but of earth being followed by that hell, 'where your worm dieth not, and the fire is not quenched.' Turn and flee before your doom is sealed; while yet the light is with you, escape to Jesus the deliverer from this present evil world, and from the wrath to come; to Jesus who came to destroy the works of the devil; to Jesus who 'turneth us from darkness into light, and from the power of Satan unto God, that we may receive forgiveness of sins, and inheritance among them which are sanctified by faith in him.' Acts 26:18.

III

MARY NOT SEEKING BUT RESISTING JESUS

'Jesus appeared first to Mary Magdalene, out of whom he had cast seven devils.'—Mark 16:9

'What have I to do with thee, Jesus, thou Son of God most high?'—Luke 8:28

THERE is a marked connection between the grace shown to Mary Magdalene in Jesus appearing to her first of all the disciples after his resurrection, and the grace previously shown her in his casting out the seven devils. This reference, obviously designed by the words themselves, is all the more noted by the circumstance that Luke, writing in another connection, simply says, 'out of whom went seven devils;' while Mark, connecting Christ's appearance to Mary Magdalene with his previous grace, states expressly that Jesus had cast the devils out of her. There is an express choice by the Lord Jesus Christ of Magdalene for his first interview after rising from the dead; this choice is founded on the ejection of the devils; and that ejection therefore stamps Mary as a model instance of grace, as a distinctive example above many others, in which the Lord would have us contemplate the character and working of his mercy in the new covenant. It is therefore important for us to inquire into the leading features of such a case of divine deliverance.

The normal case of possession in the New Testament, that wherein its working is both most malignant in itself and brought out most at large, is the demoniac among the tombs; and his also is the most detailed case in the actual outcasting of the demons. Yet he does not remain to us equally with Magdalene as the chief example of gracious deliverance from their power. He is sent to his home, preaches in Decapolis, and disappears from the Gospel narrative. He is not suffered, like her, to follow Jesus; nor have we any account of Christ's being seen by him when risen from the dead. Doubtless, when Jesus returned to Galilee after the resurrection, this demoniac of the Galilean Sea was not the least among 'the five hundred brethren, who saw him at once;' yet there is no record of the Lord's appearing to him at all. It is Magdalene, out of whom he had cast seven devils, who is the chosen example of this abundant grace.

In looking to what is more special in such an instance, let us take at present the peculiar obstacles to grace; which in her case may be brought out in these two features, that Mary does not seek Jesus, and that she resists him.

1. Mary not seeking Jesus

Although this is not expressly asserted, but only that Jesus cast the devils out of her, we are left in no uncertainty regarding the fact; because no demoniac ever sought Jesus, none in all the Gospel narrative; and the soothsaying damsel of the Acts forms no real exception.

1. The examples of demoniacs healed are both numerous and varied; but amongst them all there is *not a single instance* of one that sought deliverance for himself. The diseased often did. The lepers, who dare not draw nigh in their defilement, came and lifted up their voices afar off for mercy; the weak woman, who had spent her all for health and was only the worse, ceremonially unclean though she was and defiling all that touched her, came and pressed through the crowd to Jesus till she reached the hem of his garment; the blind man by the way-side, who could only hear the tread and the hum of the passing throng, sent his cry through the multitude till it entered the ears of Jesus. These all came for their own healing, secretly drawn by a higher power, but aided by no earthly friend. But the possessed never came; or they came not asking health, but earnestly asking to be suffered to abide unhealed.

It is so in every narrated instance; and though there is one general statement that may seem at first to be contrary, the difference is only apparent. In Luke 6:17-18, it is written, 'And he came down with them, and stood in the plain, and the company of his disciples, and a great multitude of people, … which came to hear him, and to be healed of their diseases; and they that were vexed with unclean spirits: and they were healed.' Some of the best critics read the verse, 'and they that were vexed with unclean spirits were healed;' but the passage, as it stands, does not state that the possessed came to Jesus for healing, but only that they stood in the plain along with the multitude. It is obvious also that many of the diseased were incapable of coming, and must have been brought; and this is the constant statement elsewhere regarding all the possessed. In Matthew 4:24: 'They brought unto him all sick people that were taken with divers diseases and torments, and those which were possessed with devils, and he healed them.' In Mark 1:32: 'At even, they brought unto him all that were diseased, and them that were possessed with devils'; and in Acts 5:16, 'There came a multitude bringing sick folks, and them which were vexed with unclean spirits, and they were healed every one.'

As in the general account, so in every individual instance, none of the possessed came to Christ of their own accord. A watchful mother, whose daughter is grievously vexed with a devil, hears of Jesus, leaves her child at home, pleads with him for mercy, and will not be stopped either by silence or rebuke till she obtains the children's crumbs for the dogs, and returning finds her loved one dispossessed, and resting quietly on her bed (Matt. 15:21; Mark 7:24). A tender father brings his demoniac boy, his only child, vexed from infancy with an unclean spirit; brings him first to the disciples, and then to Jesus, and prays and weeps, and believes through helped unbelief, till at the divine command the devil rends him sore, and leaves him for ever (Matt. 17:14; Mark 9:14; Luke 9:38).

2. There is one detailed case, not in the Gospels but in the Acts, that is extremely singular in respect of voluntary coming within the joyful sound of the Gospel; but only brings out the more clearly, that no demoniacs ever came to Christ or his disciples for healing. It is the case of *the soothsaying damsel in Philippi* (Acts 16:16). She waylays Paul

and his fellow worshippers day by day as they go out toward
the river-side, to 'the place where prayer was wont to be
made;' she meets them first, then falls in behind them, and
follows close after them, saying all the while, 'These men
are the servants of the most high God, which show unto us
the way of salvation.' She seems to love their company, and
to commend their mission; although it is only by means of
the unclean spirit within her that she discerns their character and calling.

She speaks not like the other demoniacs of destruction,
of the dreaded abyss, of Jesus coming to torment them
before the time; but of the way of salvation shown to
men, to herself and the Philippians. Yet she never asks to
be saved, nor to have the evil spirit cast out of her heart.
Her testimony draws no souls to Christ, and brings no joy
to his apostle; but only grieves him day by day, till in holy
indignation he commands the devil to go forth. Now she is
delivered, probably she is saved; but not at all through her
seeking either Jesus or deliverance from Satan, but only by
Christ of his own will casting out the evil spirit that had
discerned his presence. The case is probably somewhat akin
to that of Simon the sorcerer seeking to buy the Holy Ghost
for miraculous works. The wonder-telling spirit in the false
prophetess seems to have aimed at a certain outward union
with the wonder-working servants of Jesus, and at seducing the Philippians into that worst of all moral conditions,
'holding the truth in unrighteousness.'

Since, then, no demoniac ever sought Christ for deliverance, we conclude with certainty that Christ was not sought
by Mary, but Mary sought by Christ. This brings us to the
root of all salvation, that it is 'not of him that willeth, nor

of him that runneth, but of God that showeth mercy.' It is no discouragement to seek, for God uses the inquiry of our mind, and the desire of our heart; and 'every one that asketh receiveth, and he that seeketh findeth, and to him that knocketh it shall be opened.' But it strips our seeking of merit of any kind, of all desert of salvation. If we truly seek and ask, it is the grace of God initiating and moving our desires. None of us obtains salvation by effort of our own, any more than Mary could so obtain it. In the depths of our heart we are as hostile to God as she, as helpless in our chains, all our hope hanging as entirely on sovereign mercy. The 'devil led us captive at his will,' as truly as he led her; for the demons were only emissaries of their great prince. They are sometimes sunk altogether in the inspired account, and their chief alone noted; for it is said, in describing deliverance from them, that Jesus 'went about healing all that were oppressed of the devil.'

If then we have been redeemed, we are really healed demoniacs; not first seeking eternal life of ourselves, but sought and found by Jesus Christ. The poor demoniac did not seek, but no more do any of us until we are divinely drawn; for 'there is none that understandeth, that seeketh after God.' Rom. 3:11. Moved by our own natural will, or awakened by natural conscience, we may seek deliverance from wrath to come, but we never truly seek God or his Christ. In the inner depths of the soul's history our conversion, if real, is as completely of God as ever Mary's was. We have not chosen him, but he has chosen us; we have not loved him, but he has loved us, and sent his Son to be the propitiation for our sins; we have not sought him, but he has sought us like lost sheep, found us, saved us; and when we have come to Jesus Christ, it is only because we were first drawn by the Father, to whom be all the glory, world without end. Amen.

But a further view presents itself of the spiritual condition of the possessed, and we must contemplate:

2. *Mary resisting Jesus*

The evidence of this position rests on the facts that the ejection of the devils was violent in Mary's own case; and that demoniac resistance to Christ was uniform and invariable, alike in the mildest and the most malignant instances.

1. In Mary's own case the ejection of the devils was *violent*. Jesus 'cast out of her seven devils;' he threw them out by his almighty power; not by their consent, but against their will, and in spite of their resistance. It is written also, that 'they went out of her;' they were not seven diseases cured and ended, but they were seven living beings with wills of their own, and deeds wrought by themselves. The fever left the Galilean nobleman's boy at the word of Jesus, 'Thy son liveth;' and leaving him it went nowhere else, but was extinct. But the devils went out of Mary, only to go somewhere else. Some abode they must have; no longer in heaven above, since they left their own habitation; but either here on earth for a season, or in hell beneath, which they can leave no more for ever when their dreaded 'time' shall have come. They go out of Mary by their own act; yet altogether contrary to their will, and only because they are driven out by the resistless power of Jesus.

This indeed only proves that the ejection of the devils from Mary was violent, and opposed by themselves. But if resisted by the demons, we infer that it was certainly resisted by the demoniac whom they enslaved; for in every case the possessed fulfilled the will of his possessors, and mistook their interest for his own. The Gadarene's running to Jesus and kneeling before him have sometimes been taken as implying a conflict between the man and his oppressors. But on the contrary, the man identified his own case with that of his worst enemies, and looked on their ejection as his own severest doom: 'I beseech thee, torment me not.' It is not that the devils desire for themselves to flee, and the man for himself desires to pray; because except for them he has no knowledge of Jesus at all, and would be moved by neither fear nor hope at his coming. But the devils know that their conqueror and Lord had come; from him they have no power of flying, and no hope in flight; and for their own sakes they move the man to crouch and supplicate at the feet of Jesus. It is only when their abiding in their present victim has become hopeless, that the devils all present a separate petition for themselves, that they may enter the herd of swine; but while they have any hope of continuing in the man, they impel him to run and kneel before Christ, beseeching as for himself to be let alone.

In *the mildest cases* of possession the demoniac invariably resists Jesus. The general account of dispossession, applicable to all the cases that occurred, is that 'devils came out of many, crying out and saying, 'Thou art Christ the Son of God.' Luke 4:41. The full nature of this outcry is detailed in two instances; neither of them of an average character, but each occupying an extreme position among the possessed. In one the possession is extremely mild, the calmest of all recorded cases, in the synagogue of Capernaum; in the other it is extremely severe, the most violent of all, among the tombs of Gadara. Yet the attitude of both toward Jesus is exactly the same, and their feelings were expressed in the same words; which warrants us to conclude that the mental condition was substantially the same in all the other cases. The demoniac of Gadara is the most malignant example of diabolical possession, both in the multitude of devils, and in their terrible working; and his outcry is 'What have I to do with thee, Jesus, thou Son of the most high God?' The man with the unclean spirit in Capernaum is the least malignant example, and is in many respects like other men. He mingles with his neighbours, goes with them even to the house of God, and sitting in the midst of them creates no disquiet.

This case presents a remarkable and most instructive proof that a congregation, holding a form of sound words, and with the Scriptures of truth read continually to them, may be so dead, so devoid of the Spirit of God, that Satan may keep fast hold of the worshippers without being even disturbed by all that is uttered. So far is it from being true that along with the formal rehearsal of prayers, and the reading of the Bible in the house of God, by men ordained to the ministry, there must of necessity be even the least breath of the living Spirit. Capernaum is full of religious privileges, but sunk in formality and spiritual death. It is the Sabbath day, the synagogue is thronged with worshippers, this man with the unclean spirit enters the house of God, as he has done many a Sabbath before, and remains undisturbed and undisturbing. The place was built as a temple for the Holy One; but the congregation of dead souls has so nearly transformed it into a synagogue of Satan, that the Prince of darkness suffers in it no more disquiet than among the sepulchres of Gadara. As in such a case now, a few rays of heavenly light, a few words of living truth, would distract the whole assembly; so the entrance and teaching of Jesus then awoke the demoniac into hatred and fear. The moment he is disturbed by Christ's presence, his outcry in the synagogue is the same as the other's outcry from the tombs, 'What have we to do with thee, thou Jesus of Nazareth, the Holy One of God?' Mark 1:24.

But Mary Magdalene's was a much worse case than that of the Sabbath-worshipper in the synagogue; for his was a simple possession by a single spirit, while hers was sevenfold, and came nearer the case of him that had the legion. As the legion is a large yet indefinite number, so seven represents a numerical fulness of the unclean spirits within her. We have, therefore, no difficulty in realizing her wretched and hopeless condition. As a simple demoniac Mary has no will of her own consciously distinct from the overmastering will of Satan within her; and by the sevenfold possession the evil is terribly aggravated. She con founds Satan's knowledge, Satan's interest, and Satan's will with her own; she mistakes her cruel oppressor for her friend and supporter; she mistakes her great Deliverer for her foe and tormentor; she imagines her whole attainable ease to consist in continued union with the seven spirits that griev-ously vex her; she looks on their ejection as her ruin, their destruction as her doom of death. Christ comes to set her free, and to bind and judge the strong one that holds her in chains; and she takes part with her destroyer, and against her Saviour. If suffered to speak, her cry to Christ is, 'Let us alone, art thou come to destroy us? What have I to do with thee, Jesus, thou Son of the most high God? Art thou come to torment us before the time? I adjure thee by God, that thou torment me not.' Hers is not merely a refraining from seeking Christ; but it is the whole human will, and the whole satanic will within her, boiling with intense enmity against him, and bursting into hideous outcry.

How helpless, how hopeless! If help come not from a higher source than is either within herself or in any arm of flesh, Mary is lost for ever. No effort of her own can ever break those seven chains, and she has no desire to have them broken.

How similar the demoniac's condition to every believer's former state, and to the present state of all the unsaved! In every converted sinner, it is enmity subdued by grace; it is the heart's opposition broken down by the irresistible power of the Holy Spirit. Jesus comes to save us, and to destroy sin and Satan, our deadly foes. The sinner, beguiled and blinded by the old serpent, conceives that Christ has come to mar his peace and ruin his hopes, to condemn, to enslave, to torment him. The removal of your heart of stone, the cleansing of your conscience, the breaking of your idol, the casting out of Satan, these are the blessings Christ comes to bestow. But the death of your enemies you mistake for your own death, and your prayer is, 'Let me alone.' Your chain, that binds you to perdition, is taken for your support that gives you strength and peace. The Lord speaks; his word goes forth in resistless might to break your fetters; they snap asunder like flax in the fire; you sink—yet not into the dreaded abyss, but into the arms of Jesus, 'who loved you, and gave himself for you.' Amen.

IV

MARY REDEEMED BY THE
LORD'S RIGHT ARM

*'Mary Magdalene, out of whom he had cast
seven devils.'*—Mark 16:9

'He cast out the spirits with his word.'—Matt. 8:16

FROM Mary Magdalene, helpless to work or even to
desire her own salvation, and having strength only to
resist, let us now pass to Jesus having compassion and rescuing her from destruction. Let us look at Jesus vanquishing
Satan for her, casting Satan out of her, and redeeming her
with an everlasting deliverance.

1. Jesus vanquishes Satan for her

Christ fights Mary's battle and ours, without our aid, and
without our concurrence. The conflict is not between us
and Satan, but between Satan and the Son of man. Jesus
asks no help from us, and waits not for our consent; but
conquers Satan for us, first in the wilderness, and finally
on Calvary.

1. Before casting out devils at all, Jesus *contends with Satan in the desert,* and overcomes him; with a victory complete in itself, though not yet final in its issue. Satan, seeking to hold Mary bound, puts forth all his subtlety against Jesus who has come to deliver her; and Mary's battle and ours is fought in the wilderness, on the pinnacle of God's temple, and on the mountain-top of the world's glory. Mary in her own person is not there, but she is there in Jesus; to hold her Satan contends with Jesus, and for her is by Jesus baffled and put to flight. In virtue of that victory Christ casts Satan out of Mary, and still more in virtue of the final conflict and victory on Calvary. The trembling fear of Jesus in all the unclean spirits might have arisen simply from their recognition of him as the Holy One of God, full of a power to which theirs was quite unequal; but this fear must have been doubled by the experience of their prince, and by his defeat and their own in the first temptation in the wilderness. Jesus was not merely one coming to conquer, but already tried by them, and victorious over them.

This was the first onset by the powers of darkness on the Light of the world, in the very beginning or before the actual commencement of the Lord's ministry, and the proclamation of the glad tidings of the gospel. After it Satan departed 'for a season,' of what duration we are not informed; but till the end of Christ's work on earth there seems to have been no second similar assault. There are both temptation and harassing; through Peter's dissuading him from the cross, through the people pressing upon him the crown, through scribes and lawyers assailing him with questions like showers of poisoned arrows. But between the commencement and the close of the ministry, there is no record of any regular and sustained satanic assault. After the conflict in the wilderness Jesus, and not Satan, acted on the aggressive. He entered the kingdom of darkness, he bound the strong one, he broke the fetters of his captives, he rebuked, silenced, and cast out the devils everywhere; while they plied no temptation, and attempted no conflict. If they offered opposition, it was by passive resistance in the unwilling relaxing of their hold on their victims, not in active and determined onset on Jesus. In the desert Satan was aggressive; there was no kingdom of his there, no goods to hold in peace, no victims held in chains. By the Spirit Jesus was led into the wilderness, and thither Satan went with purposed assault on the Son of man. Thenceforward not Satan, but Jesus was the assailant; and to escape from him, to have nothing to do with him, to be let alone by him, was the utmost that the devils sought when he entered their domains, overthrowing by his word the proud and hitherto unbroken gates of hell.

2. But meanwhile Satan husbands his shattered strength; he cherishes his own daunted courage, and rallies his scattered hosts for *a second grand conflict,* recognized on both sides as final. The Chief of the hostile principalities and powers seems personally to have stood very much aloof from Jesus during the whole interval. He appears scarcely to have met him face to face at all, but rather to have left the broken battle-field to his minions. But now a second time as at the beginning, 'the prince of this world cometh;' now again, he waits not for Christ's coming to him, but acts on the offensive, and commences the assault by putting into the heart of Judas Iscariot to betray him.

The final conflict has now commenced, for Mary, for us,

for all whom the Father has given to the Son. On our behalf Jesus meets Satan and all his hosts in Gethsemane and on Calvary. He is weak, and they are strong; for it is the hour of his feebleness, 'this hour' unto which he has come to be crucified in weakness; and the season of their strength, 'the hour and the power of darkness.' They are many, and he is alone; for 'many bulls compass him about,' while he is forsaken by men on earth and by God in heaven; alone in the midst of the gathered hosts of hell. More than when the seven demons held Mary in undisturbed possession, or the legion revelled as masters within the Gadarene, much more now have come both 'their hour and their power.' It is the accumulating of sins that are to be forgiven, when sins are laid on Jesus; and the congregating of devils to the only spot in the universe where their battle is fought, when 'those eagles are gathered together to the carcase.' The battle lost in heaven has been gained on earth; and the world is theirs save in this one spot, and but for this one Man. And now it is no longer the devils timidly beseeching Jesus to let them alone, or flatteringly seducing him to worship their prince; but fiercely and madly striving to rend him as their prey, their legions like famished wolves gathered by the scent of blood. It is love, holiness, truth, meekness, obedience, patience in weakness; with hatred, pride, falsehood, rebellion in power. Those foaming billows cast up from the nethermost depths the mire of the horrible pit; all the floods of the abyss pass over him; yet they leave the Lamb of God unspotted, undefiled, whiter than snow. And now it is finished. God is glorified by the Son of man. The father of lies is overthrown, falls like the lightning-flash from heaven, is cast out of his usurped dominion in all the elect; out of the Gadarene, out of the Magdalene, out of you, brother, sister, and out of me. All Mary's interests were bound up in the battle, and yours and mine; but she and you and I went not forth into that field of blood. Then we tarried at home, yet now we divide the spoil.

2. Jesus casts Satan out of Mary

He casts the unclean spirits out of her by his own direct act; by the word of his power; they leave the soul of Mary for the Holy Spirit to occupy their place; and the tumult of hell within her is followed by a heavenly calm.

1. Christ, coming to Magdala, casts the devils out of Mary *by his own direct act*. In the weakness of the temptation and the crucifixion he awaits and meets Satan assaulting him, undertakes Mary's warfare, and binds her foes. In his ministry, travelling in the greatness of his strength, he goes forth to crush Satan in his own stronghold, and casts him out of the soul which he held in chains. As in the desert and on Calvary, so now on the seashore, the conflict is not between Mary and her enemy, but between Jesus her Saviour and Satan her oppressor. The devils desire to remain in their victims everywhere, in Gadara, in Capernaum, in Magdala; and they discern at once that the issue is not between them and their captives, but only between them and the Deliverer. Their power to abide in a soul, or to remain in a country, rests altogether with Jesus. As soon as Christ comes the conflicting spiritual powers meet, darkness and light contend together. Mary's own part is with Satan, though he is holding her in chains; and all the more because he is holding her chained, for he deceives all whom he destroys. Jesus and Satan both claim Mary in Magdala,

as both claim her in the wilderness and on the cross; only there is no conflict here, but the victor commands the vanquished to quit his possession.

Into all spiritual deliverance the same elements enter. The god of this world ruling everywhere, in a soul or in a country, always holds his victims fast till Jesus comes in the power of the Holy Ghost. It is allotted to believers to call Jesus to rebuke Satan, and cast him forth. His slaves desire to abide as they are; but if Christ comes and commands him to go, the blinding of the mind by the god of this world is at an end, the children of darkness believe in the light, and in believing they become children of the light and of the day.

2. As in all the other examples, so in Mary; Christ delivers her *by the word of his power.* He sends his word and heals her; the King sends and looses her, even the ruler of the people, and lets her go free; he casts out the spirits with his word; with authority and power he commands the unclean spirits, and they come out. Psa. 107:20; 105:20; Matt. 8:16; Luke 4:36. It is the same word of which it is written, 'Of his own will begat he us by the word of truth;' and of which Jesus says, 'Now ye are clean through the word which I have spoken unto you.' The simple word it is, yet the word in the power of the Holy Ghost; for Christ himself says, 'I with the finger of God cast out devils; I by the Spirit of God cast out devils.' Luke 11:20; Matt. 12:28.

It is the word of almighty power, unavoidable, irresistible; yet not in the mere exercise of might, but of justice and of truth, for to utter that word costs Jesus his life; his life at the hands of those whom he destroys by his power, for 'through death he destroys him that had the power of death.' For Mary, held fast by the powers of hell, the pains of hell take hold on Jesus; her cords of death bind the Lord of Life, and by him are snapped asunder for ever.

3. At the word of Christ, the evil spirits leave Mary's soul *for the Holy Ghost to occupy it.* Jesus enters Magdala, speaks not to Mary but to her oppressor, and the seven devils come out of her, crying, 'Thou art Christ the Son of God.' Luke 4:41. This is recorded as the cry of all the ejected spirits, and therefore also of those seven. One and all they leave her in that hour; and the Holy Spirit, by whom they were cast out, now fills her heart and mind in Christ Jesus. Previously the wicked ones never for a moment cease from troubling her; they are like the miry, unresting sea; they cannot rest themselves, and they give no rest to her. The word is spoken and they are gone; themselves are gone with all their thoughts; they are gone one and all, with their prince that ruled them. Christ by his word has quelled those raging billows, and in Mary's soul there is a great calm. The sin is finished, the wretchedness gone, the condemnation cancelled, the banishment revoked. Mary's heart is made new by the Holy Spirit, like the heart of a child, yet of no fallen child of man. Her conscience is cleansed, her crimson sins are white as snow, Christ is in her heart the hope of glory, and angels minister unto her as an heir of salvation. The world of spirits is more unveiled to her than to others, on account of the past possession. God, Christ, the Spirit, ministering angels, are seen by her more quickly and more clearly than by others of the redeemed; for, though a stranger to grace, she has been no stranger to the spiritual world through the spirits of darkness dwelling within her.

On Mary in Magdala all nature now shines anew. The fair scenes of her youth had been turned for her into the gates of hell. The deep lake, the dark mountain, the midnight heavens had been peopled in her eyes with horrid forms; and had echoed to her ears only the yells of haunting fiends. But now the sun, moon, and stars, the green earth, the blue hills, and the bright Sea of Galilee are hers as they had never been before. Hers is now the song,

> How pleasant to me thy deep blue wave,
>   O Sea of Galilee!
> For the glorious One who came to save
>   Hath often stood by thee.
>
> It is not that the wild gazelle
>   Comes down to drink thy tide,
> But He that was pierced to save from hell
>   Oft wandered by thy side.
>
> Graceful around thee the mountains meet,
>   Thou calm reposing sea,
> But ah! far more, the beautiful feet
>   Of Jesus walked o'er thee.
>
> —R. M. M'Cheyne

Hers also are the thunder-cloud and the lightning flash, the tempest and the billow; no longer to tremble at as the earnests of inevitable and eternal doom, but to admire and rejoice in as the handiwork of her reconciled God and Father. What a name to her is the name of Jesus now! How sweet above every name in heaven and in earth! It is Jesus of Nazareth who has taken the prey from the terrible; it is he who has redeemed Mary's soul; he who has sought, has found, has rescued the hopeless captive; Jesus the Saviour, Redeemer, Deliverer of Mary, of me, of you. In the freshness of the new-born soul within her, all above, beneath, around, is fresh with the unsullied dew of morn. Freed from the bondage of corruption, and translated into the glorious liberty of the children of God, her soul rests and rejoices in the peace of God that passes all understanding. What a rest to such a soul! Every believer knows it; but for Mary seven chains have been rent in pieces, seven gates of brass broken, seven howling wolves slain, seven fiery serpents cast out. Her spirit is freed 'like a bird from the snare of the fowler,' and soars out of the smoke of her torment into the light and liberty and joy of heaven:

> O that men to the Lord would give
>   Praise for his goodness then,
> And for his works of wonder done
>   Unto the sons of men!
> Because the mighty gates of brass
>   In pieces he did tear,
> By him in sunder also cut
>   The bars of iron were.
>
> —*Psalm 107*

4. The tumult of hell in Magdalene is now followed by the sweetness of *a heavenly calm*. A new song has now been put into Mary's mouth, and like the mother of Jesus she cannot but magnify the Lord, and rejoice in God her Saviour. Yet judging from the parallel case in Gadara, holy, tranquil quiet is probably the prevailing feeling in her soul; a great calm after the long tempest; the peaceful rest of heaven succeeding the boiling tumult of hell. 'They found the man out of whom the devils were departed sitting at the feet of Jesus, clothed, and in his right mind, and they were afraid.' Luke 8:35. What a picture of holy serenity and humility

and gratitude on the one hand, and of man's estrangement from God on the other! They were afraid, but not of the fierce demoniac yelling amid the tombs, and lacerating his own flesh. They had become accustomed to that terror and misery; and could live unmoved with fear or with pity, in the presence of hell possessing a portion of this earth. But that same portion of earth is now possessed by heaven; the kingdom of heaven has come into that maniac with right-eousness, peace, and joy in the Holy Ghost, and they are afraid! They can stand the horrors of hell, become almost visible before them; but they tremble at the sight of the curtain that veils heaven partially lifted before their eyes, and its holy light and quiet revealed. How akin to Satan fallen man is, and how alien from God! Satan with his legions creates no commotion in Gadara; man dwelt in by God fills the whole community with terror. So near to hell man is, and the powers of hell so readily become familiar to man; so far removed from heaven, and the presence of heaven and its power so strange and foreign.

3. Mary's is a complete and lasting cure

The departure of devils was sometimes only for a season; for the unclean spirit, after going out of a man, seems naturally to return to his old haunt, and seek a second occupation of the soul. Unwilling to leave, then driven out by irresistible power and fleeing in terror, then finding no rest elsewhere and seeking to resume his old abode. Many in the present day, as in all past times of awakening, give sad evidence of such a history. While in some the god of this world is cast out for ever, in others he is only scared away for a season, and no higher spirit occupies the desolate house. Into how many have the old lusts returned; the lust of the eye, the lust of the flesh, and the pride of life, it may be even with seven-fold power; the lusts of this world, and their father the devil, who returns along with them? How sad the spectacle; the latter end worse than the first; hope blighted, the open door of heaven closed, and earth filled again with the occupants of hell in greater number than before!

It is indeed refreshing to witness an abiding change; Satan cast out for ever, and his place for ever occupied. So it was with the demon-bound boy at the base of the holy mount, over whom Jesus gave the command, 'Thou deaf and dumb spirit, I charge thee, come out of him, and enter no more into him.' Mark 9:25. And so it is with Mary Magdalene. The devils, finding elsewhere no rest, may have returned; but they find no empty house adorned for its former masters. Christ occupies Mary's soul; Christ, who has cast the devils out, enters and fills her heart, fills it as scarcely any other heart of man, fills it as the outcast devils had never done in the plenitude of their possession, fills it leaving no void, fills it with all the fulness of God. Jesus dwells in her mind and soul, with a unity of indwelling such as she never knew when sin and Satan dwelt together there; with unity of truth and love in the vine and in the branch. Her emptied heart Christ replenishes with the same Spirit by whom the devils were ejected; with the kingdom of heaven within; right-eousness and peace and joy in the Holy Ghost displacing and excluding the kingdom of darkness. The word, that word of Christ by which Satan had been rebuked and from which he fled, now dwells in her richly; for she follows Jesus wherever he goes, that she may hang upon the words of his mouth, as 'better to her than thousands of gold and silver.'

If you would have Satan shut out for ever, you must have no empty heart inviting his return; but Christ's Spirit and living word ever in your soul. You must also 'give no place to the devil,' by any indulged sin; which at once gives him the key of your heart to make it his house again, and leaves it vacant for him by 'grieving the Holy Spirit of promise, whereby you are sealed unto the day of redemption.'

Mary healed is a living witness to Jesus the healer, and a proof to all that look on her that the kingdom of God is come with power. She is permitted to follow Jesus, and before the world to form part of the visible kingdom of heaven on earth. Satan is chained to the conqueror's chariot wheels; his shattered kingdom of darkness is dragged into triumphant light; and his rescued captive cleaves in the sight of all to her divine Deliverer. The kingdom of heaven is proclaimed, with Jesus in the midst of it; and around him the love and beauty of the kingdom are adorning Magdalene, now 'turned from the power of Satan unto God,' once 'darkness but now light in the Lord.' It was thus with Mary; it is thus with all the redeemed; is it thus also with you?

V

MARY AS CHRIST'S DEVOTED SERVANT

'And the twelve were with him, and certain women which had been healed of evil spirits and infirmities, Mary called Magdalene, ... and many others, which ministered unto him of their substance.'—Luke 8:1-3

THE brief account, that Mary Magdalene was with Christ and ministered to him of her substance, presents much information regarding her, though in few words. This simple fact implies that she gave her whole heart, her whole means, and her whole time to the Lord.

1. Mary gave the Lord all her heart

The goods may be given while the heart is withheld, but she gave herself to the Lord.

1. Men often give to Christ *their means without their heart,* and their gift is worthless. Mary Magdalene might have given all her goods to the Lord or to the poor; yet had she wanted love to himself, her work had been lost. 'Son, give me thine heart,' is a deeper and more trying demand,

than 'Go sell that thou hast and give to the poor.' In an age especially of liberal gifts, it is greatly to be feared that many even of the largest givers to the cause of Christ, and of the greatest benefactors of their fellow-men, may fall short of entering into the promised rest above. The thought is deeply affecting. Not only members of the church may they be, but honoured, influential members, and greatly helpful to the kingdom of heaven on earth. The heart is of all things the hardest to give to Christ, and that without which all things else are nothing, and the giver of them all but sounding brass and a tinkling cymbal. The gold and the silver may not be parted with to purchase heaven, but rather in the name of free gifts from the expectants of eternal life; yet the heart may not have been yielded up to the Lord, and the hope, like the hypocrite's, must perish. Often also, when we have once given the heart to God and when the other offerings to him have followed, we slowly steal out the first, great single gift, the one central jewel in the signet that gave it all its worth and beauty, and leave only the outer settings round the absent gem.

2. But with Mary *the soul* is yielded to Jesus, first and alway; and then the surrender of the substance is one of the chief fruits and tokens of the surrender of the heart. We are ever secretly reserving the inmost heart for some other object; and that object, good or bad in itself, is an idol to us. But Jesus will be deepest within the man, expressly claiming for himself the innermost chamber of the soul. Alas! when the secrets of the hearts are revealed, in how many will some treasure be found deeper than the Lord Jesus Christ? That hidden prize is certain death to the owner of the accursed thing. 'Thou shalt love the Lord thy God with

all thy heart,' is God's demand under the law, and he will not have less. This law, 'written in the heart and put into the mind,' is God's free gift in the gospel of Jesus Christ. There is indeed a law in our members warring against the law in our mind, and bringing us into subjection to the law in the members. But the law in the mind is the deeper of the two; it is the new spirit created 'within,' in the 'hidden part,' in the 'inner man.' When the deepest secret of all, the believer's heart, is opened, Christ is found there; Christ in him the hope of glory. Have none of us reason to tremble lest when the depths within are broken up and searched out, not Christ the pearl of price should be found, but that foul and loathsome reptile self? If so, a sad surprise will be ours in the great day; everlasting shame and confusion of face. 'I the Lord search the heart, and try the reins of the children of men.—Search me, O God, and try me, and see if any wicked way be in me, and lead me in the way everlasting.'

2. Mary gave her whole substance to the Lord

We are all called to the heart-surrender of our substance to Christ, and to hold ourselves ready for its actual surrender.

1. We are not commonly called to sacrifice all for Christ by an actual outward gift, but we are called to make *a heart-surrender of all our means* to the Lord. 'He that forsaketh not all that he hath, cannot be my disciple.' To one earnest candidate for heaven Jesus issues the command, 'Go thy way, sell whatsoever thou hast, and give to the poor, and thou shalt have treasure in heaven; and come, take up the cross, and follow me.' Mark 10:21. He cannot, his heart will not, his possessions are deeper within him than the love of everlasting life. The Lord may at any time lay this command on any disciple,

and his true follower holds himself ever in readiness. He has consented to have the chain that binds him to his substance broken; himself given to the Lord, and his property given, surrendered as no longer his own. Jesus does not retain it now, but restores it to him again; yet no longer in the same relation. The man was chained to his wealth, the chain is loosed and the man set free; the wealth is restored to him in charge for the Lord, but with an open link in the chain to be unhooked the moment his Lord requires it.

2. We must ever *hold ourselves in readiness with the actual sacrifice.* Mary gives herself and her substance wholly to Jesus. All are not called to the surrender in the same form; but the trying question remains, whether if called we should freely consent, and even rejoice to be servants of Christ with our persons, and with all our effects. In Mary's circumstances would you have followed her course? This question we ought to put often to ourselves, and not to reckon it settled once and for ever; for the love of the things of earth is ever stealing again into the mind; and ere ever we are aware, the heart is ensnared with the deceitfulness of riches and the lusts of other things, choking the word and rendering it unfruitful. The question requires to be repeated frequently, and to be driven deeper than before into the mind, conscience, and heart. At first the joy of the Lord oft carries us away; and without effort or conscious sacrifice we prefer Christ to all, and count all things loss for his sake. But at another time, and under no overflowing joy in the Holy Ghost, we have to ask ourselves if we are not loving the things of earth for their own sakes; or if we are receiving them simply from the Lord, enjoying them only in the Lord, and devoting them wholly to the Lord.

As Christ's stewards, yet neither called nor warranted like Mary to sacrifice all expressly and immediately for his cause, we shall find great advantage in *systematic* giving. Not that all can give alike; for the tithe, which may serve for a general rule, may be too much for one and far too little for another. But by laying up, as the Lord prospers, a suitable portion of their substance for God and for the poor, most will find that otherwise they had been giving far less then they imagined; and that by such a dedication they have more riches than before for that treasury where the moth corrupteth not, and the thief breaketh not through to steal. The discovery will create both grief and joy; grief for the past neglect, and joy at the acquisition of unexpected wealth. The richest man is not he who possesses most, but who has most to spare for the poor, for those who lack either the bread of this life or the bread that endureth for ever. The Lord also loves cheerful giving, to which nothing is more conducive than giving systematically; for in bestowing the giver feels that the receiver only comes for that which he has already laid up in his name, and in refusing the conscience is clear and the heart is not hardened by a secret sense of wrong.

3. Mary gave her whole time to the Lord

She was right in all this, for she had either Christ's command, or his permission and undoubted approval. She counted it a privilege, of which she joyfully availed herself, to give all her treasure and all her time to her Redeemer. In her place would I so account it, and would you? would I so prefer Christ to home, to family, to friends? would I so esteem his reproach better than all the treasures of Egypt? It looks well in another, it reads well in history, it is well in the sight of God, and well for ever in heaven above; but would I or you think well of it, if actually placed in our choice or enjoined for our obedience?

The substance of Mary's example remains for imitation by us. The outward form of it is exceptional, and is justified by these special circumstances; the sanction of honoured usage, the providential relief from domestic duties, and the express warrant of Christ.

1. It was *customary* for Jewish matrons or widows to travel with noted teachers of the law, to benefit by their instructions, and to supply their wants, so relieving strangers of that burden. There was, therefore, nothing unusual in the conduct of Mary Magdalene, and the other devout women who accompanied Jesus, and ministered to him.

2. With many of these there was apparently *no call for their remaining at home*. With some their families were following Christ, as in the case of Salome, whose sons James and John were amongst the apostles; with others, while they were themselves infinite gainers through Jesus Christ, their households were at least no losers; and in the case of the wife of Herod's steward, it was doubtless with her husband's consent. Their general description is that of 'certain women which had been healed of evil spirits and infirmities;' their maladies probably rendering them only a burden to their friends before their healing. Without doubt this was Magdalene's condition. Possessed by seven devils, she could only have been a daily grief, anxiety, and terror to her relatives; her safe absence would have been a boon; her healing must have been an unspeakable relief to them all; and in her own home, where she had been worse than

useless, there may have been now no demand for services which only now she was capable of rendering. Those services might therefore be bestowed on Jesus without the sacrifice of other claims.

3. The chief point of all is *Christ's implied call,* or permission to Mary Magdalene to minister to him. Such honour none appear to have taken to themselves. Christ accepted no offer of apostleship, 'but called unto him whom he would.' The demoniac of Gadara pleaded for liberty to accompany Jesus, but it was refused; the penitent at Simon's table was dismissed with a blessing. Mary Magdalene, if not called, was unquestionably permitted to attend on Jesus; her presence was not by any oversight, but with the consent and approval of her Lord.

Mary then, with his own sanction, gives her whole heart, whole substance, and whole time to the Lord Jesus Christ and his gospel. The world, without and within the church, would account this only another form of lunacy. Those who reproached Jesus with casting out devils through Beelzebub, and said of himself that he had a devil and was mad, would consider Magdalene more hopelessly and more odiously mad than before. Such a life as hers is ever full of the reproach of Christ, and the foolishness of the cross; but full also of the wisdom of God, and the power of God unto salvation in the weak vessel of his own rich mercy. And however different in form, our surrender of heart and wealth and time must in substance be the same as Mary's. The bulk of our time may not be spent in Christ's immediate service; with most of us it cannot; but it is not the less the Lord's, occupied with what pleases him, and spent therefore with as good a conscience as if in actual waiting upon him. Only let us be sure of this, that if Mary's Christ be ours, he expects the same from us as from her. There is but one heaven for Magdalene and for us, and one way for her and for us into that heaven. There is only one Jesus Christ, the way to the Father, and substantially only one way of possessing and serving Christ. He is an undivided and complete Saviour to us as he was to her, sacrificing himself wholly for us, giving himself unreservedly to us, and bestowing on each of us all his salvation. But he is also the one and only Lord over us; he refuses to be for any man one of two masters; but demands from us, as from her, all our heart, all our substance, and all our time. 'If any man come to me, and hate not his father, and mother, and wife, and children, and brethren, and sisters, yea, and his own life also, he cannot be my disciple. Whosoever he be of you that forsaketh not all that he hath, he cannot be my disciple.' Luke 14:26, 33. These commands sound harsh and severe at first; but if once obeyed, Christ's yoke is always easy and his burden light, and in every acceptance of it there is rest to the soul. Let us therefore, through Christ Jesus, present our bodies a living sacrifice to God, for it is our reasonable service; being bought with a price, let us glorify God in our body and in our spirit, which are God's; and whether we eat, or drink, or whatsoever we do, let us do all to the glory of God. Rom 12:1; 1 Cor. 6:20; 10:31.

VI

MARY AS CHRIST'S CONSTANT FOLLOWER

'And many women were there, which followed Jesus from Galilee, ministering unto him; among which was Mary Magdalene.'—Matt. 27:55, 56

'Mary Magdalene, who also, when he was in Galilee, followed him and ministered unto him.'
—Mark 15:40, 41.

HAVING considered Mary Magdalene as Christ's servant, let us now look upon her in the kindred character of his follower; for while these two merge into one, they may be profitably contemplated apart. In this connexion we may study her example as following Christ's steps, hearing his word, seeing his works, and sharing his cross.

1. Mary follows Christ's steps

From the day of her deliverance out of the power of Satan till Christ's ascension to the Father's right hand, Mary's chief characteristic was the firm resolution, or rather the intense desire that superseded the need of resolution, *never to lose sight of Christ,* or else to strain every power of mind and body to recover the loss. Among all the men and women that believed in Jesus Christ, none equalled her in the singleness and intensity of this desire. The sister of Lazarus sat at the feet of Jesus, and heard his word in her brother's house, but Mary Magdalene followed him 'whithersoever he went.' The mother of Jesus was blessed above women in believing the word of promise, yet she is never named amongst the constant attendants on Christ's ministry. Magdalene was not called to behold the glory of Immanuel in the high mountain apart, nor the midnight agony of the Son of Man in the garden. But she followed Jesus to Calvary, first 'beholding afar off' and then 'standing by the cross,' and she watched him there through the great day of atonement. She waited while they took him down from the accursed tree; and when they bore him away to the tomb 'she followed after;' and while they interred their Lord, in the attitude of a mourner she 'sat over against the sepulchre, and beheld how his body was laid.' Other devout and honourable women accompanied her, but she is named first; not by accident, but as occupying the foremost place; as without doubt the most earnest, most active, and most persevering of them all. The dark and silent Sabbath past, she is first of them all at the sepulchre on the resurrection morning; coming 'while it was yet dark,' with the one object of her soul's desire not to lose Jesus. The sight of the vacant tomb sends a sharp pang through her heart; and she runs to tell the disciples, in the hope that they may find the Beloved of her soul. They come, and finding him not, they 'return to their own home.' But Mary has no home on earth without

Jesus; and she stands weeping at the sepulchre, on the spot where she had seen him last, since she cannot discover him now.

'These are they that follow the Lamb whithersoever he goeth.' How beautiful the picture, how attractive the company, how pleasant the thought of forming one of them! Mary is their representative. Even as Israel of old followed Christ in the pillar of cloud by day and of fire by night, resting when it rested, and journeying when it journeyed; so did Mary follow the Lord Jesus on earth, and so by grace may every believer follow the Lamb now. 'As many as are led by the Spirit of God, they are the sons of God.' It is Christ leading by grace, and Christ leading by providence; but one Christ leading. Grace and providence combine in one path. Grace moves providence, controls it, uses it, blesses it; providence ministers to grace in the soul, exercises it, proves it, gives it growth and vigour. They are two parts of one portion from the Lord; and with Mary providence and grace were manifestly together, when she followed Jesus in his journeys; as they were with believing Israel when they went after the cloudy pillar through the desert.

One evening, in the capital of Bavaria, I observed a flock of sheep passing along a crowded thoroughfare, with neither shepherd nor dog following them. Surrounded with people passing to and fro in the busy street, they seemed untended and unprotected as if within a quiet fold. Wondering at the sight, I looked again, and saw their shepherd walking slowly before them; an aged man of haply fourscore years, and the number of his flock about the same. He did not strive nor cry, nor make his voice to be heard in the street by others;

but 'his sheep heard his voice and followed him;' and he seemed to call them by name, for when he looked toward a straggler, it drew near at once to the flock. In the confusion of many sounds his voice alone they heard, and not the voice of strangers; in the midst of many passengers they followed his footsteps alone, and not the footsteps of another. He ever went in advance of his sheep; he trusted them to follow, and not one ever passed before him. The charge was an anxious one through the city; and he watched them with his eye, looking from side to side as he walked onward; but he never for one moment turned back, or left his own place at the head of his little flock. 'These are they that follow the Lamb whithersoever he goeth;' among the green pastures and by the still waters, along the rough road and the weary journey, through the crowded street and the strange and hostile world, they still follow the Lamb. He puts forth his own sheep, and goes before them, trusting that they will mark his steps, and hearken to his voice; saying, 'Surely they are my people, children that will not lie: so he is their Saviour.' Isa. 63:8.

Nothing else will make up to the believer for the loss of the Lamb of God, no apparent happiness in earth, no applauded usefulness in the church or in the world. 'The Bride, the Lamb's wife,' separate from the Lamb, is a weak and vain wanderer. It is ever 'an evil thing and bitter, to forsake the Lord our God' leading us by the way. Yet how common it is, how few are guiltless of the charge, how prone our heart, and how swift our feet to depart from the Lord! and after departure, how slow to return, and how inconstant to abide! Let us strive to hold fast the promise, 'Thou shalt call me, My Father, and shalt not depart from me.' Jer. 3:19.

2. Mary hears Christ's words

She hears them in the synagogue, by the way, at the table, and in the secret conclave.

1. In *the synagogue* Mary listened to the gracious words that proceeded out of his mouth, when he opened the Scriptures. Many enter the house of God following man, and they hear only the words of man; they enter it following the world or the church, and hear little else than the voice of the church or of the world. But Mary followed Jesus into the congregation; whether in the synagogue, in the temple, on the mountain, or on the sea-shore. She heard the words of Christ's lips with her ears, and she received the words of Christ's heart into her soul. 'My sheep hear my voice, and they follow me.' She heard her shepherd's voice and followed, following because she heard; she followed her shepherd's footsteps and heard, hearing because she followed. If the worshippers were following Jesus into the synagogue, the word would run and be glorified; it would run even through stammering lips, and be glorified in many that are ready to perish.

2. By *the way* she heard Christ's words. So do all who follow the Lamb continually. His were ever the lips of the righteous feeding many, his the well-spring of wisdom like a flowing brook; passing through the fields of corn and discoursing on the Sabbath made for man, sitting by the well of Sychar and promising living water, walking through the vineyards and revealing himself as the true vine, calling his followers to look upon and consider the white lilies before them clothed by their Father's skill, and the dark ravens above them fed by their Father's care.

In listening daily to such a teacher we count Mary's privilege inconceivably great, as indeed it was great beyond all price. Yet Christ's words sank no deeper than the Spirit planted them in her heart; and if we have as much of the Spirit as Mary, we shall have as much also of Christ. In our hands are the words of Jesus, the very words on which Mary fed. And if we have his words and keep them, we have himself in them, and they will never leave us night or day; for he saith to us from of old, 'My son, bind them continually upon thine heart, tie them about thy neck; when thou goest it shall lead thee, when thou sleepest it shall keep thee, and when thou awakest it shall talk with thee.' Prov. 6:21, 22.

3. At *the table* Mary ministering ate of heavenly bread, and drank of the new wine of the kingdom. At the table of Simon the Pharisee, she is privileged to listen to the sweetest of all utterances on earth, the Son of Man absolving from all her sins one who was chief among sinners; at the table of Zaccheus the publican, she hears him announce his coming to seek and save that which was lost; at the table of Simon the leper, she learns that every good work done to the Lord will be held by him in everlasting remembrance. Jesus is the same yesterday, today, and for ever. If he is invited and honoured as a guest at our tables, the Spirit even there will bring to our remembrance some of the gracious words which flowed from his lips on earth, and which still drop sweeter than honey out of the comb from his lips in heaven.

4. In *the secret conclave* Mary hearkened to Jesus. Sometimes he took only the twelve with him, as at the Last Supper and probably on other occasions; some times he chose three out of the twelve, as on the mount of his unveiled glory, and in the Gethsemane valley of the shadow

of death; and again he selected some of the twelve along with others, as in raising the dead child of Jairus, when he took Peter and James and John, with the father and mother of the maiden. This select yet mingled character marked the company that gathered about Jesus when 'he was alone, and expounded all things to his disciples;' the twelve apostles there, the seventy disciples or part of them, and doubtless the ministering matrons who followed Jesus. These private congregations must have substantially resembled that which afterwards met in the upper room at Jerusalem, where Peter and the apostles abode, along 'with the women, and Mary the mother of Jesus, and with his brethren.' In such assemblies when 'the doors were shut,' or when the 'desert place apart' as effectually excluded the outer world, Mary Magdalene heard her blessed Lord 'opening the Scriptures, and expounding all things to the disciples,' while most of all he opened their understanding to apprehend the words of life. In such meetings of two or three gathered in the name of Jesus, all the most earnest disciples still 'speak often one to another;' and not less than in the great congregation is the mind of the Lord revealed to those who thus wait upon him.

Jesus comes into these assemblies of ours when entreated by us; but from time to time he also says to such disciples as Mary, in his own self-moving love, 'Come ye yourselves apart into a desert place, and rest a while.' Those who follow him whithersoever he goes, he invites and draws by his word and Spirit to come apart for a little season, not only out of the world, but out of his own urgent work, to hold most sweet and secret fellowship with himself.

3. Mary sees Christ's works

It is her privilege to behold the work of the Lord in others; to be herself a witness before them of his mercy to her; and to meet with cases of deliverance closely resembling her own.

1. Next to experiencing the work of the Lord in our own hearts, is the happiness of beholding that work *in others*. It is an angelic joy, for 'there is joy in the presence of the angels of God over one sinner that repenteth;' it is a divine joy, for the Great Shepherd brings home his lost one, rejoicing and saying, 'Rejoice with me, for I have found my sheep that was lost.' In partaking of it we enter into the joy of our Lord; and nothing more effectually revives our souls in first love and first faith. It is high honour and privilege to be used by Christ in any of his wonderful works toward the sons of men. It is an almost equal privilege and honour to be called by him to witness those works, to be taken along with him when he raises the dead, and opens the eyes of the blind; for it is little more that any man ever does in the salvation of others, than stand by and behold the work of the Lord. It is a great loss to the believer to have no share, even as a spectator, in such transactions. You have reason to be apprehensive about your own place among the 'friends and neighbours' of the Good Shepherd, if he never calls you to rejoice over his lost sheep found. In such a case, you have cause to inquire if you have ever been numbered with his 'friends,' reconciled to him through his blood; or to fear lest having been once a friend, you have lost your place among the 'neighbours,' the people nigh unto him, and ready to be called to participate in his joys.

2. Mary following Jesus beholds his works, being herself one of the noblest of them all, a *living witness* to his almighty power and unsearchable love. All who looked on her saw Satan triumphed over, heaven filling a heart that had been occupied by the fiends of hell. She followed Christ, a living token of his grace, a constant encouragement to the most desperate to come to Jesus, or for their friends to bring them. There is nothing more helpful to the Lord's work, than for the healed to be gathered round the Saviour in presence of the sick. When others were charging stricken ones to hold their peace, or bidding them not to trouble the Master, surely Magdalene must often have whispered to them to be of good courage. Her voice must have been among the first to carry the cheering words, 'Be of good comfort, rise, he calleth thee.' Her prayer must oft have ascended for some weak one struggling in the crowd, that she might not depart unhealed. Such are the blessed privileges of all 'who follow the Lamb whithersoever he goeth;' and especially of those who follow him in a time of refreshing from the presence of the Lord.

3. In *one instance* above all others Mary's interest must have been intense, if she was called to cross the lake to Gadara. The demoniac in the tombs was healed after Mary had begun to minister to Jesus, and she may have been present at the cure. In that case, how rapt must her spirit have been from the first to the last of the scene! In this, the only example she had ever witnessed worse than her own, when his cry to Jesus was, 'I beseech thee, torment me not,' she must have been ever breathing the secret but intense supplication, 'Lord, cast those devils out.' And when he sits at the feet of Jesus, clothed and in his right mind, she

above all others must have entered into his joy, and aided in his new song of salvation to his God and her God, his Redeemer and her Redeemer.

If we follow the Lord wholly, he will bring us to some case more akin to our own than the most; in which we may see our own features even more deeply marked, and his power more gloriously revealed; yet even then he may reserve some grace for us and not for others, and may charge us, 'Let no man take thy crown.' A more marvellous monument of grace than Mary herself, this legionary demoniac sitting at the feet of Jesus seemed to be, yet he is refused what Mary receives. This privilege bestowed on her, of following the Lord everywhere, is denied to him; and he is sent home with a blessing, to testify to his own the wonderful works of the Lord. All are not called to be apostles, or ministers, or released from earthly duties to have no work on earth but following Jesus. Great as the grace of the Lord was toward him, he did not receive such a call, nor was it even granted to his petition. He had not the calling of the twelve or of the seventy, nor even the humbler calling of Magdalene. He was charged to remain at home, while she was privileged to follow Jesus to Jerusalem, to look on his cross, to watch at his tomb, to be the first witness of his resurrection, and even to be sent by him as the messenger of his word, an apostle to the apostles themselves.

It is a mistaken conclusion, that the last must of necessity be the first; that the lowest in sin must become the highest in grace. It is often otherwise even in the most marked conversions. 'Many that are last shall be first;' but not all, nor even perhaps the greater number. We often remark, 'That man will be first of all, for his conversion is so marvellous;'

and we find ourselves mistaken. He was an extraordinary sinner, but he is converted only into an ordinary saint. The Gadarene is last; he is lower than Mary; his legion of devils are many hundred times more than her seven. They are all cast out; the power put forth is greater; the deliverance wrought more marvellous; yet to her is the larger favour, the grace more exceeding abundant. He had been last, but she still continues first; according to the measure of the gift of the Spirit, distributing to every one severally as he wills.

Nature has a character of its own, and grace a character of its own; and it is impossible to judge from the natural character what the character of the whole man will be under grace. Nature modifies grace in every instance; because grace does not confer new faculties, but renews those already existing. Grace alters and re-makes the existing man. It cleanses the conscience, enlightens the understanding, renews the affections, turns the will. Yet in so working, it also comes with a character of its own. The mould in which the man was cast at birth, distinguishing him from all other men, will remain with him for ever; the image of God resting on him, instead of the image of Satan. But grace differs as well as nature, it may be as much; and that not merely in greater or less abundance, but in variety of type. 'Of his own will begat he us by the word of truth, that we should be a kind of first-fruits of his creatures.' In this new-birth we all have gracious peculiarities, just as in our first birth we have natural peculiarities. We receive grace 'differing' according to the impress of the gift of the Spirit; not simply grace less or more abundant according to the measure given, but differing also in character according to the gift of God.

The natural qualities such as mental vigour, which ought to minister to grace, often clog and hinder it by their very strength; while the natural deficiencies, which are expected to dim the lustre of grace, often only suffer it to shine forth in its own beauty. The Gadarene is farthest from God and from Christ; yet not he, but Mary is chosen to be nearest. He is possessed with an energy so tremendous for evil when excited by Satan, that he seems equal to vast apostolic efforts of burning zeal and love, when moved by the Holy Spirit; yet he is sent back to his own home with it all, while Mary is called to follow the Lord 'whithersoever he goeth.'

4. Mary shares Christ's cross

To the multitudes following, and to her, Jesus turned and said, 'If any man will come after me, let him deny himself, and take up his cross, and follow me.' Mary accepted the condition, she denied herself, took up her cross and followed. Jesus spoke the same words to me and to you, when we commenced to follow him; and have we accepted the burden? It is first Christ's cross for us, Christ crucified in our stead; most free for all our acceptance, and most sufficient for all our guilt and all our need. But it is next, our cross after him, and glorying in the cross of Christ whereby we are crucified. Jesus adds, 'Let him take up his cross daily and follow me;' Mary accepts the daily burden, as well as the daily salvation, and she follows Jesus daily, taking up her cross and following. The burden becomes heavier; the scorn of man increases; the words of Jesus become more sharp, and his sifting more exclusive for the little flock alone, and more humbling to the carnal mind. He declares more fully that none but the elect of the Father can come to the Son, and that there is no life for any human soul except in eating his flesh and drinking his blood. Thus far many have followed Jesus, but now they turn back once and for ever: 'From that time many of his disciples went back, and walked no more with him.' Mary follows still. The words of Jesus try her, but they never turn her away; for to whom can she go, but to him who has the words of everlasting life? Even then one of the twelve perseveres in whom Satan reigns; one who is a devil, and yet says, 'To whom shall we go? thou hast the words of eternal life.' Lord, is it I?

The cross grows heavier with appalling rapidity. Jesus tells the disciples plainly that he is to be delivered into the hands of men, and to be crucified. Very dimly they discern his meaning; but when he purposes to go up to Judea, they know fully the danger of that course: 'Master, the Jews of late sought to stone thee, and goest thou thither again?' Yet they agree with Thomas, 'Let us also go, that we may die with him.' It is no triumphal marching now, with the silver trump of glad tidings confirmed by signs and wonders; it is no eager throng of sufferers pressing round the healer; it is no crowd of listeners hanging on the gracious words that proceed out of the preacher's lips. It is a little company sorrowful and silent, following Jesus who leads them now to the city 'that killeth the prophets.' It is no longer the shepherd with loving eye looking abroad for some lost sheep to be gathered in; but the Man that is God's fellow, with the sword of the Father awaking against him, setting his face steadfastly to go up to Jerusalem, and straitened till the now mingled cup has been drunk. It is no longer Jesus in the heart of the multitude, who stand before him, and behind him, and on either side. But in advance of his disciples, and alone by himself, he walks before them all; and 'they are amazed, and as they follow they are afraid.' Mary too is amazed and afraid, yet she follows. She has counted the cost, she has taken up her cross, and through astonishment, sorrow, and fear, she still advances, following Jesus.

Even thus she follows on to the end, a true cross bearer with her Lord; to Calvary with all its blighted hopes, its manifold griefs, its astounding shame; to the tomb on the eve of the Sabbath about to commence, and to the tomb on the morrow when the Sabbath is over. But soon 'for shame she has double, and for confusion she rejoices in her portion.' Her Lord is risen, and shows himself first to Mary Magdalene. He takes off her sackcloth, and girds her with gladness, foreshadowing the everlasting joy that is now upon her head in the Father's house above. There the cross has been exchanged for the palm; the Lamb in the midst of the throne, whom she followed so closely on earth, is feeding and leading her unto fountains of living water; and God has wiped all tears from her eyes. And so also we, if we follow her as she followed Christ, shall enter into his rest, and shall go no more out, but shall reign with him for ever and ever. Amen.

VII

MARY THE PATIENT SEEKER OF
HER ABSENT LORD

'But Mary stood without at the sepulchre weeping:
and as she wept, she stooped down, and looked into
the sepulchre, and seeth two angels in white sitting,
the one at the head, and the other at the feet, where
the body of Jesus had lain. And they say unto her,
Woman, why weepest thou? She saith unto them,
Because they have taken away my Lord, and I know
not where they have laid him.'
—John 20:11-13

THE chief desire of Mary's life, as we have seen, is never
to lose sight of Jesus. They lead him to the cross, and
thither she follows, beholding him afar off; they bury him in
the grave, and there also she 'beholds how his body is laid.'
But the great stone is rolled to the door of the sepulchre,
the day sacred to holy quiet intervenes, and she 'rests on the
Sabbath according to the commandment.' Before the dawn
of another morning she hastens to the tomb in search of
Jesus; and we would now consider her earnest seeking, her

mistaking gain for loss in the search, and her quiet waiting.

1. Mary's earnest seeking of her absent Lord

Mary was first found by Jesus when she was lost, and now she seeks Jesus lost by her. Many are thus found by Christ, who have not sought him; like Matthew sitting at the receipt of custom, when he is called to follow the Lamb. The word enters, and life with the word; and heart and will close with the call. But Mary is the most marked of her class; because she was first healed, before any incipient response on her part, and then called to follow. Now in many souls thus saved without long previous search, there is a great crisis when grace freely given is succeeded by grace requiring to be sought. The abundant manna falling openly round the camp is cheerfully gathered, without labour as without price. But after a season Jesus says to the soul, 'To him that overcometh will I give to eat of the hidden manna.' Rev. 2:17. It is still the bread of life as before; it is equally without money as at first; but the call now comes, 'Labour for the meat that endureth unto ever-lasting life, which the Son of Man shall give.' John 6:27. Many in this hour refuse the labour, refuse to seek and strive, refuse to obtain by overcoming. Some turn aside altogether under such a trial, proving that they had never truly tasted that the Lord is gracious. Others sadly fail in earnest seeking, and never make that progress in grace which their first start promised.

But Mary is a noble example of a soul seeking an absent Christ. None was ever more found by him without seeking at first, and none ever sought him more earnestly afterward when he was gone. This is grace, both real and abundant;

variously adapting itself to the varying lot of the soul. Having received at first with no effort put forth to obtain, she afterwards strains every nerve to find, as if all depended on the effort.

Love moves her to an early seeking; when it is yet dark, she comes to the sepulchre. 'They that seek me early shall find me,' said the Redeemer of old; with promise not of early, but of certain finding to the early seeker. Early Mary seeks, early she does not seem to find, yet she will find surely in the end. 'I sought him, but I found him not,' is now her dark complaint. Knowledge has vanished away, faith is bewildered, hope is benighted. Love alone remains unshaken and undiminished; for 'love is strong as death, and many waters can not quench it, neither can the floods drown it.' Song of Sol. 8:6, 7.

2. Her mistake of gain for loss in seeking

Mary mistakes gain for loss through unbelief; every believer does; and unbelief erases Christ's words from the memory.

1. The mistake is the fruit of *unbelief,* and of such unbelief as we should think inexcusable; yet the Lord does not condemn her for it, but rewards the seeking, and forgives the unbelief. This is a singular comfort to weak believers. There is a strange mingling of strength and weakness in the faith of the disciples, or rather of strength of love with weakness of faith. Mary believed in the Lord Jesus Christ to the saving of her soul. Yet she never fully believed his own words that he should die, till he was actually dead; and when dead she disbelieved his words that he should rise again, and that not only till he rose, but after he was actually risen. But the Lord bears with her, and with all his weak

disciples, who follow on through weakness and darkness, clinging to him in love.

The empty sepulchre filled Mary with grief, when it should have made her shout for joy. Hope was at its lowest ebb when Jesus expired on the cross, though that death was the opened door of eternal life for the lost. But with Mary hope sunk lower still; the vacant tomb was her last death-blow. The dead Christ was much to Mary, was all to her; was more than all others living. Christ living had been her life; Christ dead is still all her life; but Christ away is death. More faith would have rejoiced in the tenantless tomb; for Jesus out of the sepulchre was really a glad tiding of great joy. Yet it is the darkest passage in all Mary's life: 'They have taken away my Lord, and I know not where they have laid him.'

2. With *every believer* the valley of Achor is the manifold door of hope, from first to last through all his course. It is not merely that God gives an escape out of evil, with the temptation providing a way of deliverance; but it often is, that the seeming evil is actual good. That which we count the greatest of all ills; that of which we say, All might be borne but this; that which is dark as the gloom of midnight, with no star twinkling through it; that ultimately is the very dawning of the day. Christ in the sepulchre, so welcome to Mary, would really of all things have been the saddest for her; Christ not risen; therefore she, and we, 'of all men most miserable.' Christ out of the sepulchre is Mary's greatest good, though received by her with a new overflow of deepest, bitterest sorrow. So it ever is. Christ is resurrection and life; our death with him is only unto a new resurrection; and the Lord our God ever causeth all our darkness

to be light. Even as what we take for greatest good is oft our sorest trial, so our darkest day is oft the fullest with unfading brightness. Redemption, resurrection, salvation, transform all evil into good through Jesus Christ our Lord. That which we greatly fear, which we strive against, which we pray against, actually comes; comes in darkness and sorrow; but comes as the herald of life, health, and joy.

3. Unbelief in Christ's followers brings with it a strange *forgetfulness* of his words; and it is indeed the Spirit of Christ who brings to our remembrance whatsoever he has spoken. The enemies of Christ had heard some words of his about his resurrection; they took them in their natural sense, they remembered them well; and after they had crucified him, they could not rest without sealing his sepulchre, and watching it with a guard of armed men. But Christ's foes had more fear and jealousy of his resurrection, than his friends had hope. His disciples had heard in secret ten words for one that the Lord had publicly uttered on the subject; yet with the treacherous memory of unbelief, they let them all slip from their minds like idle tales, and lost them in the hour they needed them most. It is what all believers often do. Also even now, the words that Christ speaks through his servants, when little noticed by friends, are often fastened like goads in the heart of his enemies; and his work in its first beginnings frequently creates more opposition and fear amongst his foes, than joy amongst his followers.

3. Her quiet waiting

She waited patiently, she waited alone, she waited fearlessly.

1. Mary waited *patiently*; for her 'love suffered long' in waiting for Jesus. It was Mary's love that moved her to

wait and look for Jesus; it was ignorance and unbelief that kept her waiting in the dark; yet Jesus did not chide the unbelief, while he gave a glorious reward to the love. Faith might have saved the waiting; faith in the assurance that Christ would rise again. Knowledge might have saved it; the knowledge of the fact of the resurrection, which the sight of the linen clothes and the napkin should have added to the faith in its promise. Yet Mary's love sought more and obtained more than John's knowledge and faith. Peter and John entered the tomb where the linen clothes lay in order, and the napkin wrapped up by itself; and John at least both saw and believed. The 'place where the Lord lay,' so quietly arranged, conveyed more to his mind than to Mary's; but he was satisfied with less. He saw, believed, and 'returned to his own home;' he was assured of Christ's foreknowledge in foretelling his resurrection, and of his power in breaking the bonds of death; and he was satisfied without seeing Jesus.

Mary believed less and knew less, but she loved more. No well-ordered but empty tomb could ever satisfy her soul. She would have been content with less of Christ, but not without Christ at all. A dead Christ would have contented her for the time, seeing she could have no more; but Christ gone would never have satisfied her, till she knew that he could not be found. John believed the empty tomb, he saw and believed; yet Jesus he saw not, and he was blessed in not seeing, yet believing. He was more blessed than doubting Thomas, who believed in Jesus risen only when he saw him; yet Mary was more blessed than John, in waiting for Jesus till she found him. John did better than Mary in believing; Mary better than John in waiting; John got sooner, but

Mary got more. Love moved Mary to run to bring the apostles to the empty tomb; and love fixed Mary like a statue at the tomb, till she saw her Lord. There is a blessed believing, in simple trust even in darkness; and there is a still more blessed waiting, that will take no contentment till God shines in the heart, giving the light of the knowledge of his glory in the face of Jesus Christ. 2 Cor. 4:6.

'They shall not be ashamed that wait for me;' and the Lord makes good his word to the waiting soul, even when it waits in much ignorance and lack of faith. 'Be of good courage, and he shall strengthen your heart,' all ye that wait on the Lord; 'for the Lord is good unto them that wait for him, to the soul that seeketh him; my soul, wait thou only upon God.' Psa. 27:14; Lam. 3:25; Psa. 62:5.

2. Mary waited *alone;* waited, wept, and sought by herself. Nothing tries the soul so thoroughly. Many seek Jesus, moved by the example and company of others; it is the mind of others working in them, rather than their own. It is good to be moved to seek in any way; good to be provoked to love by those around us; but it is solitude that tests and proves the soul. Mary did not slight the company of others in seeking for Christ; she both sought their society and asked their aid. She is the first seeker on the morn of the resurrection, and she is the last; she comes early while it is yet dark, and she waits till all the others have gone. She takes the other women with her to anoint the body of Jesus; and not finding him, she runs to bring the apostles to search for him. They leave without finding, the other women also leave without finding, and Mary waits alone. She waits and weeps; she waits and stoops into the sepulchre; she waits and inquires.

Alone Mary waits. The rest are with their companions in Jerusalem, mourning and weeping; some of the women are trembling and rejoicing at what the angels have told them; but Mary weeps alone. She loved the church, but the church had not redeemed her; she loved her Lord's servants, but they were nothing to her without her Lord. She *must* find Jesus. If she find him not, she can only weep; but she will wait and weep without a single friend, if so be she may haply find. It were well for us, if we sought Christ more in solitude. 'Enter into thy closet, and when thou hast shut thy door, pray to thy Father which is in secret, and thy Father which seeth in secret shall reward thee openly.' Matt. 6:6. Mary sought and found by herself, even as she sought for herself; alone in seeking, alone in finding; and both seeking and finding for her own soul. She sought at first along with others, and in their name as well as in her own; 'They have taken away the Lord,' she said to the apostles, 'and we know not where they have laid him.' But afterwards she sought alone and for herself: 'They have taken *my* Lord,' she said to the angels, 'and I know not where they have laid him.' And it was in the personal seeking of Jesus, that she received a glorious message to carry to others. She sought and found Christ for herself, and then Christ sent her as his faithful messenger to the rest; the bearer of the words which she had heard, the witness of the Lord whom she had seen.

It is not what we seek for others, that usually profits them most. Commonly God makes us seek and find for ourselves, and then testify to others what we have seen, and speak what we know. It is the lack of this element that makes much of our preaching so powerless; for it is the God-taught man who is the God-sent messenger. It is

Christ found by us for our own souls in solitude, who is Christ preached by us on the house-tops, and so lifted up that all men are drawn to him. 'If they had stood in my counsel, and heard and marked my word, they should have turned the people from their evil way.' Jer. 23:18-22.

So it is with the ministers of the everlasting gospel in their public testimony; and so it is with every follower of Jesus by whom the Lord would send a message to a perishing soul. Have you sought Christ alone? Have you shut the door, and prayed in secret till you found him whom the Father, 'that seeth in secret,' reveals to the inquiring soul?

3. Mary waited *fearlessly;* for her love cast out fear in seeking Jesus. In more respects than one 'there is no fear in love, but perfect love casteth out fear.' In all the rest fear for the moment prevailed against love; but in Mary love banished all fear of every kind, all *natural* dread, and all supernatural. She makes no account of the terrors of the night in going out of the city to the sepulchre, while it is yet dark; she cares as little for the greater terrors of the day, when she returned to the city and back again to the tomb, and tarried there under the risen sun without the least impression of the dread of man. The others are hasty in all their movements; 'for fear of the Jews,' coming quickly and tarrying briefly. Mary ran for Peter and John to help her to find Jesus, but returning to the tomb she 'stood without,' weeping. She gives no heed to the fact that the others, brethren and sisters, all have gone away and she is left alone. 'There is no fear in love.' She cares nothing for the appearance of friend or foe, except in so far as they may tell her of Jesus. She sees a stranger whom she takes for the gardener, and his presence neither awes nor disturbs her, nor turns

her one moment from her object. She finds in him only another hope of obtaining some clue to the resting place of him whom her soul loveth. 'Sir, if thou have borne him hence, tell me where thou hast laid him, and I will take him away;' in admirable oblivion also of her own strength, so unequal to such a burden, however beloved.

But her love is even more remarkable in overcoming the fear of the *supernatural*. It is impossible to draw nigh to Jesus without coming to companies of angels, who are always ascending and descending by the Son of Man, as the ladder of their intercourse between heaven and earth. Jesus is ever in the midst of angels; in his annunciation, in his birth, in his temptation, in his agony, in his sepulchre, in his resurrection, in his ascension, and in the presence of his Father. When it is declared to us, 'Ye are come to Jesus, the mediator of the new covenant,' it is immediately added, 'and to an innumerable company of angels.' Heb. 12:22. Selected messengers from that host appeared 'in divers manners' at the tomb of Jesus on the morning of the resurrection. For fear of one of them, with his countenance exceeding terrible, the keepers trembled and became as dead men; at the sight of another Mary's companions were affrighted, and they ran with his message, silent and amazed. But Mary, stooping into the sepulchre, 'seeth two angels, one at the head and the other at the feet, where the body of Jesus had lain.' The angels at the head and the feet of Jesus agree with the cherubim at each end of the mercy-seat; looking toward each other, and bending over the mercy-seat and the ark of the covenant, into which things the angels desire to look. This attitude of the angels at the tomb suggests to us Christ as the true ark of the covenant, with the 'law within his heart,' like the tables within the ark; and Christ as the true mercy-seat, sprinkled with his own blood, over which God is seated as on his throne of grace, dispensing pardon to the guilty; 'God in Christ reconciling the world unto himself, not imputing unto them their trespasses.' 2 Cor. 5:19.

That cherubim and seraphim should wait as holy ministers around her crucified Lord, seems nothing marvellous to Mary. 'He is the chiefest among ten thousand, and altogether lovely;' he is worthy of such attendants; and their appearance does not distract her for a moment from her search, nor arrest one drop of her fast-flowing tears. Their presence had filled the sepulchre with glory and with awe to every other beholder, but to Mary they are simply ministering servants at her Lord's empty grave.

It is the emptiness of the tomb alone that she sees. Christ not there goes more to her heart than a legion of angels there can affect either her senses or her thoughts. She does not fear, she does not even wonder; for the one thought, Where is Jesus? fills her whole being, and leaves no room for a second, however great. It is ever so, that the one thing truly great absorbing the soul makes other great things little, because they are only secondary and infinitely less. The great salvation, the great Saviour sought, how little then are the great things of earth; nay, the secondary great things in heaven or in hell, how little they become! The supernatural had been more familiar to Mary than to most. The seven devils that lodged within her had not been cast out without leaving in her memory many a terrible passage of intercourse with things unseen, and many a helpful lesson for the time to come. Those glorious angels in white could not have cast one fiend of the pit out of her soul; and they are nothing in contrast with him who had cast the seven forth, and translated her out of darkness into his own marvellous light.

Mary sees these heavenly ones, their glistening raiment, their several positions. On the sad eve of the Sabbath, sitting on the ground mournfully over against the sepulchre, she beheld how the body of Jesus was laid. She knew the resting-place of her Lord's head, and the resting-place of his feet; she has now seen enough to know that he is gone, but still she stoops inquiring and weeping over 'the place where they laid him.' She takes quiet note of the angels; that the one sits over against the head, and the other over against the feet, of Jesus no more, but 'where the body of Jesus had lain.' She looks on them, enough to make sure that neither of them is her Lord, and then she seems to weep afresh with more abundant sorrow. She makes no inquiry of them, and they put one brief question to her, 'Woman, why weepest thou?'—these words depicting her whole state. They soothe not her, like the other women, with 'Be not afraid;' for such is not the comfort that Mary needs. To them the angel speaks with words of encouragement, as one excelling in strength; and then tenderly invites them to enter and examine the tomb—'Come, see the place where the Lord lay.' But to Mary the angels speak as in reverence for her grief. They see that she entertains no fear of them; that her Lord's sepulchre is more to her than to them; that she is studying for herself 'the place where her Lord lay,' without any invitation from them. They address her simply and briefly, yet respectfully, not willing too rashly to intermeddle with her grief, 'Woman, why weepest thou?' Mary replies, 'Because they have taken away my Lord, and I know not where they have laid him.' I am weeping; let earth and heaven know the cause; there is nothing worthy of men or angels to think of but this, 'They have taken away my Lord.'

O heroine among women, princess among the daughters of Israel, 'not afraid with any amazement!' Cherubim and seraphim she answers, as calmly and simply as she would a child. Other women would have thought, 'Are these bright ones looking on a weak woman; are they marking my tears; are they addressing themselves to me?' They would have trembled and been silent, or have fallen like John at their feet to worship. Mary sees nothing, hears nothing, knows nothing, but her deep heart-sorrow, and the cause of it, her absent Lord. And when the angels ask the reason of her grief, she tells it simply, then turns away, as finding nothing in them, and seeking if light may spring up elsewhere. When she had so said 'she turned back.' The tomb no longer attracts her, Christ is not there, and the Christless tomb has no charm for her. Christ is elsewhere, out of the tomb, and therefore she turns from it in sorrow; somewhere else, if she only knew where, is more attractive to her. 'The place where the Lord lay,' is not her demand, but the place where the Lord now rests; 'I know not where they have laid him.'

O wondrous, fearless love; love that nothing can diminish, nothing disturb! Glorious demonstration, that 'neither death nor life, nor angels nor principalities nor powers, nor things present nor things to come, nor height nor depth, nor any other creature, shall be able to separate us from the love of God which is in Christ Jesus our Lord.' Rom. 8:38, 39.

Yours, believer, is the same Lord Jesus that Mary loved, and the same loving Redeemer. The object of your love is equal to hers, is the very same; and his love to you is not less than to her. To Mary and to you his love is unto death for your sake, and this measure can never be exceeded. Nay more, yours is the same love as hers; it is wrought in you by the same Spirit; it comes from above, among the good gifts of the same Father. Less cherished and less abounding it may have been; but in itself it is equally true, equally intense, equally constant, equally persevering in presence and in absence. If the Holy Ghost is in you, there is in you the spirit of all attachment to Christ; and if you straiten not the Spirit, your heart will ever go out toward him even as did hers.

Meanwhile, sitting far beneath her, we honour, we love, we thank Mary Magdalene for so loving our Lord Jesus Christ; and fain would we learn to follow her in that matchless devotion to her Lord and ours, her Saviour and ours. Amen.

VIII

MARY FINDING CHRIST

*'And when she had thus said, she turned herself back,
and saw Jesus standing, and knew not that it was
Jesus. Jesus saith unto her, Woman, why weepest
thou? whom seekest thou? She, supposing him to be
the gardener, saith unto him, Sir, if thou have borne
him hence, tell me where thou hast laid him, and I
will take him away. Jesus saith unto her, Mary.'*
—John 20:14-16

THE scene last contemplated is now entirely altered; seeking is changed into finding, absence into presence, darkness into light. The scene is altered both suddenly and slowly; suddenly in fact, for Christ sought among the dead reveals himself alive; slowly in apprehension, for though seen he is at first unknown. Mary finds Jesus, but does not recognize him when found; he asks of her the object of her search, and reveals himself.

1. Mary finds Jesus

'She turned herself back, and saw Jesus standing.' Christ's

manifested presence is in answer to faithful promise, yet in sovereign mercy.

1. This remarkable example stamps with a seal of distinguishing honour *the promise,* 'Seek and ye shall find.' It is the first of the promises fulfilled after Christ's resurrection from the dead; they are all yea and amen in him, all equally sure, yet this is brought into light before any other. It is by an early, earnest, and patient seeker, that the risen Jesus is first found. This great fact speaks to us in this wise: Get as near to Christ as you can; seek for him in the closet, where he is in secret; in the house of God, that Mount Zion which is his rest; in the meeting of two or three together, where he stands in the midst of them; in the words of eternal life, by which he reveals himself. Go and seek him thus, for it is good for you to draw nigh to God. Draw as nigh as you can; and believe his promise, that in drawing nigh to him he will draw nigh to you.

2. Yet it is purely of *sovereign grace* that Jesus is revealed to Mary. 'She goes forward, but he is not there, and backward, but cannot perceive him; on the left hand where he worketh, but she cannot behold him; he hideth himself on the right hand, that she cannot see him.' The discovery of the clothes and the napkin is the simple fruit of diligent and early search; for a later inquiry might have found them disturbed or removed. But no striving and running of bodily effort, no exercise of mind and spirit, no intenseness of desire, no acuteness of thought, no fervour of love, can avail to discern or to grasp the living, unseen One. 'Who can by searching find him out?' There is a gracious bond of connexion in the promise to the seeker. But in the nature of things, Mary waiting at the tomb has no more power to

discover Jesus, than Peter and John in their own houses. In point of fact, Jesus afterward revealed himself on the way to Emmaus unto two disciples who were not seeking him; although that also fulfilled the words, that 'they that feared the Lord spake one to another, and the Lord hearkened and heard.' Yet how sovereign is it all, how helpless is man toward it, how incapable by any effort of reaching the hidden One!

Jacob at the brook wrestles with the angel, till he is blessed before the breaking of the day; for through grace inworking, the worm can so prevail with the mighty One. But how can Jacob find the One, to have the opportunity of so glorious and fruitful a conflict? Like Mary alone in the garden, Israel her father is alone by the brook, 'and there wrestled a man with him.' But how did he meet that Man? His solitude could not reveal him, his prayer cannot force him into light and sensible presence. It is of mere sovereign grace that the covenant Angel reveals himself to Jacob, 'greatly afraid and distressed.' So likewise it is to Israel's genuine daughter; not indeed afraid like her father, but like him 'greatly distressed.' In sovereign grace, love, and pity, Jesus manifests himself to Mary. Nevertheless sovereign mercy has attached itself to the faithful promise, so that the true seeker can never be put to shame. Such tears also, as Mary's, have a power to touch the heart of Jesus, which in his condescension he cannot resist, and to which he cannot but reveal himself. As Joseph can no longer refrain from disclosing himself to his sorrowing brethren; so Jesus cannot conceal himself from Jacob, when he 'weeps and makes supplication,' nor from Mary when she stands at the sepulchre weeping; nor from you, poor sorrowful suppliant, waiting for him as those that watch for the morning. Take to yourself the ever memorable words of that noble servant of God, John Knox, not by inspiration yet most aptly expressing inspired truth: 'The patient abiding of the sorely afflicted was never yet confounded.'

2. Mary does not recognize Christ found

'And she knew not that it was Jesus' is Mary's case, and the lively portrait of inquirers to this day.

1. Mary *knows not* Jesus when she finds him. She sees him and mistakes him for a stranger, she hears him and his words carry no comfort to her soul. She asks Jesus to tell her where Jesus is; she passes by Christ in order to find Christ. She seeks an absent and distant Saviour; and the Saviour present and close beside her she does not perceive. She 'seeks the living among the dead;' inquiring after Christ crucified, and not recognizing him in Christ risen. Having before her the image of what Christ to her mind ought to be, she cannot recognize him in what he actually is. Like the woman at the well of Sychar, she speaks to the Messiah present concerning a Messiah of her own conception. It is indeed good to ask Christ for Christ, in the Lord to seek the Lord, in the Spirit to pray for the Spirit. But Mary asks Christ present for an absent Christ, the true Christ for an imagined Christ; which is fruitless seeking, except for the grace of God pardoning our weakness and sin.

2. It is the vivid picture of *inquirers* to this hour. They seek a distant Christ, and reject Christ present. Jesus is near them, before them, with them; he is speaking to them in his word, he is listening to their prayer. And they are running to the ends of the earth in quest of him; turning from him

where he is, to seek him where he is not. He is not distant; and if they could reach the distance where they fancy him to be, they should not find him there, for he is not to be found except where he is. But he is near them; and the moment they recognize his nearness, they possess him. 'Say not in thine heart, Who shall ascend into heaven? that is, to bring Christ down from above; or, Who shall descend into the deep? that is, to bring up Christ again from the dead. But what saith it? The word is nigh thee, even in thy mouth, and in thy heart.' Rom. 10:6-8.

This error, which we are so expressly warned against, we invariably fall into at our first inquiry after God. We have some vague, yet stubborn idea of a Christ whom we must climb for, or dig for, or traverse sea and land for, and no other Christ will satisfy us; till we are brought back like a little child, and find Christ standing at the very spot which we were leaving in the certainty that he was not there. So also we seek his Spirit, without whom we cannot discern him; and the Spirit speaks to us in the word, convincing and leading us to Jesus; and we refuse the very Spirit which we are asking. The words that Christ speaks are 'spirit and life;' and we seek some quickening spirit apart from the words of Jesus. But the Comforter coming convinces us that our sin consists in refusing a freely given and a present Christ; and we believe and are saved.

But we oft repeat our inquiry after a distant Saviour, and refuse the Saviour who is talking with us. 'Behold, I stand at the door and knock; if any man hear my voice, and open the door, I will come in to him, and sup with him, and he with me.' Jesus stands and knocks at the door of Mary's heart: Woman, whom seekest thou? why weepest thou? Mary knows not the voice of Jesus, and opens not the door to welcome him; yet she is earnestly seeking him all the while. At how many doors is an unknown Christ now standing; of how many sinners, of how many saints? Many are asleep and heedless; but many others are blindly crossing his purposes with their own, and defeating their own desires. He stands at *your* door knocking, and it remains closed against him, because you know not his voice, nor his loving readiness to enter your heart and abide with you. You stand at *his* door knocking, it is thrown wide open to receive you, yet you will not enter in; because you believe not his loving welcome to the chief of sinners, his blessed assurance: 'Him that cometh unto me I will in no wise cast out.'

3. Mary is asked by Jesus the object of her search

'Jesus saith unto her, Woman, why weepest thou? whom seekest thou?' He ever demands of the suppliant the object of his desire; and teaches us to make our petitions special.

1. Christ knew whom Mary sought, and wherefore Mary wept, yet *asks* her whom she seeks, and why she weeps. It is the Saviour's manner, and like all his ways is full of meaning and instruction. The blind man at Jericho cries, 'Jesus, thou son of David, have mercy on me;' and will not be stopped either by Christ's silence, or the people's chiding. All know the one mercy which he needs and implores. Jesus commands him to be called, he comes, and Jesus asks, 'What wilt thou that I should do unto thee?' 'Lord, that I might receive my sight.' Mark 10:51. So here, when he is about to wipe away Mary's tears, and reveal him whom her soul seeks, he first inquires whom she is seeking, and wherefore she weeps; for it is not merely 'seek and ye shall find,' but 'ask and ye shall receive.'

Mary had sought, and is finding; Jesus will have her also ask, that she may receive. 'O my dove, in the clefts of the rock, in the secret places of the stairs, let me see thy countenance, let me hear thy voice; for sweet is thy voice, and thy countenance comely.' Song of Sol. 2:14. If believers did only believe how pleasant their asking is to their Lord, as well as profitable for themselves, they would seldomer need the reproof, 'Ye have not, because ye ask not.'

2. A lesson is given us of definiteness and *specialty* in our petitions. The blind man implores mercy; it seems humbler to make the supplication general, and to leave the special mercy to the wisdom and grace of the giver; but Christ will not have it so. He will not have it referred merely to his pleasure, but will know the man's own desire, and will hear his special petition. It is Christ alone that can work it—'What shall I do unto thee?'—but he will have the suppliant expressly name his own particular want, and utter his own definite desire. It is not 'What will Christ do unto thee?' but 'What wilt thou that I do unto thee?' A vague and general prayer may spring from a general and doubtful faith. Its result is only a vague and uncertain answer; a misty glory is all that it ascribes to the grace and power of the Lord; and a seal scarcely legible all that it stamps on the faith of the suppliant. A special prayer tests the genuineness of faith in the Lord's ear to hear, and in his arm to save. Its distinct and special answer gives unchallenged and undivided honour to Christ, unto whom or in whose name it had been offered, and sets a seal from heaven on faith in Jesus which he that runs may read.

There is often indeed a rash specialty, an offensive peremptoriness in prayer; which is apt to scare the humble soul, lest it should run into the vainglorious emptiness and provocation of such petitions. Yet the definite, and earnest expression of our own desire has in it nothing contrary to the most entire resignation, but is rather the best preparation for it. It is after uttering our own will, that we can most fully leave it in the Lord's hands and say, Not my will but thine be done. The children of God, most exercised in deep submission, will commonly be found to be the most specific in their requests, both for the greatest things and for the least. Their definite petitions are sometimes so great as to appear too bold, and sometimes so minute as to seem trivial; yet in both, wisdom justifies herself in her children.

Does some thorn in the flesh seem to you too small to trouble the Lord with, because your own hand can easily pluck it out? You try and fail; it sinks as a keen thorn into your side, as a sharp grain of sand into your eye; it becomes embedded in your flesh; and you learn to your cost, that it can only be extracted by another hand than your own. If you are to have deliverance at all, you must get it now by asking.

Inquiring soul, the Lord Jesus is saying to you in tenderest love, 'Whom seekest thou, why weepest thou?' Tell him whom you seek, open to him all your desire: 'My Lord is away, and I know not whither he is gone.' Silence may probably be all the reply; silence, and perhaps withdrawal. 'I will go and return to my place, till they acknowledge their offence and seek my face; in their affliction they will seek me early.' Hos. 5:15. Confess your sin, and seek his face, and rest not till you find him. Or if you have some burden of your own besides his absence, or a burden for others, still press to see himself first, and then tell him your sorrow. Esther, burdened unto death for her people, is asked by the king, 'What wilt thou, Queen Esther, and what is thy request?' And she first petitions, 'Let the king come to the banquet I have prepared for him,' before she opens the burden of her heart. The king first, the king's presence, the king's favour; and after obtaining that, she supplicates, 'Let my life be given me at my petition, and my people at my request.' Go thou and do likewise.

4. Mary has Christ discovered to her

'Jesus saith unto her, Mary.' He reveals himself; calls Mary to her own remembrance; grants her fellowship with himself; and speaks to us as unto her.

1. Christ *reveals himself*; 'Jesus saith, Mary.' Jesus utters one word, that word is her name, and no more; yet it is all. 'The Lord whom ye seek shall suddenly come to his temple, even the Messenger of the Covenant, whom ye delight in.' Christ is intensely desired, and diligently sought by Mary; yet in the end he comes suddenly. It is his customary manner; for he is the same yesterday, today, and for ever. It was his manner of coming yesterday to Mary; it is his manner of coming to me and to you today. He bears long, and then he answers speedily; he bears long, proving us; he answers speedily, that no flesh may glory in his presence. So it was in the first opening of the gospel kingdom; the Spirit expected and prayed for, then coming suddenly as a rushing mighty wind from heaven. So it will be in the close of this kingdom, and the ushering in of the eternal: 'As the lightning, that lighteneth out of the one part under heaven, shineth unto the other part under heaven; so shall also the Son of man be in his day.' Luke 17:24. So is it in a thousand

waiting souls today. All is distance, darkness, chaos; till in a moment Jesus rends the veil and says, 'Mary'; says, 'It is I.'

His words do not say 'I am Jesus,' but his voice declares it; and this first touches Mary's heart. It is her own name uttered, but it is her own name in Christ's lips. 'It is the voice of my Beloved; behold, he standeth behind our wall, he showeth himself through the lattice.' Song of Sol. 2:8, 9. It is not, 'Thou art Mary, but I am Jesus;' for it is 'Mary' uttered by Jesus, and Jesus rather than Mary in the utterance. It is the Shepherd's voice, and his sheep know that voice. These were indeed the Shepherd's words before, 'Whom seekest thou, why weepest thou?' the words of Jesus, but not in the well-known voice of Jesus. Christ's words oft reveal him not to the soul; the whole Bible speaks, and he is not there; but one word by the Spirit makes him known. Now it is one single word of Christ to Magdalene in his own recognized voice; and all Christ is in it. What pity, what kindness, what tenderness, what love in the utterance! All Christ's heart goes with it, pouring itself out to the sorrowing one, his redeemed. One word brings before her JESUS; all that he has done in her behalf, all that he has been to her, and all that he is in his own loveliness.

2. 'Mary' uttered by the voice of Jesus, is also Mary *recalled to her own remembrance:* Mary once 'the habitation of devils, the hold of every foul spirit, the cage of every unclean and hateful bird;' Mary in all her sin and alienation from God, in all her wretchedness in this world, in all her fearful looking for of judgment in the world to come; Mary choosing to have it so, resisting the kingdom of heaven come to her, and rejecting her Saviour and her King; Mary with the devils cast out by the Spirit of God, become as a

little child, and entering the kingdom; Mary 'following the Lamb whithersoever he goeth,' walking up and down in the name of the Lord; Mary bereaved, overwhelmed, desolate, yet weeping, watching, clinging to all that remained of her lost Redeemer; Mary distrustful and forgetful, seeking the living among the dead, not remembering her Lord's words that he must rise again from the dead the third day; Mary known and recognized by Jesus, the good Shepherd who knows his sheep, and calls his own sheep by name; Mary, her inmost name known by Jesus, all her history, all her heart, all of evil and good, of light and darkness, of sorrow and joy, of grace received and grace abused, all that gathers round that name known to Jesus as to none other in all the earth; 'Mary' uttered by the Shepherd's voice, every other voice besides only the voice of a stranger, of one that knows her not at all, or knows her only in part; but this the voice of the Shepherd, who knows her altogether. 'O Lord, thou hast searched me, and known me; thou knowest my down-sitting and mine up-rising; thou art acquainted with all my ways; thou knowest my foolishness, and my sins are not hid from thee; thou hast known my soul in adversity; O Lord, thou knowest thy handmaid; Lord, thou knowest all things, thou knowest that I love thee.'

3. It is *mutual fellowship* between the Shepherd and his sheep, when Jesus says to her, 'Mary.' 'I know my sheep, and am known of mine, as I know the Father, and as the Father knoweth me; as the Father hath loved me, so have I loved you;' Mary knowing Jesus and known by him, as only the Father knows the Son and the Son the Father; knowing and known, as in no earthly friendship however close. Her name is uttered with a tenderness of love and fulness

of meaning, such as the word never bore from the lips of
father or mother; such as never from the lips of brother or
sister; such as never from the lips of husband and guide of
youth. 'I have called you friends, for all things that I have
heard of my Father, I have made known unto you; greater
love hath no man than this, that a man lay down his life for
his friends.' John 15:13, 15.

But the soul seeking Jesus may ask, Will he speak thus *to
me,* even as he spoke to Magdalene? did not her following
him on earth make some difference of personal acquaintance? Doubtless we shall never see Jesus face to face as they
saw him on earth, till we behold him in glory. With us it
must be, 'whom having not seen we love, in whom though
now we see him not, yet believing we rejoice with joy
unspeakable and full of glory.' Yet the difference is not really
great after all. Because *first,* it is the risen Jesus that speaks
to Mary; and after the resurrection Christ never allowed the
same familiarity in his disciples. He was no longer known
by them 'after the flesh,' as he had been before; and his intercourse more resembled his present spiritual fellowship with
believers. In this resurrection state Christ addresses not
only Mary thus by name, but in like manner the doubting
Thomas, and Simon the son of Jonas. *Next,* Jesus was more
fully revealed to Mary by the Spirit, and spoke more home
to her inmost soul after his ascension to heaven than before
it; because he says, 'It is expedient for you that I go away,
for if I go not away the Comforter will not come unto you;
but if I depart I will send him unto you.' *Further,* this calling
of men by name has been Christ's manner from the beginning. The Lord, walking in the garden in the cool of the day,
asks our first and still our nearest father: 'Adam, where art

thou?' Adam, with all the glory given him, all his sin, and all his loss and fall. The Angel of the Lord accosts the fugitive bondwoman in the wilder ness of Shur by name: 'Hagar, Sarah's maid, whence earnest thou, and whither wilt thou go?' On Mount Horeb he calls to his servant out of the fire in the bush: 'Moses, Moses;' and so continually throughout his dealings with the sons of men. And although not now in visible appearance, nor by audible sound, yet as really he calls you also as if by your own name.

Son of Adam, place yourself before the Lord Jesus, till you feel his eye resting on you, and hear his voice utter your name, as he uttered 'Mary' and said no more. So listen to your own name from his lips; for it is known to him as well as Magdalene's was. You have to do with him as much as she had, though all the record of the intercourse may only be, 'I have nourished and brought up children, and they have rebelled against me.' Let your own name sound in your ears as uttered by him, and heard by you alone. It is no imagination; it is simply your listening to a constant truth, 'I have called, and ye refused; I stretched out my hand, and no man regarded.' Son of Adam, where art thou? with what fig-leaves clothed, under what branches concealed? Stand forth in the presence of your Lord, meet him, hear him. Survey your own name announced by him; examine it, weigh it, consider it round and round. Strip it of all deceitful coverings, and let it stand naked, detach it from all surroundings, and let it stand alone. It will one day be solemnly announced before the assembled universe, when the judgment is set, and the books are opened. If Jesus confess it not then before his Father, you will call in vain on the rocks to fall on you, and the hills to cover you. Listen to it now, that you may quickly betake yourself for hiding to the outspread wings of the Angel of the Covenant; saying, 'The Lord is my refuge, under the shadow of thy wings will I rejoice.'

Seeking soul, you desire to find the Lord Jesus, and you pray for his gracious appearing. 'The Lord whom ye seek shall come suddenly; behold, he shall come, saith the Lord of hosts; but who may abide the day of his coming? for he is like a refiner's fire, and like fuller's soap.' Mal. 3:1, 2. Consider this image of the fuller's soap and test yourself by it, whether you truly desire his coming and can abide it. The garment is put into the fuller's hands, to be cleansed unsparingly from every spot and stain, and made thoroughly clean and white. If you welcome this cleansing, you can abide his coming; but if you welcome not the cleansing, you cannot abide the coming, nor do you truly desire it. Mark, however, that the question is not, whether you are so clean as to endure the Lord's judgment, which will become the inquiry at his second appearing. The question is not now, if you are white and clean as the fuller's soap can make you; for then his coming would have no resemblance to the soap and the washing of the fuller. But are you willing to be subjected in your mind, soul, and conscience to this fuller's soap, or are you not? It matters not how clean you are, how few your stains; you cannot receive him, if you desire to retain one of them all. It matters not how defiled you are, how crimson and scarlet your sins, if you are willing to be cleansed from them all. Then you welcome Jesus with his cleansing blood, and purifying Spirit; you submit your soul to the searching soap of the fuller; you delight in it; you can abide his coming now; and you shall stand hereafter when he appeareth.

'Jesus saith unto her, Mary.' Jesus said of old: 'Hagar, Sarah's maid, whence comest thou, and whither wouldst thou go?' Daughter of the bondwoman, Jesus puts these questions to you, 'Whence comest thou?' It may be of godly parentage, the daughter of a praying mother, or a God-fearing father, or haply of both. 'And whither wouldst thou go?' 'I am going into the world; I love the world, and the things of the world; I delight in the worldly song, and the worldly dance, and the worldly spectacle. I have tried it, and desire to enjoy it still for a season;' or, 'I have not tasted it yet but I long to launch into it, for I weary of the dull monotony and the restraint of a quiet religious course. I go to joyous liberty, hilarity, and life.' But hear, O daughter, what your God saith to you: 'She that liveth in pleasure is dead while she liveth.' This pleasant life is only painted death; this festal hall is for you a whited sepulchre. The friend of the world is the enemy of God; and child of the kingdom, as by birth you are, you will soon 'be cast into outer darkness, where is weeping and gnashing of teeth.' How awful a change! Out of the gaiety, the excitement, the admiration, the brilliancy of the festival, into the blackness of darkness for ever! Stop, ere it is too late; hear the voice of Jesus calling you; turn and live.

Finally, let us all seek to be familiar with our own name, as in the presence of the Lord Jesus Christ; and so shall it not take us by surprise when uttered by him at the great day.

> O may we stand before the Lamb,
>   When earth and seas are fled,
> And hear the Judge pronounce our name,
>   With blessings on our head!

IX

MARY SALUTING CHRIST AS RABBONI

*'She turned herself, and saith unto him, Rabboni;
which is to say, Master.'*—John 20:16

JESUS had addressed Magdalene as 'Mary,' and she replies
to him 'Rabboni,' which is either 'Master,' or 'My Master;'
and signifies in the first instance 'Teacher,' or 'My Teacher,'
but is also near akin to 'Lord,' with which it is associated by
Christ himself: 'Ye call me Master and Lord, and ye say well,
for so I am.' John 13:13. There is an Old Testament promise
of the Messiah, which brings out fully all the elements
contained in this salutation, Rabbi or Rabboni, and which
we shall therefore employ in illustration. It occurs in Isaiah
55:4: 'Behold, I have given him for a witness to the people,
a leader and commander to the people.' These are the
words of the Father bringing in the new and everlasting
covenant, in which all the poor and thirsty are invited to
drink the living waters freely. This new covenant may be
said to commence with the resurrection; when the old has
been fulfilled and set aside in Christ, and when the Father
addresses Jesus, 'Thou art my Son, this day have I begotten

thee.' Acts 13:33. We may therefore regard with special interest this first appellation, 'Rabboni,' with which he is saluted
on his rising from the dead; and we find the elements of
the salutation in the witness, leader, and commander of the
promise. 'Witness' in the case of Jesus is essentially the same
as 'Rabbi, teacher;' 'leader and commander' is the same as
'Rabbi, master;' and we shall therefore take Teacher, Leader,
Commander, as unfolding the one Rabboni.

1. Rabboni, my Teacher

This is the first and leading idea of 'Rabboni;' Jesus is the
great Rabbi to Mary and to us, her Teacher and ours.

1. Jesus is the Teacher from whom *Mary* has learned
all the saving truth she has ever known, who led her to
God and made her wise unto salvation. He is the teacher
in whose lessons she trusts with unhesitating faith; whose
words enter her soul, and become part of her inmost being;
whose statutes have for years been the light of her path, and
the lamp of her feet: the teacher on whose lips she has hung
like a little child; on whom she has learned to depend for
the guidance of every day; and whose removal has left her
in desolation and midnight darkness: the teacher, without
whom in all her future life she must be an aimless wanderer,
lost in the wilderness, and stumbling on the dark mountains: the teacher gone and returned, lost and found, dead
and alive again; the light of her eyes, the joy of her heart,
the treasure of her soul restored; and all heavenly light and
gladness restored along with him. 'Rabboni,' my Teacher,
my one and only Master, my Way, my Truth, my Life.

2. Jesus is *our* Teacher, not in some things, but in 'all
things pertaining to life and godliness.' As a teacher, he not

only instructs by his word, but by his Spirit opens the heart to understand the Scriptures. He convinces us that we have been fools ('for if any man will be wise, he must become a fool that he may be wise'), shows us that we have been ignorant of God, and of all good; brings us down from proud men into helpless children, and praises God on our behalf, 'I thank thee, o Father, Lord of heaven and earth, because thou hast hid these things from the wise and prudent, and hast revealed them unto babes.' He teaches us how impotent we are for the inmost thought of good, 'of ourselves not sufficient to think any thing;' and leads us to pray, 'That which I know not, teach thou me.'

Blessed is the man who has found this Teacher; a teacher who can have compassion on the ignorant, and on them that are out of the way; a teacher who, before engaging to instruct us, knows all our ignorance, our folly, our perverseness, our self-sufficiency; a teacher who can bear with all our provocations, having borne them already in his own body on the tree; a teacher who endures with much long-suffering the contradiction of sinners against himself; a teacher who has himself learned obedience by the things which he suffered, and having suffered being tempted is able to succour them that are tempted; a prophet raised up unto us by the Lord our God, and who is 'made of God unto us wisdom.'

'My Teacher, whom the chief priests blindfolded and buffeted, as a blind leader of the blind; accounted blind, ignorant, and false for me; that thou mightest fulfil the end of thy coming, and open the eyes of the blind. My Teacher, without whom I know nothing, without whom I cannot take one step in the way of life, in whom I have all light and knowledge. My Teacher at every step in my progress, in every difficulty, every temptation, every snare into which I have fallen by my own sin. My Teacher, infinitely above me, yet come down to be one with me; and taking me to be one with thyself, as a branch in the vine. My Teacher, mine with no other between thee and me, thou the Teacher of me the disciple; my teacher, for 'they shall all be taught of God,' and thou art my Lord and my God; my Teacher, who didst before thy lifting up on the cross promise the Comforter to teach me all things. My Teacher, by whom all other teachers are sent to me, by whose words they are all to be tried by me, and to whom I ever return from them all; thou sendest them to me, and they send me again to thee; my first and last, my one and only, and all-sufficient Teacher.'

Follower of Jesus, fall at his feet and call to him, 'Rabboni, my Teacher.' Perishing sinner, following the teachings of your own blinded heart, fall at his feet, and call to him henceforth: 'Rabboni, my Teacher, that which I know not, teach thou me.' Come to him for wisdom, for he will in no wise cast you out. He is teacher of the ignorant, of the foolish, of the old in the stupor of age, of the young in the heedlessness of youth, of the dark mind and of the slow heart. Come, and he will not cast you out for lateness in life, for distance of wandering, for enmity, for backsliding. Bow down unto him and say: 'Rabboni, my Teacher; the language of God is high and foreign to me, my language low and strange to him; my Interpreter, my Mediator, instruct me to speak with the tongue of the redeemed, in the language of the Father's family; open my closed lips, teach me to pray, show me thy ways, teach me thy paths.'

2. Rabboni, my Leader

'I have given him for a leader and commander to the people.' In the new covenant God has given Jesus to be the Head of the family, the Leader, the Guide, the Commander. In the old covenant we had another leader, our first father, Adam; in the new, we have Jesus Christ, the second Adam, the Lord from heaven.

1. In the old covenant, *Adam* was our leader. He led the way for us, he met the foe for us, he fought the battle for us. He lacked nothing of created goodness to fit him for such headship; holiness, wisdom, and the favour of God; all outward abundance, all inward peace; health of body, health of mind, health of spirit. God pronounced him very good; very good in himself as a man, and very good as the representative man; the first, the chief, the head and leader of his family. The human race was incapable of producing a better man.

But the adversary Satan being suffered to assault him—not by overpowering force but only by seduction—our leader, trusting in his own strength, was over come in the battle; he fell wounded unto death, and was carried away captive, the prey of the mighty. Mary, following this leader, was led captive with him; and seven devils held her fast in their chains. All of us under this same headship have been overcome. It could not be otherwise; the battle has been already fought by our representative man; our leader appointed to fight our battle has been vanquished. Under him we are already overcome, before ever we begin to fight in our own persons. Under him sin has and must have the victory; under him Satan has certain conquest over us. We fight under a leader already beaten, and there is no hope, no possibility of overcoming. When we advance against some particular foe, some sin that besets us, we may seem for the moment to prevail; and not for the moment only, but during a lengthened contest. But we are only fighting at the side of the battle-field, and with a little outpost of the enemy. The great central battle has mingled elsewhere; there we have been completely vanquished; and our petty victory is swept away in a moment by the over-whelming rush of our triumphant foes.

2. But God has raised up a *Second Head,* a second Adam, a second representative Man, a second Leader and Commander for the people. Mary under the first had been led captive by many devils; Mary under the second has Satan and his hosts bruised under her feet. To the first Adam the prince of this world came, lulled him asleep by poisoned words, and led him captive away. To the Second he came, and 'captivity was led captive;' the strong one was vanquished by the stronger than he; the spoiler spoiled of his armour and of his prey. In him as our leader we are conquerors in the very hour we call him 'Master.' The battle has been fought and won for us by the 'Captain of our salvation;' and believing on him, confiding in him, trusting ourselves to him, we share at once his victory over Satan and all his works.

To us it is said, as to Israel of old, 'Ye shall not need to fight in this battle; set yourselves, stand ye still, and see the salvation of the Lord with you.' How the soul marvels to find that it gains the battle, even when most pressed by the foe, through believing that in Christ it has been fought and won already! In its hardest efforts to overcome, it was miserably foiled before; but now by singing a song of praise to God, who giveth the victory in Christ Jesus, the soul beholds its enemies all cast down and slain. For 'this is the victory that overcometh the world, even our faith.'

The moment we fall away to our old leader, we are vanquished as before. We acquire no strength from Christ Jesus by which we can overcome, if we return to fight under our old colours. In Adam we die, in Christ we are made alive. In Adam we have died, in Christ we have been made alive; and in Adam we still die, and in Christ we still are made alive; for 'in Adam all (that are in him) die, and in Christ all (that are in him) are made alive.' The headship of Adam is no subordinate help to the headship of Jesus, but is rivalry and enmity. Here, as in all things else, we cannot serve two masters; and if one is loved, the other must be hated. The old covenant is set aside when the new covenant is embraced. Any secret inclination to Adam the first ever awakes the jealousy, and draws down the chastisement of him who is now our Leader, our Master, our Rabboni.

Brother in the human family, dare to bow down before Jesus, and to call him Master; call the Redeemer, the Substitute, the Deliverer of his people, your Leader; call him who has triumphed over principalities and powers in his cross, the Captain of your salvation; and in that instant you are safe, for he is not merely the Captain of our army, but the Captain of our salvation, and to follow him is to be saved in that hour. Brother in Christ, cleave to him with your whole heart, trust in him at all times, and call him ever Rabboni, my Master, my Head, my Captain, my Leader.

3. Rabboni, my Lord

Master is akin to Lord, and the two are one in Jesus Christ: 'Ye call me Master and Lord, and ye say well, for so I am.'

None in all the earth ever more truly called Jesus Rabboni, my Lord, than Mary Magdalene. No bondmaid was ever more devoted to a master; no ransomed captive ever more grateful to his redeemer; none ever loved Christ's service more. With every power of mind, body, and estate she served him, and loved to serve; and 'master' was never uttered by lips more sincere than hers. From a cruel bondage he had redeemed her; seven relentless masters she was serving; seven devils were each ruling proudly and cruelly over her; seven deadly foes were her lords. Now she has one only Lord; he loved her and gave himself for her; he broke her seven chains, and set her free; he bound her oppressors, and bruised them beneath her feet; and her whole heart and mind and soul worship him as Lord and Master. Rabboni, my Master, my one and only Master; my Lord, my Ruler, my Owner, my King.

The risen Jesus is our Lord, and we are his servants. 'I am thy servant; truly I am thy servant, thou hast loosed my bonds.' He has purchased us for himself with his own blood; he has bought us with a great price, and we are his property. We had sold ourselves to another, to the old liar and murderer, and we were his. 'We sold ourselves for nought,' for a golden fruit we sold our souls, for a mess of pottage our birthright; yet paltry though the price was, we had consented to the sale. Jesus on the cross has purchased us again, redeemed us with his blood. He has plucked us from the hand of Satan, having first bought us from the hand of avenging justice with a great price, and now we are his.

My Lord is 'the Lord that bought me.' What we purchase is ours; the field we purchase, and the yoke of oxen bought are ours. So also we are purchased by Christ; but with this difference, that we have a will of our own that must consent to the transference. The price was paid without our consent; yet against our will the actual transference of the property is never made, for Christ has no slaves. It is, however, not a transference of bonds, but a ransom from bondage. Nevertheless we are not redeemed to be lords and owners of ourselves, but to be the servants of the Lord Jesus Christ, whose servants are all freemen. 'We are not our own, we are bought with a price;' we love to be claimed by him as our owner, and we love to serve him as our Master. We serve him freely and from the heart; yet our service is not a gratuity which we may give or withhold, but we are bound to serve Christ our Lord.

We are loosed from all other masters for this very end, that we may serve our crucified and risen Lord, who has redeemed us with his blood: 'I am thy servant, thou hast loosed my bonds.' Servants we are, yet friends of the Lord whom we serve. He calls us friends, yet adds, 'Ye are my friends, if ye do whatsoever I command you.' The believer glories in him to others as his friend: 'This is my Beloved, and this is my friend;' but to himself he never says 'my Friend,' but always 'my Lord;' 'Ye call me Master and Lord, and ye say well, for so I am.'

'Master' in the mouth of Mary, and in ours, carries two lessons; of humility of heart, and singleness of eye.

1. It demands *humility,* not only because the servant's place is a lowly one in itself under any master; but chiefly because our Master himself is lowly, and 'the servant is not above his lord, nor the disciple his master.' A service rare and singular, indeed, it is to be under a Master who

proclaims, 'Take up my yoke, and learn of me, for I am meek and lowly of heart.' Under a proud and haughty master a servant is crushed into humiliation, if not into humility; and the pride of the master, and the lowliness of the servant seem counterparts of each other. But ours is a lowly Master; a Master so meek and lowly, that all he asks of us is that 'the servant be not above his Lord.' Yet duller eyes than Solomon's may often discover 'servants upon horses, and their Prince walking as a servant upon the earth.' Our Lord never asks us to be lowlier than himself; his demand is that we be like him, for he has set us an example that we should follow his steps. And surely we may be well content, and cheerfully say for ourselves, 'It is enough for us servants that we be as our Lord, and for us disciples to be as our Master.'

2. 'Master' implies *singleness* of eye in the servant, for no servant can serve two masters. Yet what servant of the Lord Jesus Christ has not made the attempt? Who can tell how repeated, how persevering, how perversely subtle are the efforts even of true believers to combine the two services; of Christ and the world, Christ and self, Christ and Belial? The services can never be reconciled without first reconciling the masters. But the prince of this world 'hath nothing' in Christ; and 'what fellowship hath Christ with Belial?' Yet the attempted double service is deeply injuring thousands of true believers; and tens of thousands of professors are continually perishing in the vain endeavour to please both masters. Half-master and half-lord is all they really call the Lord Jesus: Master of my soul, Lord of my spirit; but not Master of my body, my tongue, my ears, my eyes, my feet, and hands: Lord of my devotions, but not of my affections, my heart, my intellect, my time, my farm, my merchandise,

my all: Master of my future, my old age, my weakness, sickness, sorrow, my death, and my eternity; but not of my present, my health, my life, my pleasure. Half-saviour for the best of men would leave them wholly lost for ever; and our complete Redeemer is likewise our absolute Lord. Jesus is meek and lowly in heart, but he will not be mocked by any man; and to every half-servant he will sternly say, 'No servant can serve two masters; depart from me, ye workers of iniquity.'

But on the other hand, the Rabboni of Mary strikes a kindred chord in the heart of every humble and single-eyed follower of Jesus Christ:

> How sweetly doth 'My Master' sound!—My Master!
>   As ambergris leaves a rich scent unto the taster,
> So do these words a sweet content,
>   An Oriental fragrancy—My Master!
> With these all day I do perfume my mind.'
>
> —*George Herbert*

X

MARY FORBIDDEN TO TOUCH JESUS

*'Jesus saith unto her, Touch me not; for I am not yet
ascended to my Father.'*—John 20:17

MARY has found the desire of her heart, the Beloved
of her soul; her weeping ceases and is turned into
joy. Having sown in tears, she now reaps in rejoicing. The
darkest night of all her earthly sorrow is changed in a
moment into the brightest morning that has ever dawned
upon her soul. Her lost Saviour is found again, and her joy
exceeds that of her first salvation. Before she knew Christ
she was sorrowful, but not for his absence; she was not
sorrowing, but merely wretched; and Jesus found her before
she sought him. Now there has been the grief of most bitter
bereavement, along with the intense desire of the mourning heart; the sorrow giving depth to the desire, and the
desire adding intensity to the sorrow. But Jesus is found,
and Jesus no more a man of sorrows and acquainted with
grief, but risen gloriously from the grave and become the
first-fruits of them that slept. She has found the same, yet
to her a greater, higher, lovelier Saviour than she had lost.

Her captivity is turned by the Lord, and she is like them that dream; for the Lord hath done great things for her, whereof she is glad. Mary had been looking back to the things that were behind; seeking a dead Christ, and grieving that it was not with her as in months past, when she followed her living Redeemer. Jesus leads her to the things that are before; to Christ more living, because now with a life that cannot die, to 'him that liveth and was dead, and is alive for evermore.'

Even so has it been with many a believer, and so with some of you. Christ may have been found through his own gracious revelation, with little or no seeking on your part. But you have lost him again, and you seek him sorrowing with all your heart's desire. You would gladly return to the things behind, and recover the Saviour whom you had lost; but Jesus leads you forward through the midnight gloom. You find at last the Saviour you had known before, yet higher, more lovely, more beloved; and your joy may be even greater than at first conversion.

But in this very moment of gladness, there is a quick restraint imposed on Mary by the command of Jesus, 'Touch me not;' a severe command it sounds, and almost stern in such an hour. We ask wherefore it is issued, and these reasons present themselves in answer: because Jesus will be highly reverenced; because Mary has no need like others to touch Jesus; because she has no occasion to touch him now; and finally, as we shall see in our next subject, because she has good reason not to touch him, but to go from him to the disciples.

1. *Jesus will be reverenced by Mary*

Her first impulse, on recognizing her Redeemer, seems

to have been the same as that of the holy women whom Jesus accosted later in the morning, when 'they held him by the feet, and worshipped him.' Mary desired to have closer, fuller, and more sensible possession of Christ. She therefore essayed to touch him, as by clasping his feet and kissing them; to honour Jesus, as he had been honoured in the days of his flesh by the penitent in the house of Simon, and by Mary the sister of Lazarus. Jesus does not suffer it, but arrests her, saying, 'Touch me not;' words which convey both a warning against unholy familiarity, and a check on holy boldness in worship.

1. This arrest includes a warning against all *unholy familiarity* in worship. God 'will be sanctified in them that come nigh to him, and will be had in reverence of all that are about him;' and Jesus, the Son manifest in the flesh, is God over all, blessed for evermore. He will have this to be known and felt by Mary, and by all believers. An address to the Father in the name of Jesus is rarely too familiar; and for a general rule that is the safer form, at least in united worship. There is, however, ample authority for the direct worship of Christ; but such worship is more prone to run into too familiar a tone of address, and calls for a stricter watch upon our lips. There cannot be a greater error in prayer, none more apt to puff up the carnal mind, and none more certain to make our petitions void. Such unholy nearness only moves the Lord Jesus to a greater distance, for he 'knoweth the proud afar off.' It is an error into which young disciples, more than others, are ready to fall; and these should specially remember their Lord's words, 'Touch me not;' worship, adore, believe, praise, love the Lord Jesus; but preserve a hallowed distance, presume not, touch not.

2. The command conveys also a check on *holy boldness*. The former lesson is less for Mary than for others; this is a warning to her as well as to us, and only too rarely required. Many believers never are so near, as to need the command to draw no nearer. It is a highly honourable restraint, 'Thus far, and no farther.' It bears the character not of reproof, but of check, and of such a check as is needed only by the nearest of the Lord's worshippers. In seasons of the soul's straits, Jesus is wont to reveal himself in greater condescension than at other times; as to the trembling, weeping Jacob at the brook of Jabbok, and now to his waiting, weeping daughter at the door of the sepulchre. In such a revelation the heart's desire, already fulfilled, seems to move the soul to seek further for that which can scarcely be granted on earth. Mary's patriarch father, wrestling with the Angel of the covenant, insists, 'Tell me, I pray thee, thy name?' and his petition is chid and refused, 'Wherefore is it that thou dost ask after my name?' Gen. 32:29; just as her own attempt to touch the same Messenger of the covenant is now forbidden. There is a holy, awful limit to the call, 'Draw nigh to God, and he will draw nigh to you;' as to Moses at the bush God called, 'Draw not nigh hither; put off thy shoes from off thy feet; for the place whereon thou standest is holy ground.' Exod. 3:5. 'Wherefore is it that thou dost ask after my name?' to Jacob, and 'Draw not nigh' to Moses, are the same as 'Touch me not' to Mary. The charge honours her with the king's award of the noblest rank ever conferred on the children of men; the distinguished position of having stood nearest to the presence of the Great King, of reaching that line which no fallen child of man has ever been suffered to overpass.

For most of us there is too little reason to fear such a restraint. Have any amongst us ever known it? Are any willing so to press into the king's presence, as to have it said even to us: 'Touch me not; why askest thou after my name, seeing it is secret?'

2. *Mary has no need to touch Jesus, like others*

The check given to Mary is of the kindest character. The disciples at Emmaus have their eyes opened to know Jesus, and he instantly vanishes from their sight; but by an act of sovereignty more trying than the simple words 'touch me not,' for he leaves them no opportunity of touching. John in Patmos beholds Jesus revealed in his glory, and he 'falls at his feet as dead;' powerless before the high and holy One, to speak, to touch, to advance. To Mary at the sepulchre Jesus neither makes himself invisible as at Emmaus, nor visible in overwhelming majesty as in Patmos; but gives the simple intimation, 'Touch me not;' a word sufficient to a friend, who will do whatsoever he commands.

Thomas is commanded to touch; the women who return from the tomb are permitted to touch; and Mary, more devoted to Jesus than either, is in holy sovereignty forbidden to touch; yet the prohibition to her is not without reason, for she has no need for touching Jesus.

1. Thomas is *commanded* to touch, to remove his doubts; but the command is the reverse of honourable to him, and conveys a marked reproof. Mary has no doubt to remove. She has heard the well-known voice of Jesus, she now sees and recognizes himself, and her desire to touch is not in uncertainty, but in affectionate devotion. Mary, not touch-ing, is nearer to Jesus than Thomas when called to handle

the Lord of life. She says 'Rabboni;' he exclaims 'My Lord and my God!' It seems more, yet it betokens less. His confession has in it the same element as in Peter's awe, when he exclaimed, 'Depart from me, for I am a sinful man, o Lord.' In Thomas there is the full recognition of the Godhead, but less perception of the manhood of Jesus. He had known that his great Teacher was truly man, for he followed him trembling to Jerusalem, and followed on sorrowing to Calvary. His language indicates, that he had with his own eyes seen both the nails driven into the hands of the living Jesus, and the spear thrust into his side after death; or else the bloody prints of the nails, and of the spear in his dead Master. He had seen those indelible marks in Christ's body, and if the same has really risen he must see them still. He had unquestionable proof that Christ was human; that he could die, and had died. He now sees the same Christ by the same undoubted tokens, and his faith and wonder burst forth in declaring his manifest Godhead. It is hard to know Christ to be very man, and to believe that he is also very God; and hard to know him to be very God, and remember that he is truly man. Each of these, yet somewhat separately, Thomas had learned for himself, and it is well; but Jesus declares that he would have been more blessed in believing his own past words and the disciples' testimony, with less outward demonstration to himself individually. Thomas is assured by Christ presented to his touch, but in being assured he is also reproved, amazed, and awe-struck.

Mary Magdalene has no doubts to be removed by more tangible evidence. She wept to lose Jesus; she rejoices to find him again; but she is not overwhelmed by his presence, and is filled with no great surprise at the appearance of Jesus risen. Her joy at the sight of Jesus himself swallows up all surprise at seeing him alive. The rest of the women fear the angelic watchers at the tomb, and fear the risen Jesus. But in Mary the same love, that had cast out the fear of angels, casts out fear in the presence of One risen from the dead; for that risen One is her own Beloved. Like the others, she had not looked for Christ's immediate resurrection; but she does not wonder at it, or at anything her Lord may do. She had seen him raise the newly dead upon the arrested bier at Nain, and the corrupting dead out of the tomb at Bethany; and she does not marvel that he has burst the bonds of his own death, and come forth himself from the grave. She does not exclaim in astonishment, 'My Lord and my God.' Even when dead in sins she knew for herself by direct discernment that Jesus of Nazareth was the Holy One of God. The seven devils within her saw and recognized the Son of the Most High; and by union with them she also saw him in his own character and glory, and trembled before him. Past knowledge was not lost by conversion, the Holy Spirit more than supplying the place of the unholy. Christ living was to her the Son of God with power, yet the loving friend of sinners; Christ risen cannot be higher than before, and she at once addresses him by the old familiar title, Rabboni. It is Jesus, the same yesterday and today; and she needs no touch to strengthen her assurance, but rather the impression, 'Put off thy shoes from off thy feet, for the place whereon thou standest is holy ground.'

2. The other women are *permitted* to touch Jesus; not because they doubted and asked for proof, but because they feared and needed consolation. Jesus saluted them, 'All hail;' and they drew near, and held him by the feet, and

worshipped him. They were glad when they saw the Lord;
but they rejoiced with trembling, they worshipped him
in fear; and Jesus comforts them, 'Be not afraid.' For their
consolation they are permitted to touch Christ's feet; and
there is no risk with them of excessive nearness, for they
are trembling worshippers; with the fearful women no risk,
and with the doubting Thomas none, whom the touching
of Jesus only made to draw back with holy awe. But Mary
has no fear to be removed by a closer approach to her Lord;
and there is no call for such approach. Without touching
she is already nearer to Jesus than the questioning disciple
and the trembling women have been brought by means
of touching; and therefore it is fit that this satisfaction be
withheld.

It is fit in the eyes of the Lord, and let it be good also in
our eyes. Faith is the gift of God; and the strong believer has
greater faith than the weak, only because he has been more
highly favoured and gifted. But we cannot expect the grace
of the strong, and the help of the weak at once. The stronger
faith can bear more, and will be more severely tried; both
to prove, and to exercise and employ its strength. You have
cause to rejoice if the Lord makes your feet like hinds'
feet, and makes you to outstrip others in the race. But if
the feet of hinds are yours, you will need all their sureness
and their speed; for he who gave them to you, will also set
you on high places, while others are suffered to advance
slowly through the valley. If much is given, much will also
be required; and if much is given in one form, much may
be withheld in another. The unquestioning, unfearing faith,
that requires less sensible witness and evidence, will be left
without it; while the weaker faith will have grace brought

down to its capacity. If you are Thomas, you are reproved and commanded to touch; if you are Salome or 'the other Mary,' you are cheered and suffered to touch; but if you are Mary Magdalene, you may be enjoined, 'Touch me not,' and that not because you are less, but more highly favoured of the Lord.

3. Mary has no occasion to touch Jesus now

There will be ample time for this hereafter: 'Touch me not, for I am not yet ascended to my Father.' This is commonly taken to intimate that there would be time on earth to salute Jesus before his ascension to heaven; as if his being not yet ascended meant that the ascension was not to be immediate. The words themselves admit of this interpretation; but not the scope of the passage, for these two reasons:

1. There is no intimation that Mary ever had *such another opportunity* on earth, and much that implies the contrary. The trembling women, returning to Jerusalem, were allowed; and Thomas, slow of heart to believe, was enjoined to touch; but we read of none others besides.

The whole character of the appearance of the risen Saviour is full of majesty, mingled with a certain distance and reserve. The recorded manifestations of Christ after the resurrection are marked with peculiar sovereignty; all perhaps with the exception of two, the one in Galilee, and the other before the Ascension. The first of these was by definite appointment, and seems to have been in the midst of no fewer than five hundred brethren. The second, also, was no doubt expressly appointed, and was in the presence of many disciples. In assemblies so formal and so large as these, the holy women would occupy no prominent place, and would have no fit opportunity of saluting their Lord. The other occasions seem to be marked by an unexpected abruptness of appearing, and sometimes by unexpected abruptness of departure; and with nothing to indicate any welcome to draw nearer, than Jesus was pleased to come of his own will.

There was indeed in this interval, along with no abatement of love, an unavoidable distance between Christ and his disciples, such as was not before his death, and will not be in heaven; arising from the fact, that Christ's was now his risen body, while they were still in their natural bodies. This will be altered, when we are absent from the body and present with the Lord; but the dissimilarity will never be done away, till our bodies are fashioned like to his glorious body. There will then be a return to a relation, similar to that which subsisted when Christ and his disciples were both in the flesh; a relation equally close, yet inconceivably more elevated, with conditions admitting an innumerable company into privileges once shared only by a few. The final condescension and nearness of Jesus Christ to his redeemed are intimated by his declarations: that he will then drink the fruit of the vine new with them in the kingdom of his Father; and that for the servants who are found watching at his coming, the Lord will gird himself, and make them to sit down to meat, and will come forth and serve them. Luke 12:37.

2. This touching is not on earth, because the whole reference in Christ's address is *to heaven*. To the other women Jesus speaks of Galilee, and he appoints to meet them there; to Mary he says nothing of Galilee or of earth, but only of heaven. It is not, 'Touch me not, for I go to Galilee, and there

shalt thou see me;' but it is, 'Touch me not, for I ascend to the Father.' The appointment is on no earthly scene, but in the high heavens above.

It is then an assurance by Jesus, that there will be ample opportunity for the closest personal intercourse with him in heaven. It will not be after an earthly manner, for Mary there is like the angels in heaven; but it will be high and spiritual. It will not be less real on that account, else Mary had been a loser and not a gainer; nor less personal to Mary and to each believer, else she had lost and not gained. Mary desires for herself to have the closest fellowship and communion with Jesus; and he assures her that this will be granted to her heart's desire in heaven, and that she need not covet it now. Mary desires longer communion with Christ now at the sepulchre; Christ denies it, but assures her of an eternity of fellowship above. He does not deny the touching, he only delays it, and transfers it from earth to heaven; that it may be the touching of Jesus risen by Mary also risen. 'Touch me not now,' for 'to him that overcometh will I grant to sit with me in my throne, even as I also over-came, and am set down with my Father in his throne.' All his followers will have a nearness to Jesus in heaven, such as Jesus himself has to the Father. What a heaven, in which Jesus will never say, 'Touch me not,' but will call us to sit down on the same throne with himself, in inconceivable, unbroken, everlasting nearness to him, whom having not seen we love, and to whom we shall be for ever like when we shall see him face to face! Amen.

XI

MARY AS CHRIST'S MESSENGER TO THE APOSTLES

*'Jesus saith unto her, Touch me not; for I am not yet
ascended to my Father; but go to my brethren, and
say unto them, I ASCEND UNTO MY FATHER; AND
YOUR FATHER; AND TO MY GOD, AND YOUR GOD.'*
—John 20:17

MARY is denied the desire of her heart in nearer
approach to Jesus, and closer fellowship with him;
but she has more than her heart's desire, and more than had
entered her mind to conceive, when Christ makes her his
chosen messenger to the apostles themselves. To be Christ's
herald is higher honour than to be Christ's worshipper.

Mary must not tarry with Jesus, but must run for him as
his messenger; and must carry to the disciples the promise of
his ascension to the Father, and of his brotherhood to them.

1. Mary must not tarry with Jesus, but run as his messenger

'Jesus saith unto her, Touch me not, but go to my brethren.'
A woman must go to the apostles; the finder of the King

must carry his word; it is better for her to go from Christ with his message, than to tarry beside him without it; and Mary has now reached the crowning transaction in her life.

1. A *woman* must go to the disciples; Mary must not stay with Christ as his friend, but in his own strength go forth from him as his messenger. A woman is Christ's first commissioned herald after his resurrection; a woman in whom seven devils had dwelt, his elect messenger to his followers; a woman not suffered to speak in the church, ambassador to the great apostles. It is God's chosen way; he takes the weak things of the world to confound the mighty, and the foolish to confound the wise, that no flesh may glory in his presence. 'He saves the tents of Judah first, that the glory of the house of David may not magnify itself.' Let therefore no woman say, 'I can bear no message for Jesus.' In your own place by God's strength you can; and if you can you must, or you will displease your Lord.

2. The *finder* of the King must carry his word to others; Christ's messenger to men must first have found Christ. Many messengers of the gospel have never come to the fountain-head, whence the message of mercy flows; many messengers have never been at Calvary to know Christ crucified, or at the tomb to see him risen. They meet the women returning, they catch the tidings from their lips, and run with them in haste and superficial zeal. 'I am against the prophets, saith the Lord, that steal my words every one from his neighbour. I have not sent these prophets, yet they ran; I have not spoken to them, yet they prophesied; therefore they shall not profit this people at all.' Jer. 23:21, 30, 32. The burden of Mary's effort lay in finding Christ; the bearing of his message then was a light and easy yoke, for

she spake what she knew, and testified what she had seen. Being sent, she could not but speak the things she had seen and heard. But the labour, the patience, and the sorrow were in seeking and finding Jesus. She must have Christ, Christ for herself, and all else follows. The Lord does not now utter new words or hidden truths, as he did of old; for he has declared all his mind in his manifested Son, and in his word given by the Holy Ghost. But without the present Spirit quickening, the word itself is but an old history, a dead letter; or rather a letter killing, having power to slay but none to make alive. But the old word, coming new from Christ himself, has all the freshness of new tidings of great joy. The chief labour, therefore, of every messenger of Jesus is to find Christ himself, and receive the law from his lips; and then all else is easy.

3. It is *good* for Mary to go from Christ; for it is better to go from him with his message, than to tarry beside him without it. The forward messengers often run unsent, but the unwilling messengers tarry unbidden. In itself it was good for Mary, it was the highest possible good, to draw near to Christ; and having found him to tarry with him. But in that hour it was not good for her, either to draw any nearer or to tarry any longer. The greater nearness, and the long abiding will be found in heaven; and one hour in time may be of more value than ages in eternity. In our Father's house above, there is time enough and to spare; time for all inquiry into Christ, and time for all enjoyment of his fellowship; but on earth 'the time is short.' It was the choicest opportunity Mary was ever to have in this world for intercourse with Jesus, yet it must be broken off for that which is greater and better; 'touch me not, but go.' Wait not for

more, but go with what you have got; take that and divide it among the brethren; the rest will be given in heaven; 'touch me not, but go.' Going in such a case is better than touching; carrying Christ's message, better than enjoying Christ's fellowship.

Fellowship is an hour of eternity anticipated; it is fore-tasting the feast of Paradise above. We need it for strength; it is given also that our joy may be full; and without it we cannot call others to have fellowship with us, because our fellowship is with the Father and the Son. But fellowship is eating the fruit of the tree of life; witness-bearing is sowing the seed, which by grace will spring into new trees of righteousness, the planting of the Lord by which he shall be glorified. Now if fellowship is fruit eaten, and witnessing is seed sown, there is a vast difference in their value.

Jesus saith, 'I am the door: by me if any man enter in, he shall be saved, and shall go in and out, and find pasture.' John 10:9. Jesus is the way in to the Father, but Jesus also is the way out from the Father; by him they shall go in, by him they shall go out, and shall find pasture in both. By Christ we go out; by Christ we leave Christ, and go into the world; by Christ we go from Christ, that we may win others to Christ, yet with himself accompanying us all the while. 'Touch me not, but go;' for going is greater than touching.

4. Mary has reached *the crowning transaction* of her life. Take it, that Mary had touched and not gone, and look at the result. Weary and heavy-laden she is indeed; for she has borne an overwhelming load of sorrow during three days and nights, having the length of years; and weighted with this burden of grief, she has been running to and fro from Jerusalem to Calvary on that desolate night and early morn.

'Come unto me, and I will give you rest, all ye that labour and are heavy laden,' is Christ's invitation to her, if ever it was to any; she comes, and finds rest to her soul. But how brief the repose! Jesus says, 'Mary;' Mary says, 'Rabboni;' Jesus replies, 'Touch me not, but go.' From the apostles in Jerusalem she had run to the tomb; from the empty tomb she had run back to the apostles; from them again she has run to the tomb a second time; and now she is hurried back by Jesus a second time to Jerusalem. 'Touch me not, but go;' draw not nearer, but go; tarry not, but go.

The great transaction of Mary's life is now in its crisis; the one great work she was ordained to do for the Lord on earth is upon the wheels, and if it is marred her life's history is blemished for ever. Someone else will take her crown, and she be made another vessel as seems good to the potter to make it. Her soul is saved; all the Lord has done for her and in her remains; but that which she might do for him is lost by her. Her high vocation is to bear this one message to the brethren, and what a message! 'I ascend to my Father and your Father, to my God and your God.' Such a message no tongue of man or angel had ever borne before, nor will ever bear again; a message which can be likened only to the words of Jesus himself before his decease; a message for all the church; a message for all the elect still scattered abroad; a message for all nations; a message for all ages till time itself is no more.

This is the crown of Mary's life, her crowning favour from the Most High, the one great work given to her above others. She had received much from the Lord; her state had been most wretched and her grace most abundant; but what the soul merely receives remains mostly with itself, and will be more seen in heaven than on earth. She had done much for the Lord, yet in common with many others ministering and following, though first among the followers. But her distinctive work had not yet fallen to her portion. Even in seeking and finding Jesus after the resurrection she was not singular. She sought and found, but the other women sought also and found; only she sought more earnestly, and found earlier. But Jesus appearing to her first, is grace to her rather than glory to him. Mary, the mother of Jesus, had her distinctive transaction when she believed the word of the Lord; and therefore all generations call her blessed. Mary the sister of Lazarus had her peculiar work when she poured the precious spikenard on the head and feet of Jesus, and her memorial is world-wide as the gospel itself. Mary Magdalene's distinctive honour is being entrusted with this lofty message for the apostles, and for all generations of mankind.

In such a case her self-denial is tried, 'Touch not;' and her obedience is tested, 'Go.' Had she remained and been so allowed, an hour of high and holy fellowship had been hers, an hour at the gates of heaven, an hour to be held by her in life-long remembrance. But what more? Nothing! It is all between herself and her risen Lord; it is the white stone with the new name, which none knoweth save the giver and the receiver. It is heaven foretasted by her, and most sweet to herself; but it is little or nothing to the church and the world, present or to come.

'Touch me not, but go,' is a word to many believers, a word to many of you. Prayer may be mistimed, communion misplaced; for something else may be neglected, some-thing else may be lost for ever, some thing greater shall we say?—yes, and better. Mary's going is better, is greater, than Mary's tarrying or touching. It is good not to go till we have found Christ; but it is sometimes good to go the very moment we find. There may be more of Christ, more of his mind, more of his heart, in going from him to carry his word to others, than in tarrying with him to converse with himself. Only let us go with a good conscience; let us not condemn ourselves in going, as if there were less of Christ, when there is really more. It is self-denial; self-denial in Mary's case, not in carrying the welcome message to eager listeners, but in tearing herself from Jesus to carry it. The self-denial in our case will probably be, in the cold or hostile reception which we fear for the message and the messenger.

Often the chief part of a believer's life is spent in going to Christ and in coming from him, not in tarrying with him; in prayer coming to Christ, seeking him, himself enabling us to seek and to find; and then in his work going from Christ, yet in Christ. Going before finding Christ, is going without him; but going after finding him, is going with him. As far as time is concerned, the seeking with Mary is longest, the going from him to others is next, and the highest fellowship is briefest. It is by no means always so; but that will often be assigned us which we are least disposed to by nature. The mind of the Spirit has prevailed within us, over the resistance of the flesh to seeking and prizing Jesus Christ. But if now we are sent to testify, the mind of the flesh may rise again; and now there is more of the Spirit, and less of self in witness-bearing than in seeking. For though a merely carnal testifying comes to nothing, brings no blessing to speaker or to hearer; yet in testifying the flesh may be more crucified than in praying, and then there is more of the Spirit in the testimony. A testimony may thus come more within the veil than a prayer, for Jesus says, 'He that confesseth me before men, him will I confess before my Father in heaven;' and that even now, as well as in the last day.

Some professed Christians appear to cultivate fellowship with Christ, and speak much of spiritual joy; yet when testimony is to be borne to Christ they fail. In such a case there is little fellowship. The same world that stops the lips in witness-bearing will grieve the Spirit of grace and supplication, and will close the heart in prayer. To profess a secret communion with Christ, and to shun open testimony, gives little glory to Jesus, brings little profit to man, and is accompanied with little life in the soul. To every such soul Jesus saith, 'Touch me not, but go'; 'speak what you have known, and testify what you have seen.' If God has lighted your candle, you must let that light shine before men. You may be seeking more oil when he would have you use what you have, and then 'to him that hath shall be given;' but he will not give you more to hide beneath a bushel. You wonder that you have not more light, but the truth is that now you need no more. The instant you hold forth the lamp of life to others, you will need more light for yourself; and be sure that you shall have it in abundance. It is true that Christ would have fellowship with you, and that without him you can do nothing; but he will have fellowship with many more besides, and he will not have your fellowship with him hinder the communion he desires with many. Your service in bringing others into his fellowship is more glory and pleasure to him, than mere present communion with yourself; and the communion you desire he will bestow, not merely in seeking his face but in doing his will.

2. Mary's message is Christ's assurance of brotherhood, and promise of ascension to the Father

1. Mary is sent with Christ's *assurance of brotherhood*: 'Go to my brethren.' Notwithstanding their forsaking and denying him, He is not ashamed to call them brethren; unmistakably not for any good or constancy in them, but simply of his own unaltering love and grace. 'Go and say unto them, I ascend unto my Father and your Father, and to my God and your God.' The order of the words is remarkable in placing Father first; and is not undesigned, but most significant. The original relation toward man was not properly Father, but God. The original relation to Christ was not God at all, but only Father; in the past eternity it was 'my Father,' but never 'my God.' After the incarnation it is both; yet so that the root-relation is Father, and the secondary relation is God; and therefore Jesus names Father first, 'my Father and your Father, my God and your God.'

It is through our Lord Jesus Christ alone, that we are privileged to call the great God our Father. This name occurs in the Old Testament, yet seldom, and mostly in the later books when the promises concerning Christ are more fully brought out. But the title 'My Father' is never addressed to God by prophet, priest, or king. In the whole book of Psalms, neither David nor any other writer ever calls God his Father. He is called the Father of the fatherless, and extolled in pitying them that fear him as a father pitieth his children; but is never either directly addressed, or spoken of simply as Father. He is God, Lord, King, Shepherd, but never Father. This is rendered the more remarkable by the fact that in the 89th Psalm, verse 26, it is expressly prophesied of Christ, 'He will say unto me, Thou art my Father, my God, and the Rock of my salvation.' Elsewhere also, when this title is introduced, it is chiefly in connexion with the grace that he gives under the New Covenant, as in Jeremiah 3:19: 'Thou shalt call me, My Father, and shalt not turn away from me.'

But if David, the man after God's own heart, does not call God his Father, very different is the language of David's Son and Lord. The expression 'My God' is used by Jesus once before his death; 'My God, my God, why hast thou forsaken me,' on the cross: once after his ascension, but repeated several times in the same passage (Rev. 3:12), 'Him that overcometh will I make a pillar in the temple of my God, and I will write upon him the name of my God, and the name of the city of my God, which cometh down out of heaven from my God;' and once in the passage before us between his death and his ascension, 'My God and your God.' These three are all the times in which Jesus calls Jehovah 'my God;' unless we add a fourth by implication in his answer to Satan: 'Thou shalt not tempt the Lord thy God.' But the other title, 'My Father,' Jesus employs at least fifty times in speaking either of God or to God; and the simple term 'Father' still oftener, using one or other more than a hundred times. From eternity it has been the great term of recognition, and to eternity it remains: 'As the Father knoweth me, even so know I the Father.' But now also it is for ever: 'Blessed be the God and Father of our Lord Jesus Christ.' Eph. 1:3.

With Christ it is 'My Father,' and then 'My God;' with us we should expect it to be 'your God,' and then 'your Father.'

But no; it is 'my Father and your Father, my God and your God.' Because it is only in Jesus Christ that we are restored to our God; and if in Christ, we are first raised to the rank of sons, and then reinstated in the relation of creatures. Man is not restored to the service of God, and then exalted to sonship; but in Christ he at once receives 'life more abundantly' than in Adam. The Spirit of the Son is sent forth into our hearts, by whom we cry 'Abba, Father;' we are adopted freely as sons into the family of which Christ is the first-born; and then accepted as subjects and servants. In Christ God is first our Father, and then our God. How full of love, how full of teaching, how full of life this message by Magdalene is! 'Go to my brethren, and say unto them, I ascend to my Father and your Father, and to my God and your God.'

2. Mary is sent with Christ's *promise of ascension:* 'Say unto them, I ascend to my Father.' The advocacy with the Father, the headship over the church and over all things to the church, and the outpouring of the Spirit are all immediately connected with the ascension. But leaving so wide a field let us revert to this one view, that Jesus ascends to the Father's right hand to meet his disciples there: 'Touch me not, for I am not yet ascended, but go to my brethren, and say unto them, I ascend.' The message by the other women is, 'I go before you into Galilee;' Jesus first and they following, to meet together in the place appointed on earth. By Mary Magdalene the message is, 'I ascend to my Father;' Jesus going first, and they following to the place he has gone to prepare for them in heaven. In his Father's house are many mansions, enough for all and fit for every one; and had it been otherwise, he would not have suffered them to hope in vain, but would have told them of it plainly.

He is now ascending to that Father's house, but will not without telling them whither he goes. Heaven is new, and seems strange to Mary and the disciples; but is neither new nor strange to Jesus, who is more at home there than the disciples are in Galilee. Heaven seems new and strange to the disciples; yet Jesus is neither new nor strange, but their oldest, best known, and most tried friend. The place where Jesus is cannot be strange to them, for he is there before to meet, to welcome, to receive, and bring in each entering soul. Heaven is not even altogether new to them, for it is 'the kingdom prepared for them from the foundation of the world;' the place in all the universe that is best suited for them, and they for it. It is expressly 'prepared' for them, and they are expressly 'made meet' for it; they sprinkled with the blood of the Lamb to fit them for heaven, and heaven sprinkled with the blood of the Lamb to fit it for them. It is the place where, for the first time, they will be altogether at home, and at home for ever.

As surely as Jesus meets his brethren in Galilee, so surely does he meet them in heaven: 'Say to them, I ascend to my Father.' The message to Peter and the apostles, to Mary and the holy women, is Christ's message also to as many as have believed in his name. His message is to me and to you, 'Say to them, I ascend to my Father.' What a meeting it will be! The family of five hundred brethren gathered round the Lord Jesus in Galilee, each meeting eye to eye and every eye meeting his, yields but a slight earnest of all the ransomed of the Lord gathered together unto him. He has gone to Galilee, and the disciples must go down to meet him there; he has ascended to the Father, and we must ascend to meet him above. 'Thou canst not follow me now, but thou shalt follow me afterwards.' Where Jesus is, there must we be also; and there we shall behold his glory, even the glory which he had with the Father before the world was. Amen.

MARY OF BETHANY

I

MARY OF BETHANY

'Lazarus of Bethany, the town of Mary and her sister
Martha. Now Jesus loved Martha, and her sister,
and Lazarus.'—John 11:1, 5

BETHANY is a small village near the south-eastern base of the Mount of Olives. It is within an easy walk from Jerusalem of scarcely two miles, or in the words of the apostle John, 'about fifteen furlongs off.' The situation is described as pleasant; and the village surrounded with fine trees.

Bethany is designated as 'the town of Mary and her sister Martha;' its being the home of this godly family constituting its chief distinction. The name of its builder is forgotten, and the memory of any men of wealth or worldly eminence that adorned it; but the record of this simple household abides, shedding a hallowed fame over the place of their dwelling, and associating it for ever with their names.

Of the two sisters the younger is before the elder, 'the town of Mary and her sister Martha;' the last first and the first last. In the earlier gospel narrative Martha has the precedence; she is evidently the elder of the two, and the head of the house. The evangelist Luke records that, when Jesus entered the village, 'a certain woman named Martha received him into her house; and she had a sister called Mary.' Luke 10:38. Then it was Martha and her sister Mary; it is now and for ever, Mary and her sister Martha. The reason is, that Mary is the greater in the kingdom of heaven. In earth she was second, Martha's sister; but in heaven, and in the annals of its occupants, she is first, 'Mary and her sister Martha.' She was the least and lowliest of the two in this world, sitting at the feet of Jesus, and therefore the most highly exalted. Lowliest she is for ever in heaven, and therefore nearest to the Lamb in the midst of the throne, whose superscription is: 'I am meek and lowly.'

'The memory of the just is blessed, but the name of the wicked shall rot.' It is interesting to remark the double working of this true proverb, even in the same individuals. The name of Mary is embalmed in ever lasting remembrance, and specially so through her anointing the feet of Jesus. Another of the holy women, often misnamed Mary Magdalene, wrought the same good work of pouring ointment on Christ's feet. But most of her life had been spent in sin, and her work is remembered but her name forgot; her much love is embalmed, but in everlasting connexion with her previous life of much sin. Some great sinners with a tardy repentance are enrolled by name in the record of the saints, like Manasseh; but then his name belonged to history irrespectively altogether of his character. But the penitent on the cross, who was that same day with Jesus in Paradise, is remembered by no name of his own; for the 'penitent thief' is his highest memorial in the church, his only designation still commemorating his sin. But Mary of Bethany, on the contrary, takes rank with apostles and confessors; for her own name not only remains, but is employed to confer distinction on the place of her birth. It is 'Bethsaida, the city of Andrew and Peter;' and in like manner it is 'Bethany, the town of Mary and her sister Martha.'

In examining Mary's character, the earthly friendship of Jesus to the family of Bethany will form our first subject of inquiry, along with a few notes on the everlasting friendship of Christ to every believer.

1. The earthly friendship of Jesus to the family at Bethany

This includes in its consideration, along with that friendship, their hospitality, their individual characters, and certain characteristic habits of Jesus.

1. The family of Bethany is honourably distinguished from all others by the fact of Christ's personal friendship toward them, preserved in the record that 'Jesus loved Martha, and her sister, and Lazarus.' The same expression is used of no family besides, and of no other individual except the apostle John, who is called 'the disciple whom Jesus loved.' The love with which he regarded the young man, of whom it is said that 'beholding him he loved him,' may perhaps be regarded as a more partial and transient form of the same human affection, going out to what is naturally attractive in human character. Mark 10:21. It proves the existence of friendship in Jesus, not irrespective of grace, yet not measured by its exact amount. Grace may have been more remarkable in John than in any other of the apostles, but there is no record to that effect, and no

reason to conclude that the friendship of Jesus toward him was founded on such superiority. Afterwards grace appears to have abounded even more toward Paul, and therefore to have been more abundant in him; but had Paul been numbered with the original twelve, John might still have been the disciple whom Jesus loved. Grace in Martha was certainly not so great as in Mary Magdalene; yet not Magdalene, but Martha Christ is said to have loved. Jesus had various near relatives, mother, sister, brother; and these he must have loved with a relative affection, independently of character altogether, and irrespectively of any reciprocity of love in them. Such domestic attachment must have been found in Jesus, for its absence would be defect and sin in us; and no manner of defect was found in him. The discovery, however, of friendship in the Messiah might have been open to question. There may sometimes be little room or call for its exercise; and such a man as John the Baptist may have found no other man, whom in this special sense he loved. Jesus came not to do his own will, but the will of him that sent him; and he declares that any one coming to him he would in no wise cast out, irrespectively of any choice or preference of his own, and on the simple ground of the wide love of the Father to sinful men. John 6:37, 38. Apart from express statement, we might therefore have conceived that specialty of friendship was excluded by his divine mission. But the Scripture leaves no doubt on this head; and human friendship forms one of the recorded elements of the character of Jesus on earth. Such friendship does not necessarily survive the grave, any more than other relations or special relative affections; and its existence in Christ after his ascension is expressly denied by the apostle Paul. Some of his fellow-Christians had been personally acquainted with Christ in the days of his ministry; but concerning any special relation to him remaining hereafter on that account, the apostle expressly announces: 'Yea, though we have known Christ after the flesh, yet now henceforth know we him no more.' 2 Cor. 5:16.

But human friendship formed part of the human character of Jesus on earth; which gives us the assurance that this particular affection is among the things that are honest, just, pure, lovely, and of good report.

2. The *hospitality* of the family is closely connected with the intimate friendship of Jesus; for that friendship probably arose, like other friendships, partly from providential circumstances and partly from the character of the friends. The fact of Christ being often a guest in the house naturally conduced to the special friendship, while the friendship would equally conduce to his acceptance of the hospitality. Hospitality itself is one of the chief elements in friendship; and this may be regarded as one of the characteristics of the family that is commended by the seal of the Son of man. Their circumstances were such as at once to enable them to exercise hospitality, and to have given them plausible excuse for its omission had they sought it. The family must no doubt have enjoyed the outward comfort which usually accompanies a wide influence; for they were well known and highly respected, not only in their native village but in Jerusalem, whence many of the Jews came to comfort the sisters on their brother's death. But, on the other hand, their means were not such as to surround them with servants, and to relieve them of the burdens of the household. The entertainment of guests entailed much personal labour on

Martha, though she could hardly have been unassisted in the more menial parts of the work.

In their cordial hospitality to godly strangers the family of Bethany found a great reward, as those 'who are not forgetful to entertain strangers' commonly do. The blessedness of entertaining angels unawares was more than fulfilled in them. When they first received Jesus into their house, even if they welcomed him as the Messiah, they could scarcely have surmised the real greatness of their guest, God manifest in the flesh, which the apostles themselves so slowly discovered. And even in this world, Jesus gave them a princely return for all their kindness. They gave him bread, and he accepted it at their hands; but the life is more than meat, and in return for bread he gave them life itself. Sudden sickness cuts down the head of the family; their joy is changed into bitter grief, and their happy home lies desolate. Jesus calls Lazarus from the grave; and with the highest of all the gifts of earth, with life itself, he repays manifold all the attentions he had received beneath their roof.

3. In the *individual characters* of the family, we know almost nothing of Lazarus whom Jesus loved, except that he was a true believer. Quiet and kindly he certainly was, with nothing of haste or forwardness in his character, else it could scarce have been hid in so large a narrative; and with extremely little of self about him, with little propensity to seek his own or to exalt himself above others. The stronger elements of character we are apt to regard as lacking; for he was not called to be apostle, though on such terms of intimacy with Christ; nor do we know that he was enrolled among the seventy disciples. But there must surely be error

in this estimate. In Lazarus, with so little of the busy Martha about him, we think there must have been much of the silent depth of his sister Mary. In the only man besides John whom Jesus is said to have loved, in the man toward whom his attachment was so marked that others called him 'he whom thou lovest,' in Lazarus the friend of Jesus, there may have been much of the quiet nobleness of soul, the deep ardour of the affection, and the magnanimous sinking of self that adorned Jonathan the friend of David. The two sisters whom Jesus loved have their characters strongly marked and widely differing from each other. That Jesus loved them was their highest honour and happiness; that he loved them both is sufficient proof that his friendship was not founded on mere likeness to his own human character. The sisters were extremely unlike; and if the one resembled Jesus, the character of the other must have presented a contrast to his. It is no surprise that he should be the friend of Mary, who sat at his feet and heard his word, and who made him the noblest offering that ever cheered the Man of sorrows in his sojourn on earth. But we are apt to wonder if he should be on terms of equal friendship with the anxious and bustling Martha, so troublesome in her very kindness. Yet so it was; Jesus loved Martha and her sister. Nor was his love estranged by her officiousness, so contrary to his own quietness of spirit; he reproves it, yet does not cease to receive the hospitality which gave occasion to the busy carefulness.

4. The welcome given him at Bethany stands in an interesting connexion with the *personal* habits of Jesus. In his last visit to Jerusalem, it is stated that for some days before his crucifixion, 'in the daytime he taught in the temple,

and at night he went out and abode in the mount that is called the Mount of Olives.' Gethsemane, whither he was wont to resort oft-times with his disciples, lay at the foot of one slope of the mount, and Bethany near the base of another. The few last nights of Jesus on earth were probably spent either on the Mount of Olives itself, or nigh to it as at Gethsemane, beneath the open vault of heaven, or with only the shelter yielded by the trees of the field or the garden. Such a resort, better even than the friendly roof, may have accorded with the great yet dark events that were in progress. This we know was the choice of Jesus on the last night of all, when he went from Jerusalem to Gethsemane at the close of the Last Supper; and his previous abiding by night on the Mount of Olives seems to imply that he entered no house. But this was probably limited to the few closing days; for the evangelist Mark narrates, that 'when the eventide was come he went out unto Bethany with the twelve.' In Bethany, and doubtless in the friendly home of Lazarus, Jesus lodged by night on his last great visit to Jerusalem; and probably also on former visits, for long before this he had been a guest in the family.

The work of Jesus led him to the busy haunts of men, and his great last work of all brought him to the crowded capital of the kingdom, the Holy City; for it could not be that a prophet should perish out of Jerusalem. But he had been brought up in the retired village of Nazareth, amid the hills of Zebulon. He ever loved the sea-shore and the hill-side for preaching the tidings of human joy, and the mountain and the desert were his chosen retreats for prayer. A fortified town like Jerusalem, notwithstanding all its population, had no spreading suburbs like our large modern cities, but

to pass without the walls was to enter at once into the quiet
of the country; and so the record runs, that when even
was come he went out of the city,' to spend the remainder
of the twenty-four hours in rural quiet ness. Early in the
morning he returned to the temple and taught, redeeming
the shortening hours of his life; but he did not therefore tarry
also till late at night in the city. The work of teaching was
over, and the residue of the time was given to conference,
to meditation, to prayer. The closing of the city gates would
indeed leave no choice between a rather early departure, and
remaining all night within the walls. There must surely have
been friendly houses in Jerusalem to give Jesus welcome, like
that of Mary the mother of Mark, where so many afterwards
gathered to pray for Peter; yet the Passover was kept by Jesus,
not at the house of any tried disciple, but of an open-hearted
stranger. But whether shut out from Jerusalem or not, he
chose Bethany for the place of his nightly rest. Along with
the hospitable home, his chief inducement must have been
the quiet of the Mount of Olives, with its lone retreats for
fellowship with his disciples and with his Father in heaven;
haply taking them forth along with him, and then bidding
them tarry by themselves while he went further to pray to
the Father. Other memories are gathered round Bethany. Its
graveyard was the scene of the resurrection of Lazarus, the
greatest of all the miracles; its pathway presented the leafy
fig-tree, whose fruitless branches called forth the curse of
barrenness, the single miracle of judgment; and its neighbourhood afforded the last resting-place for the feet of Jesus
on earth, when he led them out as far as to Bethany, and was
taken up from the Mount Olivet to the right hand of the
Father. Yet our interest in Bethany ever returns again to this

family, and our interest in them centres in the friendship of Christ, for 'Jesus loved Martha, and her sister, and Lazarus.'

2. *The everlasting friendship of Christ to every believer*

Such friendship as Christ's at Bethany could have been extended to very few of the human family; to none but those known to Jesus in the days of his flesh, and to only a few of these; not to Enoch, or Abraham, or David, or Elijah; to one only of the apostles themselves, and to few of the other disciples. This friendship, so peculiar and so rare, has now ceased for ever. But there is another friendship, deeper, closer, and more tender still, in which all believers have their share; a share essentially equal to each, and differing only in proportion to the measure of grace, in so far as it can be held to vary at all. To all his true followers, without any distinction, Christ Jesus says, 'I call you not servants, but friends.' 'Friends' he calls every one of us, and 'Friend' we are privileged to call him in return; the Friend of publicans and sinners, the Friend that sticketh closer than a brother.

There is an earthly relation that includes friendship, yet is closer and dearer. Parent and child are scarcely friends in the exact idea of the relation; brother and sister may be or may not; and these relations all want that element of friendship which consists in choice. But the relation of husband and wife, equally with friendship, is founded on choice; and when once formed, is the closest of all relations and of all friendships. Into this one only relation Christ entered not on earth. Parents he had, mother and reputed father, to whom he was subject; he had brothers and sisters; he had also friends; but Jesus Christ is the Bridegroom of all the redeemed, of the church, the Bride, the Lamb's wife.

In a deeper sense than the saying, 'He loved Martha, and her sister, and Lazarus,' every believer can say, 'He loved me, and gave himself for me.' It is not merely the sacrifice of his life for us, but the depth of his love prompting that sacrifice. As he has not spared his life for us, so he has kept back no thought of his heart from us: 'All things that I have heard of my Father I have made known unto you.' John 15.15. He has withheld from us no inward thought of love, but opened all his mind; and he has concealed no lurking ill that might overtake us, or covert snare into which we might fall. 'In my Father's house are many mansions, if it were not so I would have told you.' Jesus has kept nothing secret from us of either good or evil, which it concerns us to know. And opening all his heart to us, he invites and enables us to open all our heart to him in return. The whole church is his Bride, yet each believer is personally betrothed to him, as if there were no other. He knows his sheep every one, loves them every one, names them every one; and each one walks with him in an intimacy and a fellowship which the closest of mere human friendships can never approach. 'I know my sheep, and am known of mine; as the Father knoweth me, even so I know the Father.' John 10:14, 15. Intimacy cannot exceed this. Nor is it merely his divine knowledge of us, as with Abraham when he was called the friend of God; but it is knowledge both divine and human. The divine nature so communicates with the human in the one person of the Lord Jesus, that Christ knows each and each knows him, and he calls every one his friend. Other friends will fail you, but Jesus Christ is the same yesterday, today, and for ever; other friends may mistake you, but he knows his sheep; other friends may be estranged from you, but 'whom he loves he loves to the end.'

You are for ever friendless if you have not this Friend; for the last enemy will sever all friendships here, and in the great eternal world the lost can never find a friend among the dogs that are without. The Friend of sinners calls to you, 'Come unto me, and I will give you rest;' and 'Him that cometh unto me I will in no wise cast out.' 'Kiss the Son lest he be angry, and ye perish from the way, when his wrath is kindled but a little.' Submit to him, and he will pardon you; trust in him, and he will save you; come to him, and he will receive you, not as a servant but a friend. Then your soul will make her boast in the Lord, both now and for ever; you will triumph in him before the universe; and exulting, you will exclaim: 'This is my Beloved, and this is my Friend, O daughters of Jerusalem.' Song of Sol. 5:16.

II

MARY THE SOUL WITH A SINGLE NEED

'Martha, Martha, thou art careful and troubled about many things, but one thing is needful.'
—Luke 10:41, 42.

THE character of Mary is comparatively rare in the church in all ages, and hence there is often an unwarranted defence and exaltation of her elder sister. Christ's notice of Mary is only commendation; his address to Martha is altogether reproof,· both in form and substance. The repetition of her name, 'Martha, Martha,' is tender rebuke; and the words themselves, 'Thou art careful and troubled about many things; but one thing is needful, and Mary hath chosen the good part, which shall not be taken from her,' contain no mingling of praise. Were this the only account given us of the two sisters, we might even doubt Martha's calling into the kingdom. The contrast between the one and the many is put so strongly, and the good and everlasting portion is so expressly assigned to Mary, that we might almost fear lest it pertained to her exclusively.

That there is no ground for such a doubt, is amply proved by the subsequent narratives. These bring out both Christ's love to Martha, and her own spiritual knowledge and experience. But the Martha who turmoiled at the family feast may have been very different from the Martha who wept at her brother's grave. The character itself is unmistakably one, and with traces of the old leaven still visible; but the grace, scarce appearing in the blade at first, is bursting into the ear when discovered the second time. The words of Jesus were wont to sink deep into the hearts of those to whom they were addressed in person. In the interval between Christ's first recorded visit to Bethany and the raising of Lazarus, 'Martha, Martha, one thing is needful,' could scarcely but be deeply graven in her memory; and the words working that whereto they had been sent, consuming the hay and the stubble, would create a single heart within, and fulfil the saying of Jesus, 'Now are ye clean through the word which I have spoken unto you.' The many things cumbrous and the one thing needful to the soul, if taken exclusively in connexion with the two sisters, apply to a contrast within the church, to the entangled soul and the free. But taken in their full breadth, as Christ himself gives them, they extend to the complete contrast between grace and nature, between the church within and the world without. They are rightly received with both applications.

Let us then take Mary as the soul with a single need, over against Martha as the soul with many burdens, and let us note these two things: that man has only one need, Jesus Christ; and that Christ is near to the soul that needs him.

1. *Man has only one need, and that need is Jesus Christ*

The one great need of man is God, the one need of lost man is peace with God, and therefore the one need of every man is Christ, who is our peace and is himself Immanuel, God with us.

1. The one great need of *every man* is God. For the life that now is, man needs God; for man lives not by bread alone, but by every word that proceeds from the mouth of God. Man lives, moves, and has his being in God; without whom bread cannot feed him, and air can breathe no life into him. If God withdraw his upholding hand, man returns to his dust though all things else remain to him unchanged. If God remain with him, he can draw water from the rock beneath for his thirst, if need so be, and shower manna from heaven above for his hunger.

But still more the soul of man needs God. In his own image he created him, and for communion with himself; and with his own finger wrote it on his inmost being, that man's chief end is to glorify God and to enjoy him for ever. The handwriting can neither be altered nor effaced. Man can never sink into one of the beasts that perish. Like them in stupidity he does become; but for ever unlike in the great void that is left in his being, when man is without God in the world. Like them he may be in heedlessness of God above him and of eternity before him, but only because he is sunk in death-like torpor. Awakened out of that sleep, man is sore athirst as one perishing for want of water, and he cries, 'My soul thirsteth for God, for the living God; o God, my soul thirsteth for thee, my flesh longeth for thee in a dry and thirsty land, where no water is.' Psa. 42:2; 63:1.

The soul of man has no absolute need except God. The secondary wants may be held in abeyance; this one great first want cannot be withheld without perdition to the soul; and this one need supplied fills the soul throughout. The command is, 'Thou shalt love the Lord thy God with all thy heart, and all thy soul, and all thy strength, and all thy mind;' and the blessing is, 'My soul shall be satisfied as with marrow and fatness, when I remember thee; in thy presence is fulness of joy; at thy right hand are pleasures for evermore.'

2. *Lost man* needs peace with God. The divine favour, the forgiveness of sins, the reversal of the sentence of condemnation, the return of man into his Creator's presence, the restoration of likeness to his image; these are all included in peace with God, and that peace is now the one great need of fallen man.

3. Therefore *Jesus Christ is man's great need;* for he is our peace with God, and is himself Immanuel, God with us. This was the need of Mary's heart, and for this she left every other attraction, and sat at the feet of Jesus to hear his word. Her soul had one great want, in Christ she found that want supplied, and to him she clung with purpose of heart. In Christ she found the forgiveness of sins, in Christ the quickening of her soul into life, in Christ the image and presence of the Father, in Christ God manifest in the flesh; all that the creature craves in the Creator, and all besides that it longs for in things created. The one need is sometimes taken for the salvation of the soul which Mary sought, and sometimes for the word of life to which Mary listened; but most simply and most fully, it is Christ himself to whom Mary came, and at whose feet she sat. He was the

bread that her soul needed; so often called by himself 'the bread that cometh down from heaven, of which if a man eat he shall never die.' Martha was making ready many meats; but one alone was needed, of which Jesus had already said, 'My flesh is meat indeed.' Martha was preparing various bread for earthly hunger; but one bread for the soul was indispensable, and Jesus had announced regarding it, 'I am that living bread.'

Every soul of man needs this bread, for except we eat the flesh of the Son of Man, and drink his blood, we have no life in us. John 6:53. Till it is received by faith all is death within us, and death before us for ever. Every man needs it daily, for except in eating the flesh of the Son of Man we have no life in us; it is the only origin of life, and the only sustenance of life in our souls. And as we need this one thing, so it is the only thing that we need. All things else are lifeless to us; and having this, all things else are needless. Jesus himself certifies to us that it is our one and only need.

One of the few grand eras opens in human life when a man first discovers that one thing only is needed by him. His soul has been befooled till that time; trifled with, teased, allured, distracted. He is now awakened to one thing great, one thing needful, one thing alone for his soul, for himself. Many have seen it; I have seen it; you have seen it, some of you; you must all see it or perish. In that hour are scattered the hundred lying wants that buzz about us like bees, each calling, 'You have need of me,' and each leaving us nothing but a burning sting. 'One need,' Mary said, and leaving all things else, in the midst of the manifold preparations for the feast, she hastened to the feet of Jesus to fill the aching void in her soul. One thing needful, O dying sinner! one thing needful for you; and if not quickly found, there is before you one vast yawning want for ever.

But do I need no more? In a secondary sense you do, but not primarily, not absolutely. In real stern necessity you have one need, and you have no more; and this is one of the greatest and most practical of all truths. That same Jesus who said, 'One thing is needful,' said also, 'Take no thought, saying, What shall we eat, or what shall we drink, or wherewithal shall we be clothed? for your heavenly Father knoweth that ye have need of all these things.' In this life we need bread and we need clothing; and Christ, owning and asserting this, declares notwithstanding, 'One thing is needful;' one and no more. And why? Because bread is needed for the existence of life, and clothing for the dignity of life, but life itself is not needed. I need and you need Christ, but neither you nor I need life. Jesus says, 'Be not afraid of them that kill the body, and after that have no more that they can do.' Luke 12:4. The taking away of the bodily life he speaks of as but a little thing, a slight and surface injury to a man, leaving the great inner man himself unscathed, untouched. Truly the present life is not needful for any of us; and woe unto us if it were, for we must all soon lose it. We need not the life of the body; we need it not for a year, nor for a day, and possibly today we must part with it. Bread therefore we need not, it will soon remain before us untasted; clothing we need not, it will soon lie beside us useless. But Christ we need in life, in death, in eternity; in the body we need Christ, out of the body we need Christ; yesterday we needed Christ, today Christ, and tomorrow Christ. One need and one alone; the same to all, the same everywhere, and the same always.

But if life itself is not needed, much less do we need the varied accompaniments and comforts of life. The love of father, mother, husband, wife, brother, sister, you need it not; you need one thing only, the love of God in Christ. The esteem and praise of man, naturally so dear to us all, you need it not, but the praise that comes from God only. The countenance of friends, patrons, customers, you need it not, but only the light of God's countenance, and the light of the Lamb. The wealth, wisdom, learning, science, taste of this world, you need them not, but only to be wise unto salvation, and rich for the world to come.

In seeking first the kingdom of God and his right- eousness, there is the promise that other things will be added; and so far as they are good for us, we shall not lack them, but rather have them a hundredfold in this present life. But it is an immense relief to the spirit to come down to the great root of all realities, to ask what we truly need, and to answer, 'One thing I need and no more.' It is a great deliverance afterwards to return to this day by day, and to begin daily here, 'I need Jesus Christ, my one great and only need;' for the rest, doing everything by prayer and suppli- cation, and resolving, 'I will cry unto God most high; unto God that performeth all things for me.' Psa. 57:2.

2. Jesus Christ is near to the soul that needs him

It is nothing secondary, but in the very heart of the narra- tive, that when Jesus warned Martha that one thing was needful, *he was himself with all his fulness beside her,* within her reach, and most free for her acceptance. So it ever is under the glad sound of the gospel. The mind awakened to the sense of need, and the heart longing with intense desire for the only object that can fill it, would weary themselves in vain and soon relapse into torpor, if no relief were near. But it is rarely if ever thus with the soul of man; it may be so by man's blindness to salvation, but not by his distance from it. It is by the silver trump of the gospel that men are awakened to flee from the wrath to come, and to repent toward the living God. The call is, 'Repent, for the kingdom of heaven is at hand, and the axe is laid to the root of the tree.' The door of heaven above is thrown wide open to men, and in the same instant the sharp axe of justice is revealed to smite down the soul that will not welcome the upward call.

'One thing is needful,' is the utterance of Jesus Christ; himself the one thing needed, and close beside the soul which he warns of the need. The bread come down from heaven is freely presented to Martha, and at the same moment she is warned that she dies without it. 'There is bread enough and to spare in my father's house,' presents itself to the thoughts of the famished child of folly; and then, but not before, he dares to own to himself, 'and I perish with hunger!' Friend, there is one thing needful for you, and you die without it; but of all things it is both the nearest, with no distance to reach it, and the freest, with no price to pay for it. 'Say not in thine heart, Who shall ascend into heaven? that is, to bring Christ down from above; or, Who shall descend into the deep? that is, to bring up Christ again from the dead. But what saith it? The word is nigh thee, even in thy mouth, and in thy heart, that if thou shalt confess with thy mouth the Lord Jesus, and believe in thine heart that God raised him from the dead, thou shalt be saved.' Rom. 10:6-9.

If one thing were ever so needful, and yet by no means within the grasp of the needy, the soul might plead that there is nothing for it but to seek the many things that can profit neither much nor long, but that can at least be found. But the exact reverse is the case. The many things are hard to get, and burdensome to keep, while the one is the free and irrevocable gift of God to every one that accepts it, to every one that believes.

A man is justly condemned to die, having been guilty of a crime deserving death, and for which he has no hope of pardon; but otherwise he is not a reckless man, and his wife and children he tenderly loves. The day of execution approaches, and he is busy in his cell devising and doing all in his power to lighten the heavy blow that is to fall upon his family. From morning till night he is earnestly penning letters of consolation to all of them in the bitter prospect, writing for them to many friends who may help them in their desolation, and bequeathing to each whatever of his effects may be most valued, or most serviceable. The king's messenger enters the prison with the sovereign's free remission, on the simple condition of the prisoner subscribing the justice of his doom, and his grateful acceptance of the pardon. But how sad the spectacle! The unhappy man is so occupied, that he will not read the king's message. It will require all his time, every hour, every moment that remains, to accomplish the many things he has to do, and after all he will have to leave them only half finished. He has not a minute to spare. O wretched man! One thing is needful for you, and only one; the king's favour, your pardon, your life, and it is here. The rest are all useless; your head and hands are full of needless labours; this one grant relieves you of them all. Wife, and son, and daughter need no dying counsels, nor thoughtful bequests, nor helpful friends; for by this one gift your own life is saved, and you are yourself given back to them with all you have, and all you can think or do on their behalf. The wretched man cannot take it in; life is impossible for him; the one great good is hopeless, and he must save every moment for the many little objects that are still within his power. O benighted, miserable man! One thing is needful, and nothing more; those many things are destroying you; this one would save both you and yours.

The picture is not strong, but weak; and, earth-burdened soul, 'thou art the man.' Condemned, righteously condemned to death, with no plea to justify, with no power to escape, with no hope of a mitigated doom. A dark eternity is before you, the second death with its undying worm. Jesus Christ, with God's blessed pardon, is beside you; own the justice of God's holy law, and set your seal to the gift of his Son, and of pardon through his blood. It is the one thing you need, for all else will follow; or if otherwise, nought else is needed. Your many things burden you now, and in a few years will be gone for ever. Accept this one, and you have all. Seek first the kingdom of heaven, and the rest will follow in due time; but the kingdom will never follow second to the beggarly wants with which you are engrossed. In the name of Christ, we beseech you to let them go; count all loss for the excellency of Jesus Christ; accept of him, and he is yours, and heaven yours, and all things yours. Amen.

III

MARY THE WISE CHOOSER

'Mary hath chosen that good part, which shall not be taken away from her.'—Luke 10:42.

BEFORE considering Mary's choice let us revert again to her need, in order to gather up a fragment which should not be lost. Martha thought Christ had need of her and of her services, but Mary knew that it was she that needed Christ. In part, Martha may be regarded as occupied with the concerns of this passing life, instead of the soul's eternal wants; and on this we have nothing to add. But again, she may be taken as doing many things in the service of Jesus Christ, for the purpose of pleasing and honouring him. The case is a sadly common one; of doing much for Christ, yet caring less for Christ himself, his teaching, presence, and fellowship. Absent from Jesus she was working for Jesus, and she grudged to be left by her sister unaided in the work. She imagined that Christ had great need of her services, and that it would please him best to provide many things to honour him. But she mistook the character and calling of him who came not to be ministered unto but to minister, and to give his life a ransom for many. Jesus sought not hers, but her; he came not to receive but to give; he needed not Martha, but Martha was in urgent need of him.

Martha is like the woman at the well of Sychar whom Jesus came to save, and in whose salvation he found bread for his hunger and water for his thirst. The high-minded Samaritan imagined that it would be a boon to the weary Jew to have a cup of water drawn by her from the deep well of her father Jacob. Whereas his joy consisted in giving; and her own life was hanging on her asking from him, weary as he was, the waters of the far deeper well that springs up in the soul unto life everlasting.

Mary saw that she needed Christ; that Christ had come into their house not for their services, but for their salvation; not to receive many things from them, but to give all things to them. She needed Christ; he had come into the world for the very purpose of giving himself for her need; and it was in her owning his mission and feeding on his words, that he would see of the travail of his soul and be satisfied.

It is far easier and more natural for every one of us to seek to serve Christ, than to be willing to be saved by his service and suffering for us. The doctrinal knowledge of the truth often makes no practical difference in this respect; and the soul seeking salvation ever attempts many things to make itself acceptable to Christ. It is an exceeding great joy, when we discover that Christ has no need of us and our labours; but that we need him, and that without any works of ours he gives himself freely to us.

Martha represents the legal inquirer, Mary the believer in Jesus Christ. But Martha represents also the legal Christian, working many things that give Christ little honour or pleasure, peradventure none; and Mary sets forth the believing soul alive to its own wants, and honouring Christ by ever hungering for him, and by receiving him as the very bread of its life. Not, however, that works are to be lightly esteemed; for they are the rich fruit of the vine itself through the branches; and the soul that is fruitless of good works is only dry fuel, to be broken off and cast into the fire. But Mary was far from fruitless in holy deeds, as will come to be noted afterward; and she wrought freely and nobly for Christ, so as the burdened Martha never could.

Mary is now set before us as *the wise chooser of the good part;* and that portion we shall consider in her choice, in its oneness, its goodness, its eternity.

1. Mary's portion is *chosen* by her. Martha's also is her own choice, for neither is by necessity. There is a sense of need in both cases, with real need in one; but in both there is choice as well as need. Martha chooses many things, many cares, many burdens, and would not be happy without them. She is not happy with them, for they cannot give her peace, but neither can she rest without them. If they were not there, she would make them for herself, that she might have what delight they can yield. Without her various burdens her spirit would be unsettled, as without an object; and some minds, though not hers, are off their balance unless they have something to complain of, as well as to care for. Her burden is of choice, and not of necessity. Jesus did not thank Martha for her many things, far less for her many troubles about them; and all that was required might well have been wrought by her active hands with an unburdened spirit. But her heart loves the care, the cumbrance, and the manifold distractions. These were once the portion of her soul, and to them she is still too fondly wedded.

Christ commands, 'Labour not for the meat that perisheth, but for that meat which endureth unto eternal life,' disallowing excessive labour even for the needful things of this life. Yet it is comparatively little, that the labour of the hands interferes with the salvation and the health of the soul. It is mainly the occupation of the mind that hinders, and that chiefly in works not needful, but having at most a mere semblance of necessity. In all the excuses at the marriage feast, not one is founded on the unavoidable claims of a lawful calling; on the work of a servant to his master, on the care of a shepherd for his sheep, on the effort of a farmer to save his harvest. Christ, knowing the heart, finds the apologies either in voluntary burdens, or in lawful pleasures idolized. The marriage was not a solid reason but a mere excuse, for there was room for all, and the wife was as welcome as her husband. The land had been purchased, and there was no necessity to see it, except in the idolatrous longing of the new owner's heart. The oxen were already bought; and the proof of them could not alter one of the ten for better or for worse, but would only gratify the covetous desire of their master over his recent bargain. Not the labour of the hand, but the choice of the heart, ruins the sinner's soul.

Mary chose Christ for her portion. Doubtless she needed him, and therefore she had been a fool not to seek him; but she also chose him, and therefore sought him with her whole heart's desire. Out of her own heart, indeed, she chose only sin and earth and self; and omnipotence alone could change and create anew the deep inner springs of her heart's election. To her, with the rest of the disciples, Jesus addressed the unvarying truth, 'You have not chosen me, but I have chosen you.' Yet ordained by the Father unto eternal life, loved by the Son when she only hated him, and quickened by the Spirit when dead in sins, Mary did take Christ as the choice of her own heart; as truly her own choice, as all other things were ever Martha's.

And thus it is with every saved soul, thus even with Martha in the depths of her inner being, though the new fountain is partially choked by the old weeds around it. Christ is not the earliest, but the latest choice of the human heart, for 'the carnal mind is enmity against God;' yet he is the real choice of every renewed man. Out of all others he is preferred, selected, and held fast; without hesitation and without regret; chosen not as a mere necessity for deliverance, but as the delight and the object of the heart. So his paths and his precepts are David's choice; 'I have chosen the way of truth; I have chosen thy precepts.' Psa. 119:30, 173.

2. There is the *oneness* of Mary's choice, as distinguished from the oneness of her need. David said, 'One thing have I desired of the Lord, that will I seek after.' So Mary chose one portion; it was good, it was abiding, but it was also one, and that not through bare need but from true choice. The unity gives strength to the choice. In things of earth all are not equally distracted with many things; for some fix their heart on one object, as on some branch of knowledge, and follow it with intense desire. Yet unity of choice it is not. Along with it the praise of man, or some other end is sought; and the failure of this turns the other into disappointment and sorrow. But it is far different with the choice of Christ. The failure of other desires, one after another, only brings out more clearly and more joyfully to the soul, 'One thing have I desired of the Lord, that will I seek after; though an host

encamp against me, I will not fear; when father and mother forsake me, the Lord will take me up.' Psa. 27.

3. But further, Mary's portion is good: 'She hath chosen the *good* part.' 'The Lord is my portion, saith my soul, therefore will I hope in him. One thing have I desired, to behold the beauty of the Lord.' Lam. 3:24; Psa. 27:4. A good portion, in the highest sense of the word, is the Lord Jesus Christ, Immanuel; for there is none good but God. It is infinite gain to any creature, having no essential goodness in itself, to be called to have the good God for a portion; and so possess that which is in itself essentially and alto-gether good. What then must be the gain to the sin-laden soul, to have the Lord Jesus Christ for its part or portion! It is for man, to whom there was nothing left but evil, to be put in possession of all good; of all good, as truly as if there had been no desert of evil in him; and of all good, in such a form that the very portion received cleanses away the evil of the recipient. A sinner dare not embrace the blessed God for his portion, for this would be to clasp in his bosom a holy fire that would instantly consume him. But a sinner can embrace Jesus Christ for his portion; and find in him unabated all the goodness of Godhead, along with life to the transgressor, and certain transformation into the like-ness of the portion chosen. Great indeed is the grace, that to us who are evil a portion is freely given, so good in itself and so good for us; so good for our immediate acceptance, and so good for a lasting possession.

But let us remember, that we must choose between Mary's good part and Martha's many things; and that we cannot have at once the many things with Martha, and the good part with Mary. Christ is the one pearl of great price, for which the merchant-man sells all that he has, that he may buy the pearl. He is both the needed ransom of the soul, and the one pearl of worth and beauty for which all things else are let go. It is a captive in utmost need finding not merely a ransom, but an exhaustless treasure besides. But we cannot have the many and the one together; we must select between them. Of Martha's many things, there is not one of which she herself would say, 'This is good;' and their number alters not their character, but adds distraction to emptiness. The two are essentially different in kind. The 'many things' make up amongst them a portion, such as it is, the 'one' constitutes a portion in itself; and he who is to possess the portion must make his choice.

David, deeply offending his God, has a sad choice set before him amongst three evil things; and is in a strait which to choose, war, or famine, or pestilence. Paul, rejoicing in Jesus Christ, contemplates the choice between two good things, and is in a strait which to prefer; to have Christ with him here for a season, or to depart at once and be with Christ in heaven. Job has the evil of sin and the evil of suffering to select between; and one of his friends prefers against him the bitter charge, 'Thou hast chosen iniquity rather than affliction.' Moses has the same alternative before him; and the Holy Ghost testifies that 'he chose rather to suffer affliction with the people of God, than to enjoy the pleasures of sin for a season.'

But the great first choice set before every man is not between evil and evil, nor between good and good, nor between everlasting good and transient ill; but between partial good for an hour and real good for ever, between emptiness and fulness, between death and life, between

mammon and Christ. It is the choice set before Israel by
Joshua at Shechem, 'Choose you this day whom ye will
serve;' set before them again by Elijah at Carmel, 'How long
halt ye between two opinions? if the Lord be God follow
him, but if Baal then follow him;' set before them a third
time through Jeremiah, within the besieged walls of Jerusalem, 'Behold, I set before you the way of life, and the way of
death.' Josh. 24:15; 1 Kings 18:21, Jer. 21:8.

Christ is freely set before you for your choice, yet there
is no severing between Christ and his cross; for it is Christ
crucified that is chosen as the good portion of the soul. And
if Christ with his cross, then on that cross we ourselves are
crucified to the world, and the world unto us. Moses takes
for himself the portion of God's people; but in taking it
he chooses to suffer affliction with the people of God; not
loving the affliction, but loving the portion that involves the
affliction. Moses takes Christ for his riches, but Christ along
with his inseparable shame; esteeming even 'the reproach of
Christ greater riches than the treasures in Egypt.' Heb. 11:25,
26. You cannot divide Christ; and you may spare the trouble
of an attempt on which millions enter, but in which none
succeeds. You may assure yourself that in casting out of
your Christ his affliction and his reproach, you are casting
away God's Christ with all his salvation; that in declining
to choose the cross, you are withholding your choice from
him 'who bore our sins in his own body on the tree, and by
whose stripes we are healed.'

4. But finally, this good portion is *everlasting;* and not
merely everlasting in itself, but unalterable to every one
enabled to choose it. Mary's portion is 'that good part
which shall not be taken from her.' Alas! how few Marys

would be found with their single better choice, if Martha's many things were as lasting as Mary's one. But it is essential to the one good part, that it shall never be taken away; and equally essential to the many things not good, that they perish with the using. They are taken away; the world takes away its smile of favour, and gives in exchange the sneer of contempt; riches take to themselves wings, and fly away like the eagle toward heaven; friends, health, and life are taken away for ever. But the good part is never taken from the least of all the souls that choose it. 'Neither death nor life, nor principalities nor powers, nor things present nor things to come, are able to separate us from the love of God which is in Christ Jesus our Lord.' Rom. 8:38, 39.

How weak the hand that grasps so great a boon; how easily paralysed by sickness, how soon helpless in death! Yet the chosen portion remains. God gave it to Mary, and keeps it for her evermore; for 'the gifts and calling of God are without repentance.' There is much to provoke the giver to withdraw the gift; but whom he loves, he loves to the end. Being enemies, he loved us and gave us eternal life in Christ Jesus; being friends, however unworthy and however ungrateful, he will neither cast us away from himself, nor recall the gift of his Spirit by which we are sealed to the day of redemption. Martha's many things are gone; they perished in the using; or she was taken from them before they perished; but not one of them remains to her now. She had the root of a better portion, and that continues; but of all the rest she has taken nothing with her. Mary's portion abides, and every part of it abides, nothing taken away. The chosen Christ abides to her the same, and her chosen place at his feet abides. Christ is no more sharing the hospitality of two sisters on earth, with only one of these greatly coveting his presence; he is now in his Father's house above, with an exceeding great multitude around him which no man can number. Yet Mary is not lost in the throng.

Whatever she gained of access to the Lord on earth, whatever she acquired of knowledge, whatever she enjoyed of fellowship, is ratified for ever in heaven. No part of the good portion has been taken from her. Her spirit, now like to the angels in heaven, is for ever capable of a nearness to Jesus and a fellowship with him, which on earth were rather earnestly desired than fully attained.

Most wise was the choice of Mary, and most fully now does its eternal possession confirm the wisdom of her choice on earth. Is yours the same? Is it of one thing or of many; is it of the good or of the worthless; is it of the perishing or of the abiding? Or having through grace chosen the good part, are you letting it go again; letting it go for that which you once cast away for the sake of Christ? Will you now turn back on the road to pick up the weight which you laid aside when you ran the race set before you looking unto Jesus? Or are you seeking to have as much of earth and as little of heaven as will secure your eternal safety? Take heed lest you miscount, and fall short of life everlasting. Nothing is more common with others, nothing more likely for you.

But you complain, that you cannot choose what you know to be good. Then cry in your helplessness to him who can deliver you from yourself, and can work in you both to will and to do of his own good pleasure. Pray for the removal of your heart of stone, and for the creation of a new heart within you. Plead for the circumcision of the heart, whose praise is not of men but of God; for the fulfilment of the blessed promise, 'The Lord thy God will circumcise thine heart to love the Lord thy God with all thine heart, and with all thy soul, that thou mayest live.' Deut. 30:6.

IV

MARY THE QUIET LISTENER

*'And she had a sister called Mary, which also sat
at Jesus' feet, and heard his word. But Martha was
cumbered about much serving, and came to him, and
said, Lord, dost thou not care that my sister hath left
me to serve alone? bid her therefore that she help me.'*
—Luke 10:39, 40.

WHAT so simple as to listen and not to work? what
so easy as to hear and not to speak? what so sweet
as just to drink the words of eternal life from the lips of
Jesus, the Saviour of sinners? Yet nothing so rare, nothing
to nature so contrary and so difficult; nothing so purely
of heavenly origin, so beyond the reach of man except it
be given him from above. The carnal mind is impatient,
self-working, restless, and to be carnally minded is death;
the spiritual mind is self-helpless, looking to Christ,
learning from him, and to be spiritually-minded is life
and peace.

Martha is the picture of the soul charge-taking and restless; Mary of the soul quiet and trustful.

1. *Martha charge-taking and restless*

By looking for a little at the elder sister, we shall the better apprehend the blessed contrast in the younger. Not, however, as if this one picture of Martha developed all her character; other Christlike features in her are clearly brought out on other occasions; and on this occasion we have the central scene without the closing result. Mary sits at the feet of Jesus, while Martha is cumbered with much serving; but ere that same hour had passed away, both sisters may have sat together listening to the same Lord. It is not so written; but while the obedience to Christ's command is sometimes recorded, and sometimes the disobedience, we have often the simple command with no intimation of its effect. But in Christ's true disciples we may usually take it for certain that his precept was obeyed. Here, indeed, there is no formal injunction to Martha to follow her sister's footsteps; but Christ reproves Martha, and commends Mary to her as an example to be followed. This clear intimation of his will can scarcely have been disregarded by Martha, whom Jesus loved. It would rend many a well-woven thought within her breast, to leave off her labours in that hour, all unfinished as they were. But she, who in her own mind so sorely needed Mary's help, is certainly left without it; Mary, with Christ's approval, keeps her lowly seat at his feet, and lends no helping hand to her burdened sister. This second refusal must have tried Martha more than Mary's first forsaking of the loaded tables. It tries, probably humbles, and in that case certainly enlightens Martha's mind.

Since Mary must not leave Jesus and her one great need, to help Martha in her manifold service, is it not conceivable that Martha in that same hour may have found opportunity of leaving her many things for a little, of seating herself at the feet of Jesus, and getting some food unto life eternal? Afterwards, there is the exercise of true faith on the occasion of her brother's sickness and death, and of single-hearted service when the risen Lazarus sits as a guest. And her whole character must have been marvellously altered by the outpouring of the Spirit on the day of Pentecost. That grace so greatly needed by the chief of the apostles, even at the close of Christ's ministry, wrought in them so mightily as to make them quite other men; and the same grace descending on Martha, with the other women, must have lighted up her whole mind and heart with fire from heaven. The natural tendencies of character, which the old man perverted to earthliness, may then have been so chastened, so purified, and so directed as to make her eminently useful in the Pentecostal church, in spiritual as well as in more outward works. In a happy remark on the character of the two sisters, it has been said that 'Martha is the St. Peter, Mary the St. John of her sex;'[1] and when all the books shall have been opened, we may find peradventure the description to be as true as it is beautiful.

Yet while Mary is set before us by Christ as an example to imitate, Martha in her first introduction to us is held out as a beacon to warn. We err not, therefore, in taking the picture for our teaching in all the breadth of its unsoftened lines; a portrait not drawn by partial friends on earth, but taken at the moment with unflattering plainness, engraven by the rays of the sun from heaven.

[1] *La Famille de Bethanie*, par L. Bonnet, Pasteur de l'Eglise Française Protestante de Londres; also in an English translation.

Martha is charge-taking throughout; this element, for good or for ill, pervades her whole character, and is part of her inmost being. She takes charge with heart, with hands, with lips; she takes charge of her own house, of her brother's grave, of her sister, and of her Lord himself. She is busy with her hands preparing the supper for Jesus, assisted by Mary, and probably with some domestic aid. Hands so active as hers would leave little for her sister to do, and nothing that could be done so well, yet Mary is a charge to her. The work must be done, and Mary ought to help in doing it. Little furthering as her aid might bring, she should at least prove her interest in the work, and her respect for it by her presence. Vexed and impatient, Martha must chide her for the neglect; but with a displeasure probably mingled with self-reproach, and the inward consciousness of Mary's choice being wiser and nobler than her own.

She hastens in this mood into the guest-chamber, and finds Mary not standing near the door behind the guests, whence she might have been more easily recalled; but seated on the floor at the feet of Jesus, like one whose single business is to hear, and drinking in with intense eagerness and delight the words of the righteous One that feed many. She cannot now speak directly to Mary, and enjoin her to quit the presence of the Lord, for respect to him forbids it; but she will speak to Christ himself, who by acquiescence is sanctioning Mary's act. Jesus knew what Mary did, but had not interposed; and Martha must needs take charge of Christ's deeds, as well as of her own and of her sister's. When the disciples were caught in a suddenly excited sea that lashed their little ship with ceaseless onset, and broke over her with wave on wave, till she had sunk to the water's edge and was all but engulfing them in the deep, they cried to Jesus, 'Master, carest thou not that we perish?' And the self-same words, 'Lord, carest thou not?' come to Martha's lips in this petty tumult of household trouble; for she is tossed to and fro in a vexing sea of toil and care. Theirs was real helplessness; Jesus arose and rebuked the sea, he commanded it to be quiet, and there was a great calm. Hers is her own heart, as troubled as the restless waves, but harder to lay; Jesus rebukes Martha, and bids her be still; but we know not when the calm came. Half-worldly friends or kinswomen, vexed with the extreme devotedness of some one younger than themselves, say, 'I will not speak to her about it, but I will pray for her;' thinking they cannot possibly err in praying. Yet so did Martha; she did not speak to Mary herself, but only prayed to Christ to speak; she prayed wrong and was reproved for her prayer, while Mary for whose amendment she prayed was commended by the Lord.

How often are all believers, especially the cumbered and careful, guilty of taking not only the burden of their own affairs, which they should cast upon the Lord, but even the charge of the Lord's own acts; directing him what he should do or refrain from doing, instead of meekly waiting upon him and watching his way. It was the residue of the same spirit of charge taking, that afterwards moved Martha at the grave of Lazarus to interfere with the work of Christ, when he commanded the stone to be removed. And our own consciences testify that this proud and carnal leaven works still as busily as ever. Lord, give us the meek and quiet spirit, which is in thy sight of great price. But let us consider,

2. *Mary the quiet listener to the words of Jesus*

She sits at the feet of Jesus, and hears in lowliness, in hunger, in faith.

1. In *lowliness* Mary sits at Christ's feet. She bows beneath a deep sense of her own unworthiness, and of the honour and majesty of the Lord Jesus. Each of the three times that we read of Mary, we find her at the feet of Jesus. Here she is sitting at his feet, listening to his word, in the first recorded interview; in the next, at the mourning for Lazarus, she runs and falls at his feet saying, 'Lord, if thou hadst been here, my brother had not died;' and at the last, in the house of Simon the leper, she anoints the feet of Jesus, and in the lowliest act of all she wipes them with the hairs of her head. Blessed lowliness, which springs from a deep sense of our own unworthiness, and of the glory of the Lord Jesus Christ. Blessed lowliness, that drives us not from Christ, but draws us nearer to him; because he resists the proud, hut gives grace to the humble, and will be reverenced by all that draw nigh unto him; and because the lowliness ever seeks nearness to Jesus, for the nearer the more are we self-abased, and the nearer the more is the divine majesty seen and adored.

Martha is also lowly in her own manner; lowly in loving to be the handmaid of Christ, ministering to his wants. Yet how different the two! Martha's humility sends her away from Christ, that she may attend to his reception, and entertain him worthily of his exalted rank; and in that absence and occupation the humility cannot grow, but self takes occasion for impatience and pride; and this first choice in private goes far to fix her future place on a more public and important occasion. In the great feast after the resurrection of Lazarus, it is still written that 'Martha served.' Her work is necessary. Without the service there can be no feast at all, and none of the glorious incidents of the feast; and it is an honour to Martha, or to any daughter of Israel, to be called and made willing to minister to the earthly wants of Christ or his disciples. Yet it is Martha's first choice remaining to her, but purified and exalted; it is service still, but without care and distraction; it is service, but with no more murmuring at Mary for leaving her the second time to sit at the feet of Jesus; it is service, but in liberty and not in bondage, which differ as life from death; it is service, but doubtless with thoughts of Jesus in the midst of it, and with the hasty gathering, in passing to and fro, of some drops of the honey that flow ever from his lips. 'Martha served,' is the commendation of divine testimony; served with a meek and quiet spirit, in the midst of many things yet not cumbered by them, but in patience possessing her soul.

But Mary had made a wiser choice from the first, and it is not taken from her at the last; a higher choice in private, and it is not taken from her in public; the feet of Jesus is her chosen place at the beginning, and at the feet of Jesus she is honoured to sit at his last feast on earth.

2. Mary *hungers* for the words of Christ's lips. Martha must have bread to give to Jesus, but Jesus has better bread to give to Mary, and she must not lose it. It is a great opportunity, Mary knows this, and must redeem it to the utmost. Much of Martha's fault, and of Martha's loss, lay in her neglecting a great occasion for eternity, and taking it rather as a great occasion for time. Mary had obviously been with Martha, preparing for the fit entertainment of their guest; but Christ

being now in the house, Mary leaves her sister with her work unfinished, comes into the guest-chamber where Jesus is discoursing to his disciples, and seats herself at his feet to hear his word. Either she thinks the preparation now sufficient in the circumstances; or else her hunger is so intense for the words of eternal life, that she tears herself away from the earthly food, and must satisfy her craving for the bread of life. In defence of Mary's costly gift to Christ at the second feast, he announced, 'Me ye have not always,' as good ground for her deed; and 'Me ye have not always,' is equally the motive to her present picture at the feet of Jesus. 'Christ I have not always,' is the language of her soul; and cost what it will, she must redeem the precious hour while he is under her roof.

Mary heard Christ's discourse, esteeming the words of his mouth more than her necessary food. Martha treated Christ as if she might have him for her guest again, and again listen to his voice; but himself she may never have more, and the words he is now uttering she never again can hear. Jesus is in her house, not silent but teaching, as he ever does on such occasions. The words of life pour through his lips from the well of living water within him; every moment the living stream flows, and if not tasted by her as it passes, it is lost to her for ever. Martha can endure this, for she has many other things so precious to her heart; but Mary cannot bear it, she must hear that her soul may live.

3. Mary hears with the *ear of faith*. Faith comes by hearing, and hearing by the word of God. Nature in its strength finds good in working, and good even in effort of prayer, but finds little good in hearing. It is not doing; it therefore seems to be nothing, and to gain nothing, and at best to be a mere door to working. Hearing is indeed a door

to working, but is first a door to living, which is greater. The natural man does not hear; his ear is uncircumcised, and he cannot hearken. But Mary listens to Jesus; and look what benefits come by listening:

Through *listening* life comes to the dead soul; for the words that Christ speaks, they are spirit and they are life. The hour is coming when all that are in their graves shall hear the voice of the Son of God, and come forth to meet the Judge; and in like manner, the hour now is when the dead in sins hear the voice of Christ, and by hearing rise to newness of life: 'Hear, and your soul shall live.' It is Christ himself communicated to the soul through his words, Christ the resurrection and the life; and, therefore, his words resurrection unto life.

Through *listening* cleansing comes to the guilty conscience; for 'now ye are clean through the word which I have spoken unto you.' The blood of Jesus Christ, and it alone, cleanses from all sin. That blood is by the Spirit applied to the conscience, and this application is by the word of God. Christ in his cleansing blood, as well as in his quickening Spirit, is ever found in his own words.

Through *listening* to Christ speaking to us, he listens also to us calling on him. He threatens the proud, 'Because I called and ye refused, ye also shall call and I will not answer.' But, on the other hand, he promises the willing hearer, 'If ye abide in me, and my words abide in you, ye shall ask what ye will and it shall be done unto you.' Our ear open to Christ's words, we shall ever find his ear open in return to our prayer. Prov. 1:24-28; John 15:7.

Through *listening* the soul brings forth rich fruit unto God. The seed of the word is sown in the heart by hearing;

not otherwise. It is this living seed and this only, received by the ear of faith, that brings forth fruit in the soul. The greater the real hearing, always the more abundant is the fruit; for it is the fruitful word that brings forth fruit in the soul of man, thirty, sixty, and an hundred-fold.

Martha begins with troubled working; and being reproved, she ends with single-hearted yet homely service. Mary begins with quiet hearing, and ends with noble work, great and abiding for ever. To work is easier than to hear, because working can well be desired for its own sake. Work is an end to itself. Though not one jot of real good be done, yet there is work; and the soul, occupied with it, rests in it. Though not one tittle of the work has been accepted by God, yet the worker has pleased himself, and finds a treacherous peace. But the fruit of hearing is less easily mistaken. Hearing says nothing, does nothing, and is nothing except for that which is heard. If faith comes by hearing, if the word of the living God enters the soul, then the soul lives. But if God is silent, then the hearing is a mere aching void. It is therefore hard to sit at Christ's feet and hear. If Christ himself speaks, it is a perpetual stream of life flowing into the soul; but if Christ by his Spirit speaks not, all is death, death without even the semblance of life.

Working in the believer is the blessed fruit of life; but working otherwise is only death. 'To purge the conscience from dead works,' is amongst the chief virtues of the blood of Jesus; and the carnal mind, in its busy works, is ever doing that which requires to be covered by the blood of sprinkling. 'To him that worketh not but believeth,' lays an awful pause upon the soul. There is a solemn silence within, a death-like stillness, when the soul first dares to cease talking and stop working; and beginning to listen to the word of life, hears that it may believe in Jesus unto salvation. But how glorious the result! How different the false life wrought out from within by our own legal efforts, and the true life coming down from above through Jesus Christ! What reality and power of life are given to the soul by feeding on Christ, the bread of heaven; what freshness and eternity of life spring up as a well of living water within the heart, by the Holy Ghost given in believing; what fulness and variety of living food are received in the words of life, by every soul that 'hears and lives!' Let us therefore follow Mary; let us take her lowly seat at the feet of Jesus; and in so doing let us reckon, that 'blessed are our ears, because they hear what many prophets and righteous men have desired to hear, but have not heard.'

V

MARY THE NOBLE WORKER

'And being in Bethany in the house of Simon the leper, as he sat at meat, there came a woman having an alabaster box of ointment, very precious; and she brake the box, and poured it on his head. And there were some that had indignation within themselves, and said, Why was this waste of the ointment made? For it might have been sold for more than three hundred pence, and have been given to the poor. And they murmured against her. And Jesus said, Let her alone; why trouble ye her? SHE HATH WROUGHT A GOOD WORK ON ME. For ye have the poor with you always, and whensoever ye will ye may do them good; but me ye have not always. She hath done what she could; she is come aforehand to anoint my body to the burying. Verily I say unto you, wheresoever this gospel shall be preached throughout the whole world, this also that she hath done shall be spoken for a memorial of her.'
—Mark 14:3-9; Matt. 26:6-13; John 12:1-8.

THE scene is again at Bethany, six days before the passover when the Son of Man is to be betrayed into the hands of sinners, and in the house of Simon the leper. This Simon is spoken of as one well known at the time, but we have no mention of his name except on this occasion. He had once been a leper, and retained the designation; but he was no longer the victim of that dreadful disease, else he must have been shut out from society, and could have held no feast in his house. Though not recorded, it seems probable that Christ had healed him; and at all events he was now his confessed disciple, when to be numbered with the Galileans was becoming more hazardous every day. After the resurrection of Lazarus, Jesus withdrew with his disciples to Ephraim, on the border of the wilderness; but he had now returned to Bethany and Jerusalem, to fulfil in his bitter death the great end of his coming into the world. At Bethany 'they made him a feast,' but by whom it was made is not narrated; it would rather seem as if by Lazarus and his sisters; and the house of Simon, an intimate friend if not a near relative, was probably chosen as more commodious than their own for so large a company.

A mingling so remarkable of life and death, of good and evil, of generous sacrifice and base love of lucre, never met at one table before or since. Lazarus is there, called from the corruption of the grave to eat and drink with the living; with his friends, lately summoned to weep over his death, now gathered a second time, as for a marriage feast, to rejoice in his life. Christ is there, the Prince of life; the Son of Man, chosen out of all the flock and set aside as the lamb for the great passover; and the oil of gladness, poured upon his head at the feast, is to anoint him for his burial.

Judas his betrayer is there, grudging sore at the waste of the costly ointment; Martha in her own character is serving; and Mary with a royal munificence is anointing the head and the feet of Jesus. She it is, however, more than all the rest, that here fills the gospel narrative.

Let us then, first, consider Mary as prepared for her work at this feast; and next, as honoured and defended by Christ in that work.

1. Mary prepared by the Lord for a great work

She is fitted for her work; and in due time she accomplishes it.

1. Mary is *prepared* for her work; 'against the day of my burying hath she kept this.' A great work is required by the Lord; the Father will have a tribute of signal honour paid to his beloved Son before his death, and he will have a fit servant to offer it. Martha, the busy worker, will never suit. The thought will not enter her heart; she can do many things, but she cannot do one; the simplicity of one work will never satisfy her, and to the loftiness of this single deed her soul cannot rise. But Mary is chosen, and made ready for the work; and the work, which can by no means be left undone, is committed to her. It is allotted her for a portion, 'a good work before ordained that she should walk in it.' She will do it, she will do it well, she will do it with all her heart and soul, she will do it with queenlike nobleness, and being done it will stand for her memorial in all generations.

Mary *speaks* little. The talk of the lips, that tends only to penury, is none of hers. Of these two sisters there are seven sayings recorded, and only one of the seven, and that a brief one, is Mary's. 'Lord, if thou hadst been here, my brother had not died,' are all the words that Mary ever uttered, known to us; few words and the same as Martha's, except for her addition of more; few words, abrupt and unfinished, thoughts supplying the rest. In Martha's house Mary listens, and is silent; at her brother's grave she weeps, and is silent; in the house of Simon she works, and is silent. She speaks not, that she may hear, that she may weep, that she may work. What a blessing it would be to the church and the world, if Christian women would think of following Mary; if they would learn from her this one lesson of being 'swift to hear, and slow to speak.'

Mary *thinks* much. She has deep spiritual affections, seen in her devotion to Christ; she has deep natural affections, flowing out in intense sorrow over her brother's death. Martha goes forth to meet Christ in her own active way; but Mary waits still in the house, overwhelmed with grief, seated on the ground as a mourner. When called by Jesus she runs in haste to meet him and fall at his feet; and is followed by her sorrowing friends saying, 'She goeth to the grave to weep there.' Martha they followed not; her grief is milder, and can better sustain itself; she is thought to have gone forth on some errand of domestic duty. But for Mary they can conceive no cause of rising in haste and leaving them, except a paroxysm of grief that can assuage itself only at the grave of the deceased; and thither they follow to weep along with her. In the family at the feet of Jesus, in the desolate house with Lazarus gone, in the feast with the alabaster box of spikenard, Mary has thoughts of her own within her heart; which some chide as incompatible with the everyday work of earth, which others respect as surrounded with a heavenly halo, but which all regard as too deep for their own sympathy.

Mary by hearing *drinks in the mind of Christ* into her inmost soul. She knows that Christ is about to die. All the disciples have now heard it oft; they partly believe it, and partly think it impossible; but in none, except in her, does it take the form of practical forethought and preparation. The mother of Zebedee's children is thinking not of Christ's death, but of the splendour of the kingdom for her sons; the apostles, in the intervals of fear and sorrow, are contending which among them shall be the greatest. But the words of Jesus concerning his death have entered deep into the heart of Mary; deeper than into any other of all the disciples. That he is to die has become a fixed thought within her, which nothing can either remove or distract.

Mary resolves in her heart to honour Jesus in this death on behalf of many, and that not in word but in deed. She will honour him by no heroic, heathen act of dying over his tomb; Jesus needs not her service in life, much less her sacrifice by death, for he came to give his own life a ransom for hers. But she will honour him as dying a sacrifice of a sweet-smelling savour unto God. She has an unopened cruet of ointment, of great price and rarest odour; the bequest, it may be, of a loving parent; or long since destined for the day of her own espousals; or recently bought for this occasion. In any case it is her own; not belonging to her brother or sister or to the household, but to herself, to be disposed of as she will. Mary devotes it to the honour of her Lord Jesus in his death, and she keeps it sacredly 'against the day of his burial.'

2. Mary *discharges the work* given her to do, by anointing the head and the feet of Jesus. A day comes in Bethany, not of mourning but of feasting. It is not the foolish feasting of the

world, rapidly succeeding the decease, to drown the memory of grief; but the quiet feast of sacred joy, over the dead added again to the living. The Holy Spirit inwardly moves Mary to seize this occasion as the hour to yield the purposed honour to her Lord. It is no time for the burial of the dead; but when that time comes she may not be there, or may find no access to the corpse. At a family supper she has already taken her place at the feet of Jesus, only to listen to his words. She has won this position for herself, a 'good part,' which Jesus forbade to be taken from her; it will not be refused her at this more public feast, and her great errand emboldens her to claim it. It is a strange embalming of the dead, this festal anointing of the living. But Mary knows that Jesus is to be betrayed into the hands of sinners, and put to death; and she resolves to break the cherished alabaster-box at this feast, and pour the precious phial on his head.

There are no tears mingled with this act. The death of a beloved brother opens the heart of Mary, and makes her head to be waters and her eyes a fountain of tears; but the impending death of Jesus only draws forth the sealed and treasured oil of gladness. 'Thou hast anointed him with the oil of gladness above his fellows;' and no anointing equal to this do we read of elsewhere in prophet, priest, or king. Oil of gladness! 'She bath anointed me beforehand to my burying.' But the death of Jesus is the life of the world, the bread and the wine of joy to all his people; therefore to him also it is gladness; and he gives thanks to the Father for the breaking of his own body, and the shedding of his own blood as a heavenly feast.

Mary anoints both the head and the feet of Jesus, as noticed separately in different Gospels; the woman that was a sinner ventured only to anoint his feet; yet Mary, equally with her, wipes those feet with her hair in lowliest humility. But she mingles no tears. The penitent, in the house of Simon the Pharisee, was weeping for her sins and for the grace that forgave them all; and she washed the feet of Jesus with her tears, because the host had provided no water for his feet. In the house of Simon the healed leper, and under Martha's loving and watchful eye, purest water would be poured in plenty for the feet of the honoured guest, and there would need no gushing tears to supply the lack. Sorrow could not but lie deep in Mary's heart in that hour, but it is no time to weep. The King gives himself a free and joyful sacrifice to God for his people; and his prepared handmaid pours the ointment over him, as freely as Samuel shed the oil on the head of David when he anointed him for the kingdom.

2. Mary defended and honoured by Jesus in her work

'Why trouble ye the woman; she hath done what she could; she hath wrought a good work on me; for the poor have ye always with you, but me ye have not always.' The work is good, is well done, and is better than almsgiving to the poor.

1. The work is *good;* 'she hath wrought a good work.' It is a right noble and royal work of Mary, a deed altogether queenlike. In its first conception, in its execution, and in all its bearings, it is truly great. Martha works at the beginning, and murmurs because her sister sits and works not. Sitting and hearing in that hour are but sloth and idleness to her; out of season with one sister, because Christ needs bodily service then; in season with the other, because it is

the Lord's own precious time for ministering to the soul. But it is Mary's turn to work now, and she achieves a deed renowned through all the earth, and embalming her name through all ages; a work more grateful to the heart of Jesus than any that ever cheered him in his sorrows, from his birth in Bethlehem to his death on Calvary; a work of all others the most worthy of him, and the most exalting to his name; a work which he so prized that he sealed it with the announcement, altogether singular, that wherever the gospel shall be preached in the whole world, this also shall be told in memorial of Mary.

2. It is *well done* by her, for 'she hath done what she could.' It is little, it is nothing that any fallen child of Adam can do. She could do no work of merit in the sight of God, for no sinner can keep God's holy commandment; she could take no share in the great atonement for sin, for no mere creature can bear and survive the righteous curse of the broken law. But redeemed by Jesus Christ, she could spread abroad the savour of his name, and she did it. What she could she did. She honoured Jesus, not by words but by deed: her act declared that his name was to her like ointment poured forth, and more precious far than India's costliest spikenard. The precious alabaster, crushed by grateful hands, filled with sweetest perfume all the house in Bethany; and the record of it fills all the house of God on earth with heavenly odour. Her deed can add no fragrance to the death of Jesus, but it has borrowed everlasting fragrance from that death. Her act of anointing has been so linked with the burial of the Lord's Anointed, that it retains throughout the church the sweet savour of Christ, as fresh today as in its first hour; the odour of

Christ's sacrifice having lent its perfume for ever to the good work of Mary.

'She did what she could;' what no woman of this world ever could, and what few Christian women can. She did what Martha never could achieve, and never could imagine. Working was Martha's chosen sphere; but in working it was Mary that won the prize. A hundred works like Martha's weigh light in the balance against this one golden work of Mary's. In mere cost, which is the least, it bears the palm. Judas never murmured at a feast before, for he had never seen a costly profusion like this. 'Wherefore this waste?' the traitor asked; or more literally 'wherefore this destruction,' this perdition; fit question in the lips of the son of perdition! His own imperishable and priceless soul he casts away like dross, and then complains that the perishing ointment should be thrown away; so like to some of us, who will save anything except their own precious souls. 'This ointment might have been sold for more than three hundred pence,' that is, for more than three hundred Roman pence, or for nearly £10 of English money. It is love expending in one hour nigh three times as much as the traitor is to gain by selling his soul to Satan and his Lord to the chief priests; for the two prices set on Jesus, the noble and the base, meet singularly together by divine ordaining. But the real value of the ointment was greater; for bread was so abundant and so cheap in that land, that one of their pennies was accepted as ample wages for a whole day's work. Three hundred of those pence would therefore have hired three hundred labourers for a day; which with us would now require, not £10, but £30. So costly an anointing Mary did not count too much for Jesus.

'She did what she could;' she did it with all the faith, and zeal, and love of which her soul was capable; she grudged not the alabaster box of spikenard to Jesus; and she grudged not, that it should be expended and gone in an hour. For some more lasting good, a less free and generous spirit might have made a sacrifice; but all this cost for the fragrance of a single hour! Mary thought it not too much, and Jesus thought it not too much. Martha's many things were too much, and they only troubled him; but Mary's one he greatly prized. Jesus could easily feed the poor; he had fed five thousand by the breath of his lips blessing the bread which he broke. But he is now about to give himself to God for multitudes of perishing souls, as a sacrifice of sweet-smelling savour. This sacrifice is beyond all price in itself; the fruit of it for men passes all computation; and that ointment cannot be too costly, which is to serve for an emblem of the much incense that is now about to ascend to the Father for ever, on behalf of every one to whom Christ is precious.

3. Her work is better than *almsgiving* to the poor; better in itself, and better specially because more timely. 'Me ye have not always,' is engraven in Mary's heart from the first; and she leaves the many things, sits at the feet of Jesus, and hears his word. 'Me ye have not always,' remains engraven on her heart to the last; and she pours the precious ointment on Christ's head today, lest he should be gone tomorrow. The many things she might do always if she chose; the poor she has always, and can do them good when she will. But Christ, preferred to the many things, is equally preferred to the poor; for if set up against him, they are only some more among the many things that clog the soul. Christ is first;

before self, and before the world; before father, mother, brother, sister; before life, and before the poor.

The poor, as rivals to Christ, will gain no good from us; but in Christ honoured by us, the poor will be blessed and benefited by all who honour Christ. Christ loved the poor, gave himself for the poor, preached the gospel to the poor, and made himself poor that he might make the poor rich. If we love Christ we shall be like him, and we shall do good to the poor; even because we have them always, we shall seek always to do them good. We shall not weary of always having them, nor weary of always helping them and doing them good. We do good to the poor man, and he remains poor still; therefore we can do him good again, 'for we have him always.' We do good to the poor, and he ceases to be poor, or passes into Abraham's bosom; other poor take his place, two it may be for one, and it only fulfils the truth that we have the poor always, and may ever do them good. Great loss it were, not to them but to us, if we had them not always; for we can always do them good, not because we are always rich, but because they are ever poor. The poor can do good to those that are poorer, and are often their best benefactors.

Mary gives to Christ, it may be all she had for the poor and needy. Men will say that she may love the poor, but now she has made herself poor and can do them no good; the ointment is gone; the three hundred pence, that would so well have fed three hundred poor, are all lost in one hour for ever. But Mary remains and the poor remain, and she can still do them good; for Christ remains above for ever, and Mary will be no loser by Christ; nor will he suffer the poor to be losers. Doubtless in the great day, this one and that among the poor and needy will come forth and declare, 'Mary did me good.' Christ leaves the poor as a special legacy to her; for his words imply that at another time she will certainly do them good. He is going, but they remain with her; and the most liberal in their gifts to the Lord, are also the most generous in giving to the poor. Christ's will is Mary's; hers when she listens at his feet; hers when she anoints his head. In all her recorded acts she enters into the mind of Christ; and beyond all question, she is of one mind with him concerning the poor. Now Jesus says of her, as of others, that if she will and when she will, she can do them good. But whatever is the will of Mary, none is more successful than she in finding the way; none more resolute in accomplishing the will. Therefore we doubt not, that in the resurrection of the just many a poor one will rise to call her blessed, and to say: 'Mary wrought a good work on me, she did me good.'

Friend, have you wrought any work for Christ? any work in his name, by his strength, and for his glory? any work that will remain as fruit to your account? Begin with Mary, sitting at his feet, hearing his word, and drinking life into your soul; begin with Mary, leaving the many things and saying, 'One thing is needful;' begin with Mary, choosing the good part that shall not be taken away; and you will end with Mary in the discharge of some noble work that will abide for ever. It may be little known to men, but it will be fruit that remaineth, either among the good works that are manifest beforehand, or among those that follow after. God will prepare you through faith for his own work; and over against that grace of his in you, he will have some work ready and waiting for you in due season. If he has lighted you as his own candle in a dark world, he will not cover it with a bushel. Fear it not, but trust him for the work in his own due time. But first of all, believe in the Lord Jesus Christ for salvation, come to him for rest, cleave to him with purpose of heart, make him the one object of your heart's delight; and before your day is done, be sure that it will be recorded under your name, if not in earth yet in heaven: 'She hath done what she could; she hath wrought a good work.' Amen.

MARY OF NAZARETH

I

MARY OF NAZARETH

*'And in the sixth month the angel Gabriel was sent
from God unto a city of Galilee, named Nazareth, to
a virgin espoused to a man whose name was Joseph,
of the house of David; and the virgin's
name was Mary.'*—Luke 1:26, 27

THE angel Gabriel, the highest of all the messengers
between heaven and earth, commissioned with the
highest message ever given by God to man, is sent to
Galilee, the lowest of all the regions in the land of Israel; and
to Nazareth, one of the least of Galilean cities, altogether
unknown in the Bible record before, and starting suddenly
into note in consequence of the angelic message.

This city of Nazareth is not by the shores of the Sea of
Galilee, like so many towns of the gospel narrative, but in
the heart of Zebulon, inland and upland; not therefore a
place of fishermen, such as Bethsaida, the city of Andrew
and Peter; but of carpenters like Joseph, Mary's husband,
or haply of husbandmen and shepherds. It lies in a narrow
and secluded valley, encompassed with hills enclosing it

on every side and confining the view, yet their summits commanding a wide range with the sea in the distance. It now contains about three thousand inhabitants, but is thought to have been less populous in the time of Mary; a city as regarded its buildings, but in population only a small town.

Nazareth is the home of the Virgin Mary, and therefore also of her son Jesus. From it he takes the lowly title, 'Jesus of Nazareth;' given to him by men on earth, 'Jesus of Nazareth, the son of Joseph;' accepted and announced by him at the right hand of the Father in heaven, 'I am Jesus of Nazareth.' It is the home of Jesus because it is the home of Mary, it ceases to be his home after he commences his own work in the public ministry, and he is Jesus of Nazareth chiefly because his mother has been Mary of Nazareth. Let us there fore, in considering the history of Mary, take first some notes of Nazareth her native town. It is honoured to give Jesus the title of Nazarene; it is noted for faith and for unbelief; its guilt and its doom are exceeded in Capernaum, the second home of Jesus.

1. Nazareth honoured to give Jesus the title of Nazarene

Hitherto the city named Nazareth is as unknown as the virgin whose name was Mary; and they both appear suddenly on the record at once; for there is no mention of Nazareth in the Old Testament Scriptures. Strange it seems that a place so obscure, and quite new to history, should be chosen to confer a title on the Messiah, promised from the foundation of the world. Nazareth now emerges from obscurity, but only to be covered with contempt. The priests in Jerusalem, to whom Nazareth is unknown, cast contempt on the whole of Galilee, and affirm that 'out of Galilee ariseth no prophet.' Nathanael, the best of the Galileans, looks down on Nazareth as beneath the rest of Galilee and asks, Can any good thing come out of Nazareth?

Bethlehem, the home of David, is the fit birthplace of Jesus. It offers no more, yet is honoured to supply a manger as the cradle for David's royal Son and Lord; for 'hath not the Scriptures said that Christ cometh of the seed of David, and out of the town of Bethlehem, where David was;' and 'thou Bethlehem, in the land of Judah, art not the least among the princes of Judah, for out of thee shall come a governor, that shall rule my people Israel.' But the last is first, and the first last; the honoured birthplace sinks out of sight, while the despised dwelling-place remains conspicuous: the historical, famous Bethlehem is forgotten, and the unknown Nazareth preserved in everlasting remembrance. Men call not Christ, Jesus the Bethlehemite, but Jesus the Nazarene; and Christ calls not himself Jesus of Bethlehem, but Jesus of Nazareth.

Concerning this name of Nazarene it is written, 'He came and dwelt in a city called Nazareth, that it might be fulfilled which was spoken by the prophets, He shall be called a Nazarene:' so called not in any one prophecy, but by the prophets generally. The immediate occasion of the designation is the residence in Nazareth, but its exact character has been the subject of much question. In our translation it is always 'Jesus of Nazareth;' but in the Greek this expression occurs only twice, and everywhere else it is 'Jesus the Nazarene.' The title on the cross is, 'Jesus the Nazarene, the King of the Jews:' his own declaration at the Father's right hand, 'I am Jesus the Nazarene.' Now 'Nazarene' is nearly the same as 'Nazarite,' and we take it to be equivalent; only combining the honour that pertained to the Nazarite, with the contempt attaching to the man of Nazareth. Jesus the Son of God is despised of men; and he takes the ignominy of a despicable name. Jesus the Son of man is honoured by God, and he has given to him a name above every name; a consecrated, dedicated man, devoted to the Lord. 'Nazarene' unites both the reproach with men and the honour with God that invariably attach to the crucified Christ.

The objection that Christ was not a Nazarite like Samuel, or Elijah, or John the Baptist, only confirms this interpretation. On account of his spiritual dedication Jesus is no outward Nazarite, lest the ceremonial should hide the real. He cherishes no long hair of consecration, no seven locks fit to be woven in a web like Samson's; he feeds not on locusts and wild honey, but the Son of man comes eating and drinking; he dwells not in the desert like John, but is brought up in the city in the midst of men. Those were the shadows of consecration, while his is the substance; and the shadow is set aside on very purpose that the substance may be manifest. As he is neither of the house of Aaron, nor of the tribe of Levi, yet an High Priest consecrated for evermore, so with no outward token, he is the one true Nazarite to the unseen God of Israel. He sanctifies himself unto the Father; and in the midst of men he is holy, harmless, undefiled, and separate from sinners.

But let us not forget that it is for our sakes he has sanctified himself, that he might present us holy and without spot to God; and that by the will of God 'we are sanctified through the offering of the body of Jesus once for all.' And if consecrated by his blood and accepted by his Father, we shall be like him, and in the world as he was in the world. We also are Nazarites, marked with the circumcision whose praise is not of men but of God; and like him we shall be despised of men, if like him we are to be honoured by God. Our first name, as well as his, was Nazarene; for 'the sect of the Nazarenes' was our contemptuous appellation. We bear now the honoured name of Christians; both after Christ our head, and as anointed with the same anointing as our Messiah. But he casts not his first name away, but says from heaven, 'I am Jesus the Nazarene.' And if we are his, we must be sharers in his reproach; we must consent to be called Nazarenes; to belong to a peculiar people, consecrated unto God, obscure and contemptible in the eyes of men; and if our name should ever be mentioned with honour by our friends, we must expect to be taunted with the reply, 'Can any good thing come out of Nazareth?'

2. Nazareth is noted for its faith, and noted also for its unbelief

It is noted for its *faith.* The testimony to Mary is, 'Blessed is she that believed;' her remarkable faith we shall consider afterwards, and only at present remark that this faith was found in Nazareth. The faith of Mary was altogether singular. Other faith may have equalled hers, but no other had ever such an opportunity of exercise; and from the beginning of human history faith never on earth received so great a recompense of reward. And this faith was found in Nazareth. By her faith Mary has earned the name of 'blessed in all generations;' and by it the city of her birth has been raised into renown for ever.

'With God nothing shall be impossible,' was announced by Gabriel in Nazareth; 'With God nothing shall be impossible,' was accepted by Nazareth through one of its youthful daughters. Noble Nazareth! where else in all the world could such faith have been found? Nor was Mary alone in believing. Her betrothed husband was familiar with things spiritual and divine. 'In dreams, in visions of the night, when deep sleep falleth upon men, God was sealing his instruction.' He was no man of mere earth, and of things seen and temporal, but deeply conversant with the spiritual and eternal. He was not simply virtuous and irreproachable before men, but a man living by faith of things unseen, and entering within the veil. And Joseph was a Nazarene. How many more believers the little town contained we know not; but it possessed at least two noble witnesses for the God of Israel, two souls that waited for the great Redemption.

But one generation goes, and another generation comes in the Galilean city; faith also goes away, and *unbelief* arises in its room. Thirty years pass over Nazareth; Mary is numbered with its matrons, and Joseph seems to have slept with his fathers, for we hear of him no more. The child, then unborn, now preaches in the synagogue of his native town, full of grace and truth; and the multitude marvel at the gracious words that proceed from his lips.

But how sunk is Nazareth now! not one soul within its walls to apprehend and welcome Israel's Saviour! It had been his home, and doubtless would still have enjoyed his presence, had there been even a few to detain him by faith and prayer. So far from detaining him, the multitude quickly pass from wonder at his words of kindness to anger at his words of truth; and with a universal infatuation they rush to seize him, and to thrust him headlong from the rock on which their city stood.

Capernaum has few believers; so few that Jesus upbraids it for its unbelief, and foretells its ruin. Yet varied faith for mighty works is found within that city. Innumerable cures are wrought there, and many of a notable character. One of its nobles asks Jesus to come and heal his son at the point of death, and himself believes and all his family; one of its foreign military commanders requests Jesus not to come to his house, but to speak the word only and his servant shall live; four of its working men have faith to unroof the house where Jesus is, and obtain health and pardon for their palsied burden. There also, it seems to have been, that one of the synagogue rulers believes for the resurrection of his dead daughter, and she lives again; that one of its reputable daughters, impoverished by many physicians, touches the hem of Christ's garment and is whole; and that one of its wretched outcasts, in her sin abounding, believes in his grace much more abounding and is saved. Many unbelievers there are in Capernaum, almost all unbelievers; yet strong faith is also there, giving glory to God, and therefore mighty works are wrought there by Jesus.

But Nazareth, poor, blind, dead Nazareth! Jesus marvels at its unbelief, and in it can do no mighty work. Certain sick folk he heals, cases both few in number and feeble in character, but not one great work is wrought there. Not one leper is there in all the town, like Naaman the Syrian, to wash and be clean; not one widow of Sarepta, to obtain a new term of life for herself and for hers; no Mary now, to say that 'with God all things are possible.' She may be there still, but it is not now her time; and in all her family, and in all her city, there is not one like her to draw forth or to welcome the mighty arm of the Lord. Yet Jesus is there; with all his power and all his love he is there; able to heal every stricken one in Nazareth and willing, but straitened and limited by unbelief. Grieved and wondering, he goes forth from the town of his youth; his power and his pity go forth with him; and they are left in their sins. Thirty years ago the mightiest of all the mighty works of the Lord had been wrought in Nazareth, and there was faith to grasp it; faith to grasp the incarnation of the Son of God; that one mighty work which stood the centre and root of all mighty works together, and included them all with itself. Now there is no mustard-seed of faith for a single work of might!

Three lessons present themselves in this history:

1. That the boyhood and youth of Jesus were quiet, without show, and without marvels. He did not strive, nor cry, nor cause his voice to be heard in the street. The Nazarenes knew him; his face and his gait they knew, but they knew nothing wonderful about him. Doubtless they did not care to inquire, else they had heard enough to make them ponder and hope. But there had been nothing to startle the town; a boyhood and youth, quiet and unostentatious, had marked the early years of Jesus of Nazareth. If you have light more than others, you need not force into notice. God, who gives it, will bring it out in his own due time.

2. That the Lord had not given Jesus any friend of youth ready to believe in him as the Redeemer of Israel; not even the members of his own family, his brothers and sisters. They were converted in the end; but at the beginning of his ministry, his brethren did not receive him as the Christ of God. Nor were any of his own youthful townsmen, or

companions, his friends in the gospel. Such friends were given him not in the course of nature, but in the course of his holy ministry; not among the people of Nazareth where he had been brought up, but in John the fisherman of Capernaum, and in the family of Bethany far from Galilee. It was Christ under the law as yet, and not Christ in the gospel mighty to save. It was the sowing of that seed, whose fruit was soon to fill the whole earth. Youthful disciple, if you have to stand alone, be not discouraged; you walk in a path which the youthful Jesus trode before you.

3. That faith disappears where once it flourished. Thirty years ago faith was found in Nazareth, such as not in all the earth besides; and now in Capernaum, in Chorazin, in Bethsaida there is faith for mighty works, but in Nazareth none. One believer out of ten in Capernaum might have brought a blessing to Nazareth, and there was not one. We imagine that Mary's own faith could hardly have been in lively exercise at this crisis; else even she might have found in Nazareth some great object of compassion to bring to Jesus; and the helpless sick would certainly have detained the willing Physician. 'Thou hast a name that thou livest, and art dead,' warns each one of us to beware of resting on the faith of a past generation, or on our own faith in years now gone by. With the great exception of 'that holy thing, the Son of God,' there seems to be too much truth conveyed in the taunt, 'Can any good thing come out of Nazareth?' But this was its character in Galilee thirty years after Mary's first faith; during all that age, the town seems to have been sinking in grace and sinking in public esteem; till at length, the expectation that nothing good can come out of it is

sadly justified by the fact that it cannot furnish one living soul to welcome its kinsman Redeemer.

3. Nazareth loses grace, yet escapes desolating judgment

How deep and mysterious are the ways of God! Nazareth by unbelief loses the privilege of the mighty works of Jesus in the midst of it; it loses Christ's presence and favour by its own provocation. But again, the very want of the mighty works and the absence of the Worker seem to diminish the guilt and mitigate the doom of Nazareth, as compared with other more favoured cities. Yet this is not actual mercy, but mere lessening of judgment; and abundant faith would have ensured great salvation.

'Then began he to upbraid the cities wherein most of his mighty works were done, because they repented not: Woe unto thee, Chorazin! woe unto thee, Bethsaida! for if the mighty works which were done in you had been done in Tyre and Sidon, they would have repented long ago in sackcloth and ashes. But I say unto you, It shall be more tolerable for Tyre and Sidon at the day of judgment than for you. And thou, Capernaum, which art exalted unto heaven, shalt be brought down to hell; for if the mighty works which have been done in thee, had been done in Sodom, it would have remained until this day. But I say unto you, That it shall be more tolerable for the land of Sodom in the day of judgment, than for thee.' Matt. 11:20-24. Woe unto thee, Capernaum! woe unto thee, Chorazin! woe unto thee, Bethsaida! Why? Because mighty works were wrought in them, and they repented not. Mighty works were wrought, because a few believed unto life everlasting; and the impenitent had the benefit of the gospel, both fully preached and confirmed by signs and wonders. Therefore they are doomed to righteous destruction. But Nazareth is not included in the judgment, and it remains to this day; for Jesus said not, 'Woe unto thee, Nazareth!' In the deeper motives, it may be that he tenderly refrains from denouncing the city of his childhood and youth, guilty as it was, and cruel toward him beyond all the others. But the immediate ground of exemption is evidently this, that Jesus denounces only the cities that had witnessed his mighty works, and Nazareth is none of these; for no mighty deeds could he work there through their unbelief.

On the cities so highly privileged the woe of the merciful one has fallen heavily. 'The Lake of Gennesaret descends in judgment to a lower level than the cities of the Dead Sea.'[1] 1 It is more tolerable for Sodom than for them. Chorazin is no more; Bethsaida, the city of Philip, Andrew, and Peter, is no more; the traces of them uncertain or gone, and their sites disputed. Capernaum, the most privileged of all, the city of Jesus, the centre of marvels of grace, is gone; and only some doubtful ruins remain. 'We passed,' says Robert M'Cheyne, 'some ruins near the fountain, which I believe to be all that remains of Capernaum. How vividly this brought to mind, "Thou, Capernaum, that art exalted to heaven." We looked in vain for Chorazin and Bethsaida. What a striking lesson for our flocks these places teach! They were small, ordinary sized towns; the people were like our people; their privilege the same, to hear a free gospel from day to day; they neglected the great salvation; and where are they now? Such is the end of those that obey not the gospel.'[2]

[1] John Peter Lange, *The Gospel According to Matthew: Together with a General Theological and Homiletical Introduction to the New Testament* (New York: Charles Scribner, 1857), p. 211.

[2] Letter to the author (unpublished).

Those days are past! Bethsaida, where?
    Chorazin, where art thou?
His tent the wild Arab pitches there,
    The wild reeds shade thy brow.
Tell me, ye mouldering fragments, tell,
    Was the Saviour's city here?
Lifted to heaven, has it sunk to hell,
    With none to shed a tear?
                        —*R. M. M'Cheyne*

From such examples these great lessons remain for all generations:

1. The actual witnessing of the wonders of the Lord is a singular privilege. It brings with it a most special responsibility, and involves all the unconverted in aggravated guilt and in a more dreadful doom. The last generation was a more ungodly one than the present, and the Lord Jesus Christ was too commonly refused in the church and in the land; but it will be more tolerable in the great judgment for the impenitent of that day, than for the impenitent now. We have all heard the gospel message, which had scarcely sounded in the ears of many of them; and we have all witnessed the transforming power of the gospel in many monuments of grace. There were ten in Capernaum to receive and to retain the Saviour; it was a heavenly boon to the city, and all its people saw what kings and prophets were not permitted to behold. There were not ten in Sodom, and they refused the Lord; there were not ten in Nazareth, and they refused him. But in the day of judgment it is least tolerable for the lost in Capernaum, who saw what might have been to the salvation of their souls, and yet believed not; who saw, and repented not unto life everlasting. So with us; let us be thankful for our

great privilege, but let us tremble for the results; let us bless God for the saved, but let us tremble greatly for the lost; let the lost tremble greatly for themselves, for it shall be more tolerable in the last day for Sodom, for Sidon, for Nazareth, than for the now impenitent in Britain.

2. Familiarity with holy things often tempts men to despise them. Nazareth receives in the person of Mary the greatest message ever sent from God to men; and in the childhood, youth, and early manhood of Jesus, it harbours for thirty years the Lord of glory, the Saviour of the world. What an honour, what a blessing, yet on this very account he is refused! A stranger might have been welcomed, but a fellow-citizen is rejected; he comes unto his own, and his own receive him not. God is near to Nazareth, as not in the whole earth besides. The Son, manifest in the flesh, dwells in Nazareth for all those thirty years. The eye of the Father rests on Nazareth during those years, as not on Jerusalem or any city in the world besides; as not on all the earth beneath; as not on heaven above with all its worshipping angels. Yet Nazareth all the while is departing from God; it is further from grace at the close of the thirty years than at their commencement. At their beginning the Son of God becoming incarnate, taking to himself a true body and a reasonable soul, finds faith in Nazareth, finds a believing Mary to welcome him. At their close, he comes to his own and his own receive him not; the Son of Man comes, and finds no faith in Nazareth.

The immediate occasion of the prevailing unbelief was their familiarity with the Holy One of Israel. 'Is not this the son of Joseph?' One so well known cannot be one so great. Jesus tells them that strangers welcome salvation, while the children of the kingdom refuse it. The Syrian

Naaman believes, the Sidonian widow believes, and the people of Nazareth refuse their own prophet. And now as of old the same is ever occurring. Year by year strangers in the midst of us hear, and believe, and are saved. Year after year, the hearers of the gospel from their youth harden their hearts under the goodness of God, that should lead them to repentance. Yet it need not be. The gospel is preached, beginning at Jerusalem; Nazareth itself is among the first of the cities where Jesus preaches the acceptable year of the Lord. Children of the kingdom, 'unto you first is the word of this salvation sent; turn ye, turn ye, why will ye die?'

3. Nazareth teaches God's holy and awful sovereignty. A blessing is ordained for the Syrian leper, a blessing sent to the Sareptan widow; while the lepers in Israel are left all uncleansed, and the widows in Israel all unvisited. So Jesus is sent to Capernaum, to Chorazin, to Bethsaida, but not sent with a blessing to Nazareth. Christ's own city is as needy as any of these. Its sicknesses are as sore, requiring the healer; and its sins are as great, that its sinners being forgiven much may love much. As the loss is its own, so the blame of the loss is its own, the unbelief all its own; but the grace to the others is not of themselves, but from the Lord. Man's guilt alone destroys him, yet God's grace alone saves. Nazareth's sin leaves Nazareth unhealed in the midst of salvation; but the Lord's sovereign mercy, and not its own righteousness, brings salvation to Capernaum. If you have tasted that the Lord is gracious, see that you render to him all the glory; for 'it was not you that willed, nor you that ran, but God that showed you mercy.'

II

MARY THE THOUGHTFUL CHILD
OF THE COVENANT

*'He hath holpen his servant Israel, in remembrance
of his mercy; as he spake to our fathers, to Abraham,
and to his seed for ever.'*—Luke 1:54-55

O F the birth, childhood, and early years of Mary we
have no information whatever. But from her own
lofty hymn, while we can glean nothing of her history, we
may gather much of her previous character and thoughts;
of the character therefore and thoughts of her early youth.
That hymn supplies sufficient evidence that long before the
angel's annunciation Mary was a thoughtful child, having
her mind stored with the word of God, her heart imbued
with love to Israel, and her soul hoping for the great promise
of the Covenant.

1. Mary had her mind stored with the word of God

Moved by the Holy Ghost, she gave utterance to one of
the noblest songs in all the Scriptures. This song, though
prophetic of the future, is also full of reference to the past;

and while consisting of Mary's own thoughts and words, inspired in her by the Spirit, is replete with allusion to the Old Testament Scriptures. It does not, indeed, contain verbal quotations from the prophets, but the whole song is expressly founded on the Lord's promises spoken to the fathers; and it is imbued throughout with the thoughts, the words, and the images of the ancient seers of Israel. The songs of Moses, Miriam, and Israel over the Egyptians engulfed in the Red Sea; the song of the once weeping, but now triumphant Hannah on the promised birth of Samuel; and the Psalms of David, her own illustrious father, must have been familiar to the mind, and deeply graven on the memory of the virgin mother of Jesus.

The fact of Mary's intimate acquaintance with the Scriptures, is full of interest as regards herself, and still more as regards the childhood of Jesus.

As regards Mary *herself,* it shows the honour that is attached to the knowledge of the holy word. God added always to his own word, till all the testimony by his Spirit was finished; but he ever proceeded on the principle, that 'to him who hath shall be given, and he shall have more.' The new words were never communicated to men of new nations, but only to the sons of ancient Israel who already possessed the old, in order that nothing might be lost. No new building is reared, but on the old foundation new stones are laid. Mary is privileged to add her portion, but the new with her is still engrafted on the old; it is a New Testament song on an Old Testament foundation.

God prepares a chosen vessel for the highest honour ever conferred on woman; announces her to whom all the past looked forward, and to whom all the future looks back, as 'blessed among women;' and she is one who from earliest childhood is conversant with the lively oracles of truth. Her song of praise proves long intimacy with the sacred page, and an acquaintance therefore with it from early infancy. Let parents note it as an additional incentive to stimulate them in imbuing the minds of their children with Scripture, and children as a motive to treasure its riches in their own hearts.

But Mary's knowledge of the word possesses still deeper interest as regards *the childhood of Jesus.* He spake himself as never man spake; and his own words uttered on earth, and written in the inspired record, must be estimated at a price not lower than that of the whole volume besides. If any man was independent of the written word, it was Jesus the son of Mary. With nothing in him from infancy to censure, to prune, to correct; yet with a heart delighting in the word, he fashioned himself according to it from childhood to manhood, through life and in death. In action he honoured all its precepts; for direction he embraced all its promises; by suffering he bore all its penalties; and all these not in substance merely, but with express reference to the written word, even in the sorest agony on the cross, 'My God, my God! why hast thou forsaken me?' Now in youth he was subject to both his parents; but in infancy more dependent on Mary his mother. And the fact is full of interest, that she, from whose lips he was first to hear the language of earth, not only walked with God herself, but was deeply imbued from her earliest years with the words of the holy oracles; and able therefore to impart those oracles to the holy child, on the first opening of his infant mind.

Knowledge such as Mary's could scarcely have been obtained otherwise than by personal and continual searching of the Scriptures; by reading the word of life for herself. We know that her cousin Elizabeth, the wife of Zacharias, could read. She was aware that it was her husband's will that her son should be called John. But from the moment when Zacharias learned that name in the temple at the mouth of the angel Gabriel, he was struck dumb for his unbelief till the day of the child's circumcision; and could only communicate the name to his wife by writing on a tablet, as afterwards to the other relatives. Among eastern Jewesses at the present day reading is a rare qualification, even where there is abundant wealth. But at the time of our Saviour's birth, and afterwards during his ministry, the Hebrew women were evidently not inferior for their sex to their fathers and husbands; but had their fair proportion of mental strength and cultivation. And some learned men have maintained that Mary's song was committed to writing by her own pen, which is not unlikely, though incapable of proof. Having read the words of life so carefully for herself, the mother of Jesus would zealously obey the command of teaching them diligently to her children. To such a first-born son she would read the lively oracles with singular delight, ere he was of years to search them for himself. The infant trust and longing expressed in the words, 'I was cast upon thee from the womb, thou didst make me hope when I was upon my mother's breasts,' would increase month by month and year by year, as the child 'grew in wisdom and in stature.' The virgin mother must herself have marvelled at the law of the Lord as she read it to that son, while his eager listening betokened such thoughts as these within him: 'Mine ears hast thou opened; thy statutes are sweeter to me than honey and the honey-comb; I opened my mouth and panted, for I longed for thy commandments; I have eaten my honey with my honeycomb, I have drunk my wine with my milk; I have meat to eat that ye know not of; I esteemed the words of his mouth more than my necessary food.'

Few sons have had such a mother for their teacher, yet some have enjoyed the privilege; but never had mother such a son for a learner, to hear the law of the Lord from her lips. What took place in his boyhood, with other teachers in the temple at Jerusalem, must oft have occurred in his childhood in the humble home at Nazareth; Jesus sitting at Mary's feet 'both hearing and asking questions.' The effect on her must have been the same as on them, and day by day she must have been 'astonished at his understanding and answers.'

2. Mary's heart was imbued with love to Israel

She loved Israel as her own people; still more as the Lord's people; and with a love strengthened by Israel's solemn feasts.

1. Mary loved Israel as *her own people.* Her thankfulness for the singular grace toward herself is what might be expected in any believer; but the outburst of gratitude, 'he hath holpen his servant Israel,' proves that the national welfare was deeply rooted in her heart. Her song is more like the psalm of an aged Anna, waiting long for the consolation of Israel which has now come at last, or the ode of a struggling and weary patriot now at length victorious, than the hymn of a youthful maiden in the humble quiet of an obscure Galilean town.

The royal blood of Israel's ancient kings, flowing in her veins, doubtless quickened the patriotic fire within her. Mary, as well as Joseph, could certainly claim descent from David; that king among the sons of Abraham, by nature, by grace, and by divine election to the throne. There are, indeed, certain difficulties in the genealogies; into which we enter not, but limit ourselves to the single remark that the assurance given to Mary by the angel Gabriel, that *her* son should inherit the throne of his father David, admits of no satisfactory explanation except on the ground that Mary herself was David's daughter, as well as the betrothed bride of David's son. The knowledge of her royal lineage would serve to enlarge her interest in the whole house of Israel, as the kingdom of her illustrious ancestor.

But Mary's national love has its root far deeper than in any specialty of her own family. It is the same as in Simeon, in Anna, in Zacharias, without any such peculiarity. We value it, but without surprise, in aged saints whose other ties are broken or weakened by the lapse of years; leaving this love to the nation to gather into itself the strength of many affections. In the youthful maiden, with the ardour of other affections all unchilled, we highly prize this love to Israel, and meet it with a tribute of earnest admiration; for she presents in early youth the ripe fruit of a maturer age.

2. Mary loved Israel as *the elect of God;* 'he hath holpen his servant Israel in remembrance of his mercy.' It is Israel written in Mary's heart in earliest childhood; it is Israel, the subject of her thoughts by day and of her dreams by night; it is Israel highly favoured in the past, Israel glorious in the future; but Israel for the present oppressed, broken, scattered, ranked no more amongst the free sons of the Most

High, but numbered with the bond-servants of men. But it is specially the Israel of God. Sons of Belial, she knew, there were ever in the midst of the people, men of Israel who yet were not Israel. It is Israel, Jehovah's servant, his elect, the children of promise, the seed of Abraham, the church of the living God. Mary belongs to God's Israel, and God's Israel belongs to Mary. She is part of it, and it without her is not complete; it is one with her, and she without it maimed and imperfect. Israel and Mary are members one of another; Israel the vine, and Mary one of the branches.

3. This love to Israel, inherited by Mary, was doubtless cherished by her *frequenting the solemn feasts* at Jerusalem, whither the tribes went up, the tribes unto the God of Israel. By law, the males alone were bound thus to present themselves before the Lord; but many of the Hebrew women, and probably all the more devout amongst them, went up to the feast once a year. Hannah went yearly with her husband Elkanah to Shiloh of old; and Mary, after the birth of Jesus, went every year with Joseph her husband to Jerusalem. The same had probably been her practice before her marriage; for young women went up as well as matrons, and children often accompanied their parents. Jesus went with Joseph and Mary to Jerusalem, and Elkanah took all his sons and his daughters with him year by year to Shiloh. Luke 2:41; 1 Sam. 1:3, 4.

In this connexion it should be remembered that there was no poverty in Mary's circumstances such as to prevent these journeys to the holy city, and debar her from its cherished privileges. Poor she was undoubtedly, for a scion of the royal family of Judah; and so was Joseph her husband, for one springing from the same stock. Poor both of them also were, inasmuch as they belonged to the working classes of the community, but not poor in those classes. Joseph the carpenter was poor, not like Paul making tents when special necessity required, but working regularly for his daily bread. Joseph and Mary owned themselves poor and claimed the privilege of poverty, when they presented a pair of turtle-doves and not a lamb in the temple, along with the child Jesus. They were not rich, like Joseph of Arimathea or like Nicodemus; but there is no appearance of destitution in their lot, any more than in that of Peter and the Galilean fishermen.

In like manner, Mary was in no abject poverty before her marriage. She appears to have been in circumstances of no great disparity with those of Elizabeth her cousin, the wife of Zacharias the priest, whom she visited after the annunciation suddenly and without previous notice. That visit proves that Mary was under no necessity of hiring herself out for bread, that she was engaged in no servile work, but had the command of her own time and her own actions. After Gabriel's announcement she left Nazareth hastily, as one not required to give account of herself to others; she took a long journey into Judah, and remained there with Elizabeth for the space of three months;—facts all consistent with a life of the utmost simplicity, but having no aspect of excessive poverty.

Similar circumstances in childhood would enable Mary to go up with her relatives to Jerusalem's solemn feasts. The sacrifices in the temple would bring vividly before her youthful mind the great truth that without shedding of blood there is no remission of sins, and might move within her the prayer, 'Purge me with hyssop, and I shall be clean; wash me, and I shall be whiter than snow.' The paschal lamb, with the unleavened bread and the bitter herbs in the upper room in Jerusalem, would remind her of Israel's exodus from Egypt, and draw forth a sigh for the deliverance of the holy city from the rule of the heathen.

How soon the grace of God began to give life in the soul of Mary to rites otherwise dead, we cannot even conjecture. But to be nurtured in the love of the Lord's house and of his people is no vain training for a thoughtful child like her, and greatly furthers grace when given. Many of the daughters of our own land in former days, who afterwards excelled in grace, were so brought up in the nurture and admonition of the Lord; and next to grace itself, there is nothing better for our children than to be trained to love God's people and heritage, and to count their own interests one with the good of the church of Christ in the earth.

2. The great promise of the covenant was the hope of Mary's soul

The words of Mary are very remarkable, when she refers to God remembering his mercy, 'as he spake to Abraham, and to his seed for ever.' There is nothing of this in the angel's message; no reference to Abraham at all, but an announcement that Mary's son should be the Son of the Most High, and that he should inherit the throne of his father David. The child was to be the expected Messiah, the promised King of Israel; but it is Mary's own mind that traces the promise up to its source in the covenant with Abraham. She uses the very words afterwards employed by the apostle Paul, 'to Abraham and his seed;' and alludes to God's own words to Abraham in the original covenant, 'In thy seed shall all the nations of the earth be blessed.' Gen. 22:18.

These are not thoughts of the moment in Mary's soul, but must have been the long cherished aspirations of her heart. Her hopes, like those of all true Israelites, had been concentrated on the one great promise, the promised Seed. It was from the beginning 'the seed of the woman' that was to bruise the head of the serpent; it was specially limited afterwards to 'the seed of Abraham;' and for that promised seed all the godly in Israel were earnestly looking. Old Simeons and Annas were waiting with eyes that almost failed with looking long, yet with faith and hope that could not be put to shame. But the youthful Mary, also, was numbered with those who looked for redemption in Israel, and waited for the promise 'to Abraham and his seed.' The tidings took her by surprise, that she was the chosen mother of that blessed Seed; but the promised child himself had long been the object of firm and settled expectation in her heart.

In all the preparation of this elect vessel by nurture in the word, by love to Israel, and by the hope of the Messiah, the divine wisdom shines brightly. Mary occupying a place altogether singular in the human family and in the church of God, as the mother of Jesus, is singular also among the saints by the crowning event of her life occurring in early youth. Youthful believers had from the beginning formed a noble cloud of witnesses, as children of the covenant made with their father Abraham; but in Joseph, in Moses, in David, the crowning events of life were not in youth but in manhood, after a long and fiery trial of their faith. So it was also in the peculiar exercise of faith for the promised Deliverer. To Eve the 'man from the Lord' was neither through her first born Cain, nor through the righteous Abel; but when both were lost in one day, it was through Seth, given to her in his martyred brother's stead. To Abraham the child of promise came not, till old age had left himself as good as dead. Mary's own cousin Elizabeth is stricken in years before she is honoured to be the mother even of the Messiah's forerunner, John the Baptist. But with Mary herself all this is reversed. It is not nature exhausted and then miraculously revived; but nature anticipated, set aside. It is not faith tried by a succession of disappointments; hope deferred till the heart is sick and it becomes hope against hope; but it is gift unforeseen, blessing of which there had been no forethought, unlooked-for favour and grace. But while Mary's peculiar blessedness was unexpected, it did not find her unprepared, as we have seen already in various important respects, and as we shall yet further consider in more distinctively gracious exercise.

Meanwhile, let us remember that the promise to 'Abraham and his seed' will never be completely fulfilled, till Abraham's own children are blessed among the nations of the earth, and 'all Israel shall be saved.' As adopted children in Abraham's family, let us plead for the recovery of his children after the flesh, for their engrafting into their own olive tree. And let us all learn in this example to honour 'the things that accompany salvation,' to store our memories with the words of eternal life, to value godly upbringing for ourselves and others, to seek to be 'companions of all them that fear the Lord,' to identify our own interests with the prosperity of Christ's kingdom amongst men; and let us covet to have our names enrolled in the number of those who wait for the consolation of Israel, who look for the Lord Jesus, when 'he shall come the second time without sin unto salvation.' Amen.

III

MARY THE EARNEST INQUIRER

*'He hath regarded the low estate of his handmaiden
... His mercy is on them that fear him from generation to generation. He hath showed strength with his
arm; he hath scattered the proud in the imagination
of their hearts. He hath put down the mighty from
their seats, and exalted them of low degree. He hath
filled the hungry with good things, and the rich he
hath sent empty away.'*—Luke 1:48, 50-53.

THE general character of Mary in early youth, as one
brought up in the nurture and admonition of the
Lord, we have already considered. We now proceed to
examine the more special exercises of soul, by which she
was prepared for the signal favour vouchsafed her from
on high. These exercises, as described in her own words,
are not of the nature of transient emotions, but of abiding
habits; not desires newly sprung up in the mind, but of long
continuance and ever increasing in strength.

As gathered from her own song, Mary's characteristic
features were the fear of God, a heart humbled before him,

and a soul hungering after him. There is another element, faith, greater than any of these and the root of them all; but this will fall to be taken up afterward, because it is brought out in immediate connexion with her own peculiar honour as the mother of Jesus. Reviewing, then, these others we have,

1. Mary's fear of God

Humbly, yet without hesitation, Mary claims this character for herself. The fear of God was in her, and she knew that she was numbered with such as fear him. 'His mercy,' says she, 'is on them that fear him.' She has just received a signal token of that mercy; but she had already been taught the fear of the Lord, and been made partaker of the new covenant promise, 'I will put my fear in their hearts, that they shall not depart from me.' Jer. 32:40. There is a peculiar fitness in this fear to Mary's high calling, and its possession is a good portion for us all.

1. There is a remarkable *fitness* that the impression of holy fear should have sunk, both early and deeply, into the heart of one who was to be brought into so peculiar a nearness to the living God. Fear is an essential element in all approach to the great Jehovah, and the nearer the access the deeper always the fear; not the fear that hath torment, but sacred awe, filial fear, holy reverence. 'God is greatly to be feared in the assembly of the saints, and to be had in reverence of all that are about him.' In the angels excelling in strength that minister before him, in the cherubim and seraphim that stand in his presence, holy fear is the chief characteristic of worship. With their wings they fly; but with their wings they cover their face, as afraid to look on God Almighty;

and with their wings they cover their feet, as ashamed to be looked upon by him; and their voice of praise is, 'Holy, holy, holy is the Lord of hosts.' Isa. 6:3.

In like manner the promised Seed of the woman that is to bruise the serpent's head is to be distinguished above all the children of men by pre-eminence in godly fear. The first Adam cast off the fear of God, and did not tremble at his word. The dark brand thenceforth impressed on him, and descending on all his children, on Mary and on every other, reads thus: 'There is none that understandeth: there is no fear of God before their eyes.' Rom. 3:11, 18. But for the kinsman Redeemer, for the second Adam, for the rod which through Mary is to spring out of the stem of Jesse, and for the branch to grow by her out of his roots, the promise had been given of old: 'The spirit of the Lord shall rest upon him, the spirit of wisdom and understanding, the spirit of counsel and might, the spirit of knowledge and the fear of the Lord, and shall make him of quick understanding in the fear of the Lord.' Isa. 11:2-3. Jesus the son of Mary, Jesus near to the Father as no man is, near as is no angel in heaven, is above men and above angels to be filled with the fear of the Lord; to have quick understanding in that fear, which is of all things essential for nearness to Jehovah.

Now Jesus derives no holiness from Mary. He is indeed that 'holy thing born of her;' but holy not from her, but because he is the 'Son of God.' From her otherwise would only have been derived that body of sin and death, which she had inherited from her father Adam through her father David. 'Behold, I was shapen in iniquity, and in sin did my mother conceive me,' is the confession of David, the man after God's own heart. 'Behold, I was shapen in iniquity, and in sin did my mother conceive me,' is equally, and was no doubt constantly the confession of his noblest daughter Mary. With Jesus it is all the contrary. Human nature he derives from his mother Mary and his father David, being of the seed of David according to the flesh; human nature, but no taint of human sin, which is the corruption of nature. Behold, he is shapen in holiness, and conceived without spot or blemish; 'that holy thing that shall be born of thee.'

But though not for the end that any holiness in the mother should descend to the holy child, there is special fitness, and indeed necessity, that the fear of God be deeply written on the heart of her who is brought so nigh, so within the holy place of the Highest. Irreverence there had surely been death; in that inmost sanctuary, the censer filled with strange fire must surely have called down swift destruction. As in heaven above, so in the revelation of himself on earth, God will be had in deepest reverence: 'Honour and majesty are before him, strength and beauty are in his sanctuary; o worship the Lord in the beauty of holiness, fear before him all the earth.' Psa. 96:6, 9. Mary, the handmaid of the Lord, humbly records that this fear was hers; she was among 'them that fear him.' But 'the salvation of the Lord is nigh them that fear him;' and beyond all her thought it is near to her. 'The secret of the Lord is with them that fear him, and he will show them his covenant;' and suddenly she is taken into the Lord's secret, and his covenant is singularly revealed. 'The angel of the Lord encampeth round about them that fear him;' and about Mary in Nazareth, fearing the Lord, his angel gloriously encamps and salutes her, 'Hail, thou that art highly favoured.'

2. It is good *for us* to be partakers of this fear. If you are to be wise unto eternal salvation, then this fear of the Lord is the beginning of your wisdom. If you are to be happy in time, then you must be in the fear of the Lord all the day long, for 'happy is he that feareth alway.' If you are to enter the inner house of God on earth, and stand within the door of heaven's temple, it will be in saying, 'How fearful is this place! This is none other than the house of God and the gate of heaven.' If you are to walk in holiness and truth, it must be through the fear of God, for 'the fear of the Lord is clean, enduring for ever.' If you are to be much in the secret of the Lord, in the clearer revelation of himself, in the closer intercourse of more special communion and fellowship, it will only be through continuance and growth in the fear of the Lord; for it is ever true with us as with Mary, that 'the secret of the Lord is with them that fear him, and he will show them his covenant.' If you are from time to time to have a new song put ever again into your lips, it will be in cultivating the fear of God; for it is written, 'Praise ye the Lord, all ye that fear him.' If you are to enjoy special tokens of his favour, gifts of grace, interpositions of providence, bounties of mercy, it will be through the fear of the Lord; and Mary's song will be yours, 'His mercy is on them that fear him, from generation to generation.'

John Bunyan in his *Holy War,* in describing the recovery of the backsliding child of God, conceives with his own singular wisdom that the keeping of Mansoul was at that crisis of begun recovery committed to Godly Fear; and adds, in words most instructive to all, that he had sometimes thought that the keys of the town should always be entrusted to his care.[1]

[1] 'I have wished sometimes that that man had had the whole rule

2. Mary's humiliation of heart

She is both humble like every child of God; and appears to have been the subject of special humiliation.

1. Mary is *lowly* like all God's children. The 'low estate' and 'low degree' of Mary may refer in part to her outward condition of simplicity; or in the eye of the world, meanness and poverty. Her condition in life was low for one of the royal blood in Israel, low in contrast with the throne of her father David. And if mean in contemplation of the past, it was still meaner in prospect of the future. The daughter of a line of kings, ancient and now remote, reduced to be the bride of a carpenter, was less rare than for the carpenter's bride to become the actual mother of a king, of God's own promised King and Saviour in Israel. For an honour so high and so immediate to herself, Mary's estate was truly one of low degree. A poor maiden, in an obscure village, was the last whom man would have selected for so distinguished a position; and Mary could not but marvel at the Lord, thus 'choosing the base things of the world to confound the mighty; and the things that are not, to bring to nought things that are.'

But as 'the hungry' in Mary's song are not such as are starving in this world, so those 'of low degree' are not chiefly the outwardly poor. The low estate which God regards is the 'humiliation of his handmaid;' the same term being also applied to the Lord Jesus Christ; 'in his humiliation his judgment is taken away.' In Mary it is not mere poverty; for many of the poor are never brought down with any real humiliation, but live and die among the proud whom

---

of the town of Mansoul' (*The Holy War,* chap. 15).

the Lord scatters in the imagination of their hearts. Mary herself had once been numbered with the proud whom she now renounces. Nicodemus was one of them even unto old age; and then he was 'born again,' converted and humbled into a little child. So Mary by nature was 'proud in the imagination of her heart,' till God brought down within her every high thing that exalted itself against the knowledge of Christ, of Christ that was yet to come. By grace she had now been numbered amongst the little children that are heirs of the kingdom of heaven; amongst the meek that inherit the earth.

2. But Mary appears to have been the subject of more *special humiliation*. There must have been much more in her than the initial humbling, which is indispensable for all in entering the kingdom. 'The humiliation of his handmaid' must refer to a deeper teaching, more varied and more prolonged. It is true, indeed, that the whole expressions are prophetic of the future under the Messiah. 'He hath scattered the proud, he hath exalted the lowly and meek, he hath filled the hungry, he hath sent the rich empty away,' are all prophetic of what God is ever to do under the reign of his anointed King. But not the less are the words descriptive also of the past, of what had actually been wrought in Mary's own person and experience. What the special reference may be we cannot conjecture; but Mary's expressions, so closely resembling Hannah's of old, are much more like the utterance of a soul deeply tried through a succession of years, than of one in the comparative ignorance and inexperience of youth.

There is no reason why there should not already have been deep experience in Mary's history, and much reason from her own words to infer that there was. If we suppose her to have been in early womanhood when she was betrothed, her conversion may have taken place in child-hood, and she may have walked many years with God. But if that spiritual change occurred in youth, a few years afford ample time for much exercise of heart, and for many a descent into the valley of humiliation. The first three or four years after conversion have often more varied teaching than any other part of the Christian course, which usually becomes quieter as it advances, though not always flowing in a fuller and deeper stream. The providential leadings of youth are also as eventful as in any portion of human life; and the outward history tells deeply on the inward teaching. Mary's words indicate that in her youth she had tasted that bitter cup, the contempt of the proud around her; and that in her own soul she had undergone a humiliation, so severe that the Lord from heaven 'regarded' it,—a deep humbling which prepared and fitted her for the high exaltation that was to follow.

This is unwelcome teaching to every soul of man, but it is doubly blessed; in yielding pleasant produce to the Lord of the vineyard, for the richest fruit ever grows nearest to the ground; and in receiving abundant favour from on high, for God ever resists the proud and gives grace to the lowly. The reproof from the Lord that humbles, we have too rarely courage to ask; although 'the reproofs of instruction are the way of life,' and the humbling word would save us from the scourging rod. The stroke that humbles we dare not ask, and are not called to desire; but it is sure to reach us unasked, if we are only wise to welcome and to use it, neither despising the chastening of the Lord nor fainting beneath his rebuke. The long trial that humbles, in the soul discouraged because of the way, or the hope deferred till the heart is sick, is the hardest of all to bear and the sweetest of all when borne. 'It is good for a man that he bear the yoke in his youth. He sitteth alone and keepeth silence, because he hath borne it upon him. He putteth his mouth in the dust, if so be there may be hope. For the Lord will not cast off for ever; but though he cause grief, yet will he have compassion according to the multitude of his mercies.' Lam. 3:27-32.

Even so, it would seem, must Mary have borne 'the yoke in her youth' and put her mouth in the dust; else she could scarcely have uttered those words of praise, 'He hath regarded the low estate of his handmaiden, for behold, from henceforth all generations shall call me blessed.'

3. Mary's hunger for righteousness

In the ministry of the Lord Jesus Christ, these were among the first of all the words he uttered, 'Blessed are they which do hunger and thirst after righteousness, for they shall be filled.' And Mary describes herself as partaking of that hunger and sharing in that blessedness; for the hunger of which she speaks has no reference to outward want. We have already seen that she was not in penury; and if she had been, there was nothing in Gabriel's message to meet the case of outward poverty. It left her all as she was, as regarded present means of subsistence. But hers had been a soul hungering for what earth could never yield, and the Lord fulfilled the desires of that soul. Mary we call an earnest inquirer, because her heart cannot feed upon itself, but goes out in intense longing after the Lord.

1. Hers is a heart that *cannot feed upon itself,* and be satisfied. The hearts of most men seek such food, and in part they find it. 'God, I thank thee I am not as other men are; I fast, I pray, I give alms,' is the heart seeking and finding food in itself. It knows nothing better than itself, and desires nothing better. A better self it can imagine and desire and aim at, but nothing beyond itself; and on self with its manifold husks it feeds, and is full. 'Woe unto you that are full, for ye shall hunger,' is the awful curse of him who came to bless; full of the world and the things of the world; full of the pleasures of life; full of the cares and sorrows of life; full of the lusts of other things. Eternal hunger with no morsel of bread, everlasting thirst with no drop of water, fill the portion of your cup. 'Ye shall hunger,' with everlasting longing for many things, not one of which you can obtain; with the deep craving of a heart that gnaws itself for ever, and can find no other food but this bitter wormwood and gall.

'He hath sent the rich empty away;' they come full and they go empty. They come full of themselves, and they go empty of God and of Christ; they come full of the mind of the flesh, and they go empty of the Spirit; they come full of their own righteousness, and they go empty of the righteousness of God. They come full of earth, and they go empty of heaven; they come full of many things, and they go empty of the One. They come rich, and they depart poor; they come with bread, and they leave with a stone; they come satisfied, and they depart hungry for ever and for ever.

2. Mary's heart goes out in *longing for the Lord;* she describes both the desire and its fulfilment in the words, 'He hath filled the hungry with good things.' It is not the desire

of a day or a week in Mary, but a deep and long desire of the heart, the hunger of the soul, the craving of the inner man. Her father David knew it well, and often gave it utterance: 'My soul thirsteth for God; my heart and my flesh crieth out for the living God.' So Mary longed. She had tasted that the Lord is gracious; she had found the Lord; she had been humbled as a little child, and entered the kingdom. But such a tasting of grace only whets the appetite for more. What once she had tasted of the Lord's goodness may also for a time have been taken away, to create the longing for a greater goodness as yet untasted. But however it was, the angel's message found Mary hungering; longing for a nearness to God she had not yet known; for a fullness of soul satisfaction, as with marrow and fatness, which she had not yet experienced. And 'with good things' the Lord filled that soul; with more and higher and better than all her conception and desire.

All this is the more remarkable in such a crisis of Mary's life, in a time when the world is so apt to enter the heart. A bride, betrothed, espoused, and about to be married, Mary is not thoughtless of heaven in the prospect of a new home on earth, but abides in the fear of God; she is not lifted up with foolish joy, but is lowly before the Lord; she is not satisfied with any outward portion, but continues to hunger and thirst after righteousness.

How few there are amongst us that hunger and thirst after righteousness; and how few, after having tasted, continue to hunger and to thirst more intensely than before! How many of you are 'rich and increased in goods, and in need of nothing; and know not that you are wretched, and miserable, and poor, and blind, and naked'! How foolish the fancied spiritual wealth, how wise the spiritual poverty! How miserable the fulness; how empty and void; how utterly unsatisfying and vain; in the end how accursed! How happy the hunger; how sure of satisfaction; how pleasant in its very exercise, because it is healthy hunger for living bread! How blessed now, because it cannot be disappointed but is sure to be filled; how blessed for ever, because it is God, it is Christ, it is the Spirit that meets the heart's desire! The soul is filled with bread that can never cloy; with living water that is ever fresh; with satisfaction which instantly creates more desire and longing; with hunger which is ever met by soul satisfaction. Longing believer, to all eternity you will join Mary in her song, 'He hath filled the hungry with good things.' God in his mercy grant that none of us may have cause for ever to say of ourselves, 'But he hath sent the rich empty away'!

IV

MARY THE SIMPLE BELIEVER

'And in the sixth month the angel Gabriel was sent from God unto a city of Galilee, named Nazareth, to a virgin espoused to a man whose name was Joseph, of the house of David; and the virgin's name was Mary. And the angel came in unto her, and said, Hail, thou that art highly favoured, the Lord is with thee: blessed art thou among women. And when she saw him, she was troubled at his saying, and cast in her mind what manner of salutation this should be. And the angel said unto her, Fear not, Mary; for thou hast found favour with God. And, behold, thou shalt conceive in thy womb, and bring forth a son, and shalt call his name JESUS. He shall be great, and shall be called the Son of the Highest; and the Lord God shall give unto him the throne of his father David: and he shall reign over the house of Jacob for ever; and of his kingdom there shall be no end. Then said Mary unto the angel, How shall this be, seeing I know not a man? And the angel answered and said unto her, The Holy Ghost shall come upon thee,

*and the power of the Highest shall overshadow thee:
therefore also that holy thing, which shall be born of
thee, shall be called the Son of God. And, behold, thy
cousin Elisabeth, she hath also conceived a son in her
old age: and this is the sixth month with her, who was
called barren. For with God nothing shall be impossible. And Mary said, Behold the handmaid of the
Lord; be it unto me according to thy word. And the
angel departed from her.'*—Luke 1:26-38

*'BLESSED IS SHE THAT BELIEVED: for there shall
be a performance of those things which were told her
from the Lord.'*—Luke 1:45

BLESSED IS SHE THAT BELIEVED, is the grand distinction in Mary's character and the crown of all her life.
All generations were to call her BLESSED; all generations to
come, and in all the nations of the earth. Mary's own generation, or that which followed in her own lifetime, began the
award of praise; yet, like so many generations afterward,
they erred from the true mark in the exclamation of the
marvelling Hebrew mother, 'Blessed is the womb that bare
thee, and the paps which thou hast sucked.' Jesus corrected
that blessing with the reply, 'Yea rather, blessed are they
that hear the word of God, and keep it.' But the generation
immediately preceding her own had already touched the
true keynote of the blessing, in the declaration of the wise
and godly Elisabeth, 'Blessed is she that believed.'

Mary believed the word of God, and her faith was the
root and crown of all other grace within her. Whatever other
grace she had, of holy fear of the Most High, of lowliness

before him, or of hungering and thirsting after him, had all its root in simplest faith. Faith alone was first and most and all; but true faith never remains alone, but is the fruitful mother of every grace in the believer. And as all gracious exercises within her had their root in faith, and sprang from that one grace alone, so did they all return into faith again, and had their fruit and crown in that first gift of God and first living element in the soul. Mary believed, and feared, and was humbled, and hungered after righteousness. Mary trembled before God, and bowed down beneath his hand, and hungered for him as the portion of her soul; and in all these she returned to that simple faith, 'without which it is impossible to please him.'

Faith is the great distinction of her father Abraham, of Mary herself, and of all the redeemed in Christ Jesus.

1. Faith is the great distinction of Abraham

The great distinction of all saved souls is faith in the Lord Jesus Christ. This it is that severs them from the world that perishes; 'for he that believeth shall be saved, but he that believeth not shall be damned.' There are other distinctions in believers as amongst themselves, by which one is known from another; but faith is the great distinction between the souls of the living and the dead in the human family. So also in the history of the church collective, the chief element of all is faith; or rather, faith is that on which alone turns the whole history of the church of the living God. She rests indeed only on Christ, is built on that one rock; her walls, her gates, her battlements, her palaces and pinnacles lean all on that one foundation; her strength is out of herself altogether. But that within herself by grace, which cleaves to this one foundation, is faith; Christ the stone laid in Zion, and he that believeth on him not ashamed.

Previous to the incarnation of Jesus Christ, there are two great turning-points in the history of the church as regards the promised Seed; and so far as we perceive, there is not a third exactly of the same character. There was faith in the promise of the Redeemer throughout. All other promises were yea and amen in that one promise; all other faith centred in that one faith; and all true believers hoped in the coming Messiah. But there were comparatively few acts of faith directly for the incarnation of the Son of God. From the hour of the first promise, of the seed of the woman to bruise the serpent's head, earth was probably never altogether void of faith in the coming One. But there is no record of the acting of Adam's faith in the promise; and in most of the ancient believers the recorded faith is not immediately for the incarnation of the Messiah, but rather for salvation through his name. Noah believed for the saving of his house, and built the ark for a refuge; Moses believed for the redemption of Israel, and led them through the Red Sea; but these were not Christ, but deliverances through faith in him. Hannah believed for the gift of Samuel, and Manoah's wife for Samson; but these were only types of the Messiah. So in most other cases; the belief in the Child of Promise, and of manifold redemption through him was common to all; but direct faith for that promised Child was confined to comparatively few.

The first record of this distinct and special faith is in Abraham, who is therefore called 'the father of all them that believe,' whether his own children or not, whether Jews or Gentiles; and all believers are numbered among his children, for 'if we be Christ's, then are we Abraham's seed and heirs according to the promise.' Rom. 4:11; Gal. 3:29. We are not called children of godly Seth, or of Enoch who walked with God, or of Noah who found grace in the eyes of the Lord; but of Abraham who believed, and it was imputed to him for righteousness. All the hope held out to him was in his promised Seed, in whom all nations of the earth were to be blessed. Other promises there were, as of the promised land; but all centred in the promised Child, for without that Child they must all be void. Isaac was an essential link in the chain of promise, but was not himself that promise; for Abraham was expressly told that meanwhile his children should be afflicted four hundred years; and looking down beyond that distant term, 'he saw Christ's day afar off, and was glad.'

2. Faith is Mary's great distinction

Abraham is first in this special belief, and perhaps we may number Mary second. There is indeed a third, an interven-ing link in the person of David. Mary herself goes right up to Abraham, and names none between herself and him, 'in remembrance of his mercy (as he spake to our fathers) to Abraham and to his seed for ever;' but Gabriel announces that Jesus is to 'inherit the throne of his father David.' Now God expressly promised to David that he would 'raise up his Seed after him, whose throne he would stablish for ever.' 1 Chron. 17:11, 12. David believed and rejoiced in that promise; and Christ, the seed of Abraham, is equally called the seed of David. But there is this difference, that David received the promise of the future Messiah as coming in the line of his family, and was blessed in so believing; but he was not called to exercise express faith for the birth, either of the Messiah, or of that son of his own from whom Messiah was to descend. His faith is similar to Jacob's, who believed that the Christ was to spring from one of his sons, and foretold that out of Judah Shiloh was to come. But Abraham expressly believed for the incarnation; he believed for life to Isaac yet unborn, and to Isaac bound upon the altar to die, from whom the Messiah was to spring.

Taking it more generally, we have Abraham, David, and Mary; and taking it more specially, we have Abraham and Mary with none intervening after the same model. Now that which is important is this; that Abraham believes, and that Mary believes, and that faith is the great element in each. Abraham believes for the incarnation through himself, but afar off; Mary believes for it through herself, personally and immediately. When God would have the great promise embraced he raises up Abraham, the father of all the faithful; when he would have that promise at length fulfilled he raises up Mary, Abraham's like-minded, believing daughter. In great passages of the church's history God honours the wrestling Jacob, the meek Moses, and the zealous Elijah; but in the very greatest he puts the honour on faith alone, on believing Abraham and on believing Mary. These other graces are through faith in him in whom all fullness of grace dwells; the true wrestler with Jehovah, the one truly meek and lowly, the Son whom the zeal of his Father's house consumed; and faith lays hold on all the treasures that are hid in Jesus Christ. Among all men Abraham bears the title of 'he that believed;' it is the one great note of his character. Among all women Mary obtains the designation 'she that believed,' as the one great feature

in hers. Abraham is Mary's father; and in the faith Mary is
Abraham's first-born and noblest daughter.

The end of Mary's faith is the same as her father Abraham's; it is trust in God for the incarnation of the Messiah.
But the trial of her faith is even greater than it was, at
least in the first instance, with Abraham. Nothing could
exceed the faith that trusted God for raising Isaac from
the dead; but the resurrection of a dead son must be held
as a greater marvel than the birth of a son in extreme old
age; and the faith that was equal to the less did not stagger
at the greater. The righteous Zacharias had a trial of faith
similar to Abraham's, when both himself and Elisabeth
were 'well stricken in years.' It was the same in kind, but
far inferior in degree; for their years must have been few
when compared with the ninety and the hundred years of
Sarah and Abraham. The trial was also greatly lessened
by being no longer new. The foundation of Israel's history
was a matter of daily familiarity with the pious priest, and
might well have saved him from staggering at the promise
of God to himself. But his faith was not equal to the
trial, and he could not simply accept the promised boon.
Reason prevailed over faith, nature over grace, earthly
wisdom over spiritual simplicity.

Mary's trial was much greater, both in itself, and in the
fact that it was altogether without example. It was even
that unprecedented marvel of which it was written of old:
'The Lord hath created a new thing in the earth.' After the
miracle of Isaac's birth, after all the signs and wonders of
Egypt and the desert and the promised land, this was still
without precedent; it was altogether new in the history of
Israel and of man. 'The Lord himself shall give you a sign:

Behold, a virgin shall conceive, and bear a son, and shall call his name Immanuel.' Isa. 7:14; Jer. 31:22.

In announcing it to Mary the angel's own declaration is this: 'With God nothing shall be impossible:' There is nothing so new, so great, so hard, as to be impossible with God; if anything, this might have been, but with God all things are possible. Such is the test of Mary's faith; not the rare, the hard, the improbable, but that which is impossible to nature, to man, to angel; and possible only to the omnipotence of Jehovah. It is foolishness to sight, to reason, to human wisdom; and can be apprehended and received only by simple, unquestioning faith in the unseen and almighty God. Yet the youthful maiden does not doubt like Zacharias; but believes and staggers not, even like her father Abraham of old.

The promise to Abraham has been kept in abeyance till now; not broken nor forgotten, but delayed. It is now to be fulfilled for ever; to be promise no more, but accomplished fact; to be faithful offer no more, but actual gift. And the last link in the chain must be as bright and golden as the first. Abraham believes that with God nothing shall be impossible; and the first great link is fastened between the believing soul, and the promised but distant Redeemer. Mary believes that with God nothing is impossible; and the last link of the chain is welded into the Rock of Ages. Old Abraham believes, and staggers not; youthful Mary believes, and staggers not. Abraham believes for that which then is new and unknown; Mary believes for that which is still unheard of and unhoped for. Abraham believes God for the resurrection of nature, exhausted and dead; Mary believes God for that which is above nature, contrary to it, and possible only to the supernatural, divine, immediate working of the almighty Jehovah. She believes in God, she looks to God, she sets aside all but God. Like Abraham she 'considers not;' she overlooks earth and sense and all created things, and looks only to the great unseen Creator of all. By faith she sees the Invisible One; to the angelic message she nobly replies, 'Behold the handmaid of the Lord, be it unto me according to thy word.' And 'Blessed is she that believed;' blessed by God in the act of believing; the happy instrument of blessing for all the nations of the earth; and thenceforth to be called Blessed by all generations.

1. Faith is the distinction of all the redeemed

It is interesting to mark how all real believing in Jesus Christ is substantially the same as the faith of Abraham and Mary; it is ever faith in the power, in the goodness, and in the truth of God revealed in Christ.

1. Faith in Jesus Christ is belief in God's *power;* it is ever trust in God for doing that which is impossible with man. His character in redemption is, 'God who quickeneth the dead, and calleth those things that be not as though they were.' Rom. 4:17. With Abraham it is God 'quickening the dead;' with Mary it is God 'calling the things that are not as though they were;' and with every believer it is one of these two or both. It is easy to believe in Christ as our life, so long as we have some life in ourselves. But when all human strength is gone, when all hope of life in ourselves is lost, then faith finds its place in trusting in the living God for resurrection and life through Jesus Christ, and he that believes is never put to shame. We ever begin with trusting in ourselves, more openly at first, more covertly afterward.

Prop after prop gives way, refuge on refuge fails us, till at last all goes together, and we ask with the disciples, 'Who then can be saved?' But Jesus answers us, 'With men it is impossible, but not with God; for with God all things are possible.' Mark 10:27. Our salvation is possible only because all things are possible with God; we believe for the redemption of our own soul, as Mary believed for the promised Saviour, that with God nothing shall be impossible; and over us, as over her, it is written, 'Blessed is he that believed.'

Mary believes in the power of God; which, simple as it appears, is rarer far than is thought. David speaks of it as a special revelation to himself, 'Once have I heard, yea twice, that power belongeth unto God;' because it is a truth known and believed by few, when our own strength is gone, that power belongs to him. But he adds, 'unto God also belongeth mercy,' connecting love with power; for knowledge of mere divine power would bring no hope.

2. Even so is it with Mary; she believes in the power, she believes also in the *goodness* of God; like David, she too declares that his 'mercy is on them that fear him.' She believes in his mercy and she accepts his goodness: 'Hail, highly favoured'—'Be it unto me according to thy word.' The gift of God's great goodness she receives in simple faith; that as nothing is too hard for the Lord to do for the weakest, so nothing is too good for him to bestow upon the vilest. It is believing submission to the gracious pleasure of God, believing acceptance of unmerited goodness.

Such is all true faith. It is belief in the free favour of God through Jesus Christ; with nothing in us to call forth that favour, but everything to provoke wrath. It is belief in the forgiveness of sins, under the confessed desert of condemnation. It is not, however, a mere general faith in the forgiving God; but the acceptance of the pardon that is freely given. Mary believes in the Lord's goodness; but she accepts the blessing for which she believes: 'Behold the handmaid of the Lord; be it unto me according to thy word.' So for us all, God is in Christ 'reconciling the world unto himself, not imputing unto men their trespasses.' In Christ he says to every believing soul, 'I, even I, am he that blotteth out thine iniquity for mine own sake, and will not remember thy sin;' and with believing Mary the soul replies, 'Lord, be it unto me according to thy word.'

We accept the offered pardon, we receive the grace freely given, and in that moment it is ours. We are pardoned, accepted, beloved; and from that hour onward we live, for 'he that believeth in him is not condemned, but is passed from death unto life.'

3. Mary, believing God's power and goodness, confides also in his *truth*. 'Be it according to thy promise,' is the expression of her faith. The whole transaction is strange and unexpected to her; but she is not a stranger to God and his word; and the inquiries she makes are not in unbelief, but in holy simplicity and faith. The angel's appearance is new and marvellous in her experience, and she is troubled at first by an event so wholly unexpected. His glorious tidings are also strange and unlooked for; and the manner of their fulfilment incomprehensible. But she never doubts the truth of God's word. She had already firmly believed the word of promise made to Abraham, and confirmed to David. That word was settled in her mind as the infallible truth of the living God; and she waited for its fulfilment in due season. Now the promise made to her fathers is

suddenly brought home to herself. She accepts it without hesitation; for her question implies no doubt whatever of the truth and certainty of the fact announced, but simply an inquiry into the manner of its accomplishment. A few months earlier, the faith of the aged and experienced priest had stumbled at the promised birth of John the Baptist; but ampler grace is given to the mother of Jesus, that in this as in all things else Christ might have the pre-eminence. She believed the truth spoken of old to Abraham; and she believes the truth spoken now to Mary. How many of the daughters of Zion would have failed in such an hour! Would one other amongst them all have equally proved herself to be Abraham's child?

Does not the like trial constantly find many of us wanting? We believe the truth of God's words to others, but are slow to believe them for ourselves. We believe that Jesus Christ came into the world to save sinners; sinners in general, other sinners, any other except ourselves. We believe the saying to be faithful and worthy of acceptation by all; yet we oft distrust it, as if not worthy of our acceptance. This did not Mary; she believed that the word of God, true to Abraham, was true also to her; and blessed she was in believing. The like faith in us will receive the same blessing. Let us not put it from ourselves by unbelief; but let us take God at his word, let us trust his truth, let us accept his promise. In believing we shall be blessed now, and we shall not be put to shame world without end; for there shall for ever be 'the performance of the things spoken unto us by the Lord.' Amen.

V

MARY THE MAGNIFIER OF THE LORD

*'And Mary arose in those days, and went into the hill
country with haste, into a city of Juda; and entered
into the house of Zacharias, and saluted Elisabeth.
And it came to pass, that, when Elisabeth heard the
salutation of Mary, the babe leaped in her womb;
and Elisabeth was filled with the Holy Ghost: and
she spake out with a loud voice, and said, Blessed
art thou among women, and blessed is the fruit of
thy womb. And whence is this to me, that the mother
of my Lord should come to me? For, lo, as soon as
the voice of thy salutation sounded in mine ears,
the babe leaped in my womb for joy. And blessed is
she that believed: for there shall be a performance
of those things which were told her from the Lord.
And Mary said, My soul doth magnify the Lord, and
my spirit hath rejoiced in God my Saviour. For he
hath regarded the low estate of his handmaiden: for,
behold, from henceforth all generations shall call me
blessed. For he that is mighty hath done to me great
things; and holy is his name. And his mercy is on*

them that fear him from generation to generation. He
hath showed strength with his arm: he hath scattered
the proud in the imagination of their hearts. He hath
put down the mighty from their seats, and exalted
them of low degree. He hath filled the hungry with
good things; and the rich he hath sent empty away.
He hath holpen his servant Israel, in remembrance
of his mercy; as he spake to our fathers, to Abraham,
and to his seed for ever. And Mary abode with her
about three months, and returned to her own house.'
—Luke 1:39-56.

AFTER the annunciation by Gabriel, the Virgin Mary
'arises in haste,' and goes into the hill country of Judah
to visit her cousin Elisabeth, the wife of Zacharias the
priest. The place of his abode may either have been Hebron,
or one of the neighbouring towns, which had been allotted
by Joshua for the residence of the priests.

But no name is given, and no designation except 'a city of
Judah;' and tradition places the house of Zacharias nearer
to Bethlehem. In any case it was a long journey for Mary
to undertake; for the 'city of Judah' must have been nearly
a hundred miles from Nazareth, with the whole breadth
of Samaria between; either to traverse, or else to avoid by
crossing and recrossing the Jordan, as Jewish travellers
often did on account of the enmity of the Samaritans. But
while executed in haste, it was not entered upon rashly. It
was the haste of decision, the haste of holy earnestness and
zeal, the haste of taking counsel only with the Lord and her
own heart, the haste of energy and laborious effort. Such is
the haste of her father David when he sings, 'I made haste

and delayed not to keep thy commandments.' Such haste in a holy cause is highly acceptable to God, and singularly helpful in furthering the gospel of Christ on earth. Yet both with Mary to those around her in Nazareth, and with us in the sight of men, it will seem uncalled for and unaccountable. Toward God there is in it the most childlike humility; but toward men there is the independence of not consulting with flesh and blood.

The journey was made without delay, but not without thought or sufficient warrant. The annunciation of the angel Gabriel, besides the promise of Immanuel to herself, contained only one reference to an earthly friend and occurrence. That friend was Elisabeth, and that occurrence the approaching birth of John the Baptist. It was fit that Mary should congratulate her cousin on the Lord's great goodness to her; it was right for many reasons that she should make known his still more marvellous grace toward herself; and the intelligence communicated regarding Elisabeth by the angel directed Mary's thoughts to her above any one else in the world. God himself had made them both the subjects of his miraculous interposition; and the revelation to Mary of the coming birth of John seemed to warrant or invite her to visit Elisabeth. The event amply proved that in so doing she rightly interpreted the mind of the Lord.

This visit was the occasion of Mary's noble hymn of praise; in which we shall consider her joy in God's goodness, her joy in the Holy Ghost, and her noble thanksgiving.

1. Mary's joy in the Lord's goodness

Mary's noble outburst of joy is not in Nazareth, but in the house of Zacharias; not in Galilee, but in the hill country of Judea. Like the birth in Bethlehem this seems not to be accidental, but divinely ordered. As the birth of Jesus is to be in the land of Judah, so is also this song of praise for the incarnation; Christ being of the tribe of Judah, and Judah signifying praise.

There is joy in Mary for the favour shown her, but with no mingling of pride.

1. Mary rejoices in *the great goodness* bestowed upon her: 'He that is mighty hath done to me great things; from henceforth all generations shall call me blessed.' Her heart overflows with joy for the distinguishing favour of which she is the subject. It is a glorious exalting for one in circumstances so humble, to be the chosen mother of the Lord's anointed King. All past generations have been looking forward to the promised Redeemer; and all Israel's matrons and maidens have looked to the mother of the Messiah as the happiest and most honoured of women. That highest of all distinctions has fallen to the lot of the lowly Mary. All future generations will look no longer forward to some unknown daughter of Abraham, elect unto that honour; but will look back on Mary of Nazareth, as having already found this favour with God. It is astonishing and over-whelming joy that has alighted on this humble maiden. The mighty one has done great things for her; greater than for Sarah, the honoured mother of the nation, or for any princess in Israel since. The greatest goodness the Most High had to bestow in all the earth has been allotted to her; and well may she be filled with gladness, and sing, 'My heart rejoices in the Lord, for he hath filled the hungry with good things.' Her heart is full of the Lord's loving-kindness; her whole inward being filled with holy joy.

2. And with this joy there mingles *no pride:* 'He hath regarded the low estate of his handmaiden; he hath exalted them of low degree.' The signal favour is received with the deepest humility under the consciousness of her own unworthiness and unmeetness. Goodness so great as to remove all plea of desert does not uplift but humbles. If the favour is less or the merit more, so that the disparity between the two is not so marked, pride finds occasion to enter. But when the distance is extreme between the gift and the recipient, the effect is to humble the soul under a sense of unworthiness.

So it is with Mary in receiving Christ; and so also with every soul that receives the forgiveness of sins through his name. The distinction above others in Mary's case was greater; but the joy in itself could not be more, than when a condemned sinner is forgiven through Christ's blood, and has the full sense of the pardon of sin. Nothing can exceed the change from being a child of wrath, into becoming a child of the most high God; from a fearful looking for of judgment, to be begotten again to an inheritance eternal in the heavens; from being condemned and accursed of God, to being justified, accepted, beloved. A change greater than this, if fully realized, cannot take place upon the soul of any son of man; nor can stronger reasons for joy be stated or conceived. Christ himself declares that Mary's own happiness was not so great: 'Blessed is the womb that bare thee, and the paps which thou hast sucked,—Yea rather, blessed are they that hear the word of God, and keep it.'

Be assured of this; that there is not a more groundless imagination, than that by which you refuse the free favour of God lest its reception should fill you with pride.

The pardon of your sins, and the knowledge that all your sins are pardoned; adoption into the family of God, and assurance of your adoption; the heirship of heaven, and the full persuasion of your inheritance, will not lift you up with pride but most certainly humble you in the dust. Our natural hope of partial blessing may elate us, because we trust to meet half way the favour shown us. But God's own grace is so great to us so vile, that the firmer our assurance of it, and the closer home it comes to us, we are only the more ashamed of ourselves. 'That thou mayest remember, and be confounded, and never open thy mouth any more because of thy shame, when I am pacified toward thee for all that thou hast done, saith the Lord God.' Ezek. 16:63.

2. Mary filled with joy in the Holy Ghost

There is the seal of the Spirit to Mary's faith; and this gives her great joy in the Lord.

1. There is the *seal of the Spirit* to Mary's faith. These words of the apostle Paul are full of instruction: 'In whom, after ye believed, ye were sealed with that Holy Spirit of promise.' Eph 1:13. At first it will often be true, in the language of Luther, that 'faith is a certain dark confidence.' It is trust in that which we see not; and for that which we do not feel. It is confidence in the bare word of God. Fruitless hitherto in the soul that word may have been, yet it is received as true. The soul rests upon it as God's truth; not because the word is working love in the heart, or filling the mind with light, but simply because it is God's truth. Hundreds of inquiring souls believe not, because they feel not; looking for the fruit, and the seal of faith in order to believing, instead of simply believing the word itself, and leaving the rest to

follow according to the will of God. 'After we believe, we are sealed with the Holy Spirit.' It is the Spirit that works faith in us; but the conscious gift and seal of the Spirit follow, for we 'receive the Spirit by the hearing of faith.'

There is certainty in the Spirit's seal to faith in Christ Jesus, because 'him hath God the Father sealed.' He hath sealed Christ in his own wondrous person, and in his glorious work; and he seals Christ wherever he is, and in every soul that receives him. But there is sovereignty both in the time and the manner of the seal. With Mary, there is manifest sovereignty in the *time* of the Spirit's seal. It is not immediately on the angel's departure, but after the lapse of days or weeks. Calm and childlike confidence would seem to have been the state of Mary's mind in Nazareth, without any outburst of holy joy. There was simple and unwavering faith; but the Spirit's full seal to that faith seems not to have been given till Elisabeth had saluted her, 'Blessed is she that believed, for there shall be a performance of those things that were told her by the Lord.' The Spirit working as he wills, like the wind blowing where it lists, then sealed Mary's previous faith, and filled her with joy in the Lord.

The *manner* of the seal was also sovereign; for it was not in the solitude of Mary's chamber, as we should have expected, but in holy fellowship with a sister saint. The two meet together in the name of the coming Messiah. Elisabeth calls the unborn child 'my Lord;' which she must surely have done, only because she owned him as Immanuel, God with us. She is filled with the Holy Ghost for herself; full of the Spirit, she addresses Mary; and Mary is filled with the Holy Ghost, and breaks out into her glorious song.

THE MAGNIFIER OF THE LORD

So in substance it is to every believer in Christ Jesus. The faith is sealed to each according to the measure of the gift of God, and according to his holy sovereignty in time and manner; but always the simpler and stronger the faith, the more full will be the seal of the Spirit, because the simplest faith most owns and honours Christ, whom alone the Father seals.

2. Mary's joy is *in the Lord.* She rejoices on account of God's great goodness, and also in that goodness. But the joy does not rest in his gift and favour, however great, but in the Lord himself the gracious giver: 'My spirit hath rejoiced in God my Saviour.' Her joy is that of a poor lost sinner needing salvation, and finding it in the Lord's mercy; she rejoices in God her Deliverer, Redeemer, Saviour from sin and death. If it be God the Father she refers to as the Saviour, it is the Father saving her through his promised Son. But the name of Saviour was so given at this time to the Messiah, that it seems unlikely that Mary should use it without application to him. She was 'to call his name Jesus, because he should save his people from their sins;' and the angels at his birth speak of him to the shepherds as 'a Saviour which is Christ the Lord.' And if the angel foretells of John, that he should 'turn many of the children of Israel to the Lord their God, going before him in the spirit and power of Elias,' speaking of Jesus as God; and if Zacharias calls his infant son 'the prophet of the Highest, going before the face of the Lord to prepare his ways,' speaking of Jesus as the Lord (Luke 1:16, 17, 26); and if Elisabeth by the Holy Ghost already calls Christ 'her Lord;' it may well have been that Mary, who was told that her son should be the Son of the most high God, may now in her song have called Jesus

'God my Saviour,' even as his name was given by prophecy, 'Immanuel, God with us.' Luke 1:16, 17, 26, 43.

Mary's joy is great in itself, but it is joy in the great Lord God. There is no joy to men so high, so pure, so holy as this; not joy merely from the Lord, but joy in the Lord; and as there is none so pure, so there is none so full and so exultant. 'My spirit hath rejoiced in God my Saviour;' it hath rejoiced, and doth rejoice with a joy the greatest that language can utter. Mary's word for rejoicing is what is else-where translated 'being exceeding glad.' It is greater than can be expressed in words, for, 'believing in him, we rejoice with joy unspeakable and full of glory.' It is the human spirit filled with joy by the Lord's great goodness; then filled with joy by the Holy Ghost occupying the soul; and then plunged besides into an ocean of joy, deep and wide, even into the joy of God himself and into God as the soul's joy, the spirit exulting in the Lord. This joyful experience of Mary is not only lawful for us, but is expressly and strongly enjoined on every believer in Jesus by the lips of Paul: 'Rejoice in the Lord alway; and again I say, Rejoice.' Phil. 4:4.

3. Mary praises the Lord

She extols the Lord, and in a song divinely inspired.

1. Mary, enjoying the Lord's goodness, rejoicing in the Lord himself, gives *praise* and thanks unto his name. The Lord had exalted her, and she uses her exaltation only to exalt the Lord. The Mighty One had done great things for her, and she extols him alone as mighty: 'My soul doth magnify the Lord.' All else are forgotten, for He only is great, and greatly to be praised. It is not Mary that is great through the great things done for her, but the Lord that does

them is great. Mary does not magnify herself in receiving great things; does not magnify her people Israel on whose account she receives them; does not magnify her father David through whom they come to her; but Mary magnifies the Lord. We have noted this last, but it is greatest, and with her it is first. With her the favour shown to herself is last, her own joy in the Lord precedes it, and the Lord's own greatness is first of all. 'My soul doth magnify the Lord,' is the first outburst of her song, and it is an outburst of praise and blessing unto God most high. The mighty One, the only mighty One, he that is mighty; the holy One, the only holy One, Holy is his name; the merciful One, with his mercy on them that fear him; and the faithful One, as he spake to Abraham and his Seed. If man is great, God is but little in his eyes; if the world is great, all that is of the Father and not of the world is of small account; if the creature is great, the Creator blessed for evermore is but lightly esteemed; if self is great, the living and true God is set aside as drawing forth no admiration. 'My soul doth magnify the Lord, and my spirit hath rejoiced in God my Saviour,' is the utterance of a heart whose 'chief end is to glorify God, and enjoy him for ever.'

2. Mary is privileged and enabled to give God praise and thanks in Christ Jesus, and so is every believer; but she is privileged and exalted to utter the thoughts of her heart, as *moved by the Holy Ghost,* in words abiding for all generations. This is an honour accorded to few in any age, and to no woman but herself in the New Testament record. Other holy women utter brief sentences, that remain as precious pearls to us; but Mary alone is inspired by the Holy Ghost to utter a psalm or song of praise. The distinction is great

in itself; great as implying much fulness of the Spirit in her soul; and great as honouring her to edify the church in all ages. The Holy Spirit uses her heart and her lips; and she speaks as she is moved by the Holy Ghost.

Yet Balaam, who served two masters, sang wondrous songs by the Holy Spirit concerning the coming Messiah; of whom he confessed so sadly for himself, 'I shall see him, but not now; I shall behold him, but not nigh.' And Mary's blessedness consisted chiefly, not in the miraculous inspiration of the Spirit, but in her own heart made new by the Holy Ghost. Have you ever believed as she believed, and have you had the seal of the Spirit to your faith? Have you believed for any one thing from the Lord, and have you obtained it in the performance of the things spoken by the Lord? Have you ever accepted of the Lord's goodness, of the life and favour that flow so freely from him; and have you ever had the seal of the Spirit to your own acceptance by God in Christ? Have you ever rejoiced in the Lord; not in yourself, not in man, but in the Lord; and has your soul ever magnified his holy name? If so, take Mary's words for your own; unite with her and sing: 'My soul doth magnify the Lord, my spirit hath rejoiced in God my Saviour; for he that is mighty hath done to me great things; and holy is his name. He hath filled the hungry with good things, and hath sent the rich empty away.'

VI

MARY THE PATIENT ENDURER

'Now the birth of Jesus Christ was on this wise: When as his mother Mary was espoused to Joseph, before they came together, she was found with child of the Holy Ghost. Then Joseph her husband, being a just man, and not willing to make her a public example, was minded to put her away privily. But while he thought on these things, behold, the angel of the Lord appeared unto him in a dream, saying, Joseph, thou son of David, fear not to take unto thee Mary thy wife: for that which is conceived in her is of the Holy Ghost. And she shall bring forth a son, and thou shalt call his name JESUS; for he shall save his people from their sins. ... Then Joseph, being raised from sleep, did as the angel of the Lord had bidden him, and took unto him his wife; and knew her not till she had brought forth her first-born son: and he called his name JESUS.'—Matt. 1:18-21; 24, 25

MARY'S own hymn of joy was in due time followed by the birth of John, and by the noble prophecy of

Zacharias, the first-fruits of his miraculously opened lips. In that scene of holy gladness she was probably herself a partaker. It seems unlikely that she should remain so long in the house, and depart immediately before that great event; and the fact of her returning home may well have been narrated first, merely to conclude that portion of Mary's history. That John was to be the forerunner and herald of Jesus, she must have already known from Elisabeth through Gabriel's message to Zacharias. But Zacharias's own announcement to the infant John that he should go before the face of the Lord, must have aided to confirm Mary's faith; while the presence of the Spirit, in the midst of the little company assembled at the circumcision, would avail much to increase her joy and strength in the Lord, and to send her home to Nazareth with the fresh power of the Holy Ghost resting upon her.

But we now turn to a scene strangely different, and follow Mary through waters of bitter sorrow; exposed to reproach for the sake of Christ, leaving her cause with God, and delivered only by divine interposition.

1. Mary exposed to reproach for Christ's sake

The echoes of the Virgin's songs have scarcely died away among the hills of Judah, when a dark cloud overshadows all her life, and her bright morning of joy is turned into a night of bitter weeping. Through the Lord's singular goodness to her, and through her childlike faith in him, she is like to become an outcast in the eyes of men, as one that has forsaken the guide of her youth, and broken the covenant of her God. A darker cloud never rested upon a child of God on earth, purely for the sake of Christ; a sorer trial could not fall to the lot of any child of man. There is much, indeed, to support the youthful sufferer; yet the crisis is dark in the extreme.

1. There is *strong consolation* to Mary's soul in her sorrow. First of all, there is the answer of a *good conscience* toward God; for hers is no buffeting for sin, but doing well and suffering for it. Christians often suffer, not for Christ's sake, but for their own sins; and when they suffer for the Lord's sake, the mingling of the will of man with the work of God often aggravates their sorrow, and furnishes their foes with an excuse for evil-entreating them. There is nothing of this with Mary; her faith and obedience are the only cause of her reproach. The sting is thus taken out of suffering. When there is no secret rankling of conscience, but all is clear toward God, there is much to lighten the heaviest load of grief.

The case of most believers is substantially the same as Mary's; blessed in believing, and rejoicing greatly in the Lord; but when Christ is formed in us the hope of glory, soon exposed to reproach for his name. We must all take up the cross if we are to follow Christ, and through tribulation we must enter into the kingdom, suffering with him before we reign with him.

Next, there is the *favour of God,* which is ample compensation for the loss of human esteem; the favour of God previous to the reproach, and producing it; and the favour of God consequent on the suffering for his sake, and healing it. 'If we be reproached for the name of Christ, happy are we, for the Spirit of glory and of God resteth upon us.' 1 Pet. 4:14. Christ's cross borne by us ever draws down Christ's Spirit; and prayer itself is not more effectual for this end.

The joy of the Lord is then most of all our strength, when other joy is taken away; for Christ has promised 'not to leave us comfortless, but to come unto us,' when without him all comfort would be gone. When others cast us out for his sake Jesus himself ever seeks and finds us, nor will he leave us while our need remains.

Further, in the providence of God there are some tried and honoured *friends,* who will stand by her in the hour of need; friends both proved by herself and respected by the whole community, whose countenance and testimony are invaluable to Mary, when thus called 'to bear the yoke in her youth.' Among these Zacharias and Elisabeth are known to us; and those two are themselves a noble shield over her head, from their character, their years, and their standing in Israel. But through them there must be others, such as the circle of witnesses at the circumcision of John, and of hearers at his father's prophesying; and the Simeons and Annas, to whose longing hearts the godly priest and his wife would speak of Gabriel's announcement to Mary.

2. But the other side of the picture is *dark in the extreme.* These sources of alleviation were all present to Mary, and must have availed much to mitigate her grief, and enable her to endure the singular severity of her trial. The light of God's countenance alone will sustain the soul under any amount of suffering. But they know little who imagine that this and all other supports would make the trial, while it lasted, other than full of excruciating pain and fearfully dark to Mary's soul. The alleviation also of earthly friend-ship is weak for the present; for the godly friends in Judah are far from Nazareth, and can only help by their prayers. And further, the very clearness of the conscience suggests

the temptation, wherefore the Lord himself should cause such grief to the innocent. The high favour of God moves the soul all the more to ask why his own hand should plunge his loved ones in the ditch; and the heart is tempted to refuse the very joy of the Spirit, when all around is so full of wretchedness, and life itself has become bitter.

There is one friend who is more to Mary than all the world besides; he has heard that she has been unfaithful to him, and has made up his mind to repudiate his betrothed. Two courses are before Joseph; she does not know which he may adopt; but has every reason to apprehend that he will take one or other of the alternatives. The first, which is the more regular and more likely course for him to pursue, is to renounce her by a public divorce. In that case by the law of Moses Mary is worthy of death; and being found guilty, she must die without mercy. Deut. 22:24. In the presence of friend and relative, of stranger and foe, of judge and councillor and priest, of hoary patriarchs and venerable matrons, of the young men of Nazareth, and the maiden companions of her youth, and before the face of her betrothed bridegroom, Mary must be dragged forth as the vilest of criminals, and stoned to death; made 'a public example,' that others may fear and sin not. And where, o Virgin highly favoured, are now thy hopes of honour, wide and lasting as the world? where now the generations that are to call thee blessed? where thy loud exultings, and thy lofty hymns of praise? where all the great things wrought by the Lord for thee?

Such would be the procedure and its consummation according to the Mosaic law; such the course which most men would in the circumstances follow, and which Mary must prepare herself to meet. But Joseph is a 'just man;' he will not proceed to this extremity, and he probably takes means to inform her of his milder purpose. He knows the hitherto spotless honour and high tone of Mary's character; he knows her own declaration of innocence; and thinks it only righteous that in such a case Mary should have all the advantage which spared life and longer time can yield for the vindication of her character. But he is not himself persuaded of her innocence; or at least has no assurance of it, such as either to restore his estranged affection, or to influence him to take upon himself the responsibility of shielding and justifying the character of his betrothed. Not willing, on the one hand, to make her a public example, he is on the other 'minded to put her away privily;' that is, however, not informally, but by a private divorce, regular and judicial, effected in the presence of two witnesses.

Joseph has not yet proceeded to put this intention into execution, nor taken any actual steps toward it. But he has 'thought upon it,' and now intends to take the eventful step; for such is the force of the expression, 'minded to put her away.' The case rests entirely with him; none other can interfere; he has considered it, and made up his mind; and in the natural course of events Mary will within a few days be divorced as an adulteress.

How altered her position and prospects; how sadly fallen in the eyes of men! A little while ago, and all ages were to call her blessed; and now she is to become a by-word and a curse. She had been exalted into the first of Sarah's daughters, and of all the daughters of Eve; honoured and happy above all women in earth, past, present, or to come. And now the meanest of Nazareth's maidens will not stoop to occupy her place. The highest angel in heaven had saluted her as the highly-favoured of the Lord; and now she is to become the song of the drunkard.

Mary is about to be marked before men with a treble brand of infamy, as a sinner, a hypocrite, and an imposter. She is to be branded as a *sinner,* who has shamefully broken the vows of her espousal, forsaken the guide of her youth, and violated the covenant of her God. There is the still darker brand of *hypocrisy.* She is to stand arraigned before her people as a vile hypocrite, who took religion only for a cloak of wickedness; who covered a life of sin and shame with the garb of superior sanctity; who, by professing great love to God and delight in his law, only sought the more effectually to conceal her secret course of iniquity. But the blackest brand of all, and the hardest for a holy mind to endure, is the charge of *blasphemous imposture.* It is not mere devotedness to the Lord that Mary has professed, but she has avouched that the great Lord God, the Holy One of Israel, has visited her with special favour; she has laid claim to visions and revelations of the Most High; and has dared to screen her own infamy before men by desecrating the thrice holy name of Jehovah. If Mary of Nazareth is an imposter, there never lived, before or since, so bold and hardened a blasphemer. But let us look at,

2. Mary leaving her cause quietly with God

Foul crime, base hypocrisy, and horrible blasphemy are about to be laid to Mary's charge in Nazareth, in Galilee, in Israel. What a weight of sorrow, what a load of shame; now unequal to such a burden would most maidens in Israel have been! Of her conduct in this fiery trial we know this only, that she appears to have said nothing and done nothing to vindicate herself; but there is enough in this simple fact. The record indeed does not declare so much, and is only silent; but the fact of God's express interposition warrants the conclusion that Mary did not interfere in her own behalf. Doubtless, when demanded she would state the truth for God's glory and her own justification; but otherwise she abides in silence and in meekness. She believed at first, and was blessed; she believes now, and does not make haste. She does not strive nor cry, nor make her voice to be heard in the streets; she complains not to man of wrong, and appeals not to man for pity, but in patience possesses her soul.

Yet they know little of the human heart, who conceive that under this outward calm all is quiet within; and they know little of the mind of God, who think that in such a case he spares his own from present tribulation because he is soon to send them deliverance. But a soul that can praise as Mary did, and as so few others could, can also pray as few besides. The lips that can so well adduce the ancient promises in a song of thanksgiving can likewise plead those promises in earnest supplication. The heart that so brings forth its treasures in an ecstasy of joy will pour itself out like water in an agony of grief. Mary, not interfering for herself with men, will all the more enter into her closet and plead, 'Unto thee, o Lord, have I revealed my cause.' With the wrestling Jacob she entreats: 'O God of my father Abraham, the Lord which saidst unto me, I will deal well with thee; I am not worthy of the least of all the mercies and of all the truth which thou hast showed unto thy handmaid; deliver me, I pray thee.' The complaint of the weeping prophet has become her own: 'I am a derision to all my people, and their song all the day; he hath filled me with bitterness, he hath made me drunken with wormwood; thou hast removed my soul far off from peace; I forgat prosperity.' The prayer of her father David pours itself through the daughter's lips: 'Save me, o God, for the waters are come into my soul. Because for thy sake I have borne reproach, shame hath covered my face; they that sit in the gate speak against me, and I am the song of the drunkard; plead my cause, o Lord, with them that strive with me, take hold of shield and buckler and stand up for my help; draw out the spear, and stop the way against them that persecute me; say unto my soul, I am thy salvation; make haste, o God, to deliver me; make haste to help me, o Lord, for I am poor and needy; thou art my help and my deliverer, o Lord, make no tarrying.' And as to her father of old, so now to Mary's heart, thus broken in youth, supplication will at length have been turned into confidence and hope: 'The Lord hath heard the voice of my weeping; the Lord hath heard my supplication; the Lord will receive my prayer.' Gen. 32, Lam. 3; Psalms 6, 35, 69, 70.

3. Mary is delivered by divine interposition

What man cannot do for Mary, and what Mary cannot do for herself, the Lord does in her behalf by direct and miraculous interference. While Joseph is thinking of these things, the angel of the Lord appears to him in a dream by night. It was in no dream that Gabriel appeared to Mary, but in open day, with a commission too great for any midnight dream, and with a message that required not mere obedience, but the response of liveliest faith, and the earnest concurrence of mind and heart and will. With Joseph the transaction is less. It is to assure him on a point on which there had been doubt, and to secure obedience to the simple injunction to acknowledge and receive Mary his espoused wife. To Joseph, the son of Jacob, God manifested himself in dreams more than to the other patriarchs, speaking in divers manners to the fathers; and to Joseph, the husband of Mary, he reveals himself both now and afterwards 'in a dream by night, when deep sleep falleth upon men.'

The interposition is urgently needed, yet is in ample time; in God's 'due time' he delivers, though it often seems so late to man. Joseph has purposed to put Mary away, but has taken no step whatever regarding the divorce. Now he is at once obedient to the heavenly vision; in the morning he awakes out of sleep, and on the instant he does as the angel of the Lord has commanded. Without fear, or hesitation, or grudge, but cheerfully and in full assurance, he takes Mary into his own house, and into her peaceful happy home. All her fears are gone, and are turned again into joy and thanksgiving; God himself has wiped away all tears from her eyes; her mouth is filled with laughter and her tongue with singing, for the Lord has done great things for her, whereof she is glad.

This 'work of the Lord is perfect;' and his handmaid Mary is now, and ever after, kept from the strife of tongues. Mary is honoured in generations to come, and honoured also in her own without a shadow of reproach on this behalf. In all the bitter calumnies against Jesus there is never a taunt cast upon his birth, except that he is a Naza-rene. And so is it unto this day; those who patiently endure the cross and despise the shame, in starting on the heavenly race, are enabled to outlive it, till 'for their shame they have double, and for confusion they rejoice in their portion.' God knows the things that we need before we ask. All that we are exposed to through our own folly, much more all that we suffer for his sake, is ever before him; and he is a very present help in the time of need. Not before that time, and often when it appears in man's judgment too late, he interposes for our help. Then we see 'the end of the Lord,' that he is very pitiful and of great compassion. Our interfering for our own deliverance brings us ever into deeper waters, and moves the Lord to leave us to redeem ourselves. But in leaving our cause with him, he ever draws near in the day when we call, and in the crisis of our need says to us, 'Fear not.'

In conclusion, let us remember that the nearer we are to Christ, the nearer are we to his cross. The glorious revelation of Christ to Paul is accompanied with the intimation, 'I will show him how great things he must suffer for my sake.' But if we suffer with him, we shall also reign with him; if we bear his cross, we shall also wear his crown. Mary's joy would seem to many all too little to compensate her sorrow. But the joy is not simply good, and the grief simply evil; but from the Lord both are good, and both are among the 'all things' that work together for good to them that love him. The sorrow indeed is usually more fruitful than the joy; and therefore 'whom the Lord loveth he chasteneth, and scourgeth every son whom he receiveth.' The believer, rejoicing in the hope of the glory of God, has received therewith a golden secret which turns all darkness into light, and all the bitter into sweet. For not only do we rejoice in the hope of glory, 'but we glory in tribulation also, knowing that tribulation worketh patience, and patience experience, and experience hope; and hope maketh not ashamed, because the love of God is shed abroad in our hearts by the Holy Ghost given unto us.'

Are you a stranger to the reproach of Christ? If so, you have reason to fear that Christ has never been formed in you the hope of glory. Has that reproach once tasted become again a strange thing to you? Then you have reason to inquire if the cross of Christ has not lost its power within you. Christ and his cross are never far apart; and the absence of the cross may be warning you to seek an absent Christ.

VII

MARY THE QUIET PONDERER

'But Mary kept all these things, and pondered them in her heart. ... But his mother kept all these sayings in her heart.'—Luke 2:19, 51

AFTER Joseph's dream and Mary's entrance into his house, there is an interval of silence in the gospel narrative till the enrolment, ordered by the Roman emperor, summons them both to Bethlehem. It must have been to Mary an interval of blessed peace; of gratitude, of joy, of hope, of prayer. To Joseph and Mary together it was doubtless a season of much quiet waiting on the Lord, of humble inquiry into his mind and will, of supplication for grace and wisdom in the nurturing of the Child who was to redeem the Israel of God. The mother of Jesus is a Nazarene, but Jesus himself is to be born in Bethlehem, the city of his father David. Bethlehem is the 'house of bread;' fit birthplace for him who is 'the bread of God, that cometh down from heaven, and giveth life unto the world.'

But Jesus is also the fountain of living water for the sons of men, bearing this inscription, 'If any man thirst, let him come unto me and drink.' Nor is the type of this living water lacking in Bethlehem. It was the place of David's birth and boyhood; and in his manhood of hardship and war he longed to drink of the well from which in earlier years he had so often quenched his thirst. He is in the cave of Adullam with his hardy comrades in arms, long shut out from the house of the Lord, and sighing, 'As the hart panteth after the water brooks, so panteth my soul for thee, o God; when shall I come and appear before God?' Sighing thus for the present in vain, another desire takes possession of his soul, another thirst, which it is hard yet not impossible to gratify. It is in no want of water for himself and his followers, for in that case other measures had been adopted. But it is a spiritual longing, going out in recollection of the solemn feasts of the Lord; in remembrance of his youth in Bethlehem, where he had gone with the multitude that kept holy days. He longs to recall those days by some lively token; and his heart-thirst takes the form of thirsting for the fountain at Bethlehem, of whose clear waters he had so often drunk in happier times, and which haply in the sacred feasts had been poured out before the Lord. David longed and said, 'Oh that one would give me drink of the water of the well of Bethlehem, which is by the gate!' 2 Sam. 23:15. In gratification of his desire three of his mighty men fetched him the precious draught through the army of the Philistines; but David poured it out unto the Lord and asked, 'Is not this the blood of the men that went in jeopardy of their lives?' He looks on it as water holy to the Most High; he calls it blood, rather than water; and as if really blood and therefore sacred, he pours it out untasted to God. It is the precious emblem of that living water, brought to us by the great Captain of our salvation through the hosts of earth and hell, not by jeopardy of his life, but by its sacrifice; it is the significant type of that blood which is 'drink indeed.' This well, by the gate of the House of Bread, perfects the typical fitness of Bethlehem for the birthplace of Immanuel.

To Bethlehem then, the city of David, Mary must repair with Joseph for the birth of Jesus, David's son and Lord. Great events occur, and marvellous sayings are uttered at this time; and of these it is written, that 'Mary kept all these things, and pondered them in her heart;' and again, after the lapse of years, it is recorded of other wondrous words, that 'she kept all these sayings in her heart.' She keeps them all in her memory, and she ponders them all in her mind.

1. Mary remembers the great things of the Lord

She retained all the words of the Lord, and all his dealings in her memory and heart; for 'all these things' include both. If limited to one, it would be the 'words,' but it is all these 'matters', including both word and work.

1. Mary keeps the Lord's *words;* his words spoken by his messengers concerning herself, or her holy child and Saviour; and afterwards, the child's own words.

First of all, she *has* such words to keep; for Christ says, 'he that hath my commandments, and keepeth them.' The first great point with her and with us is to possess the words of life. Many, in the multitude of holy words around them and even within their memories, never possess one of them for themselves; and 'from him that hath not, shall be taken away even that which he hath.' The words of life shall be taken from them for ever, because they have them not. They both have, and have not; they have them in their lips and in their hands, yet they are never truly theirs in the heart, and from them they are taken to all eternity. But blessed is he that hath even one saying of the Lord; that hath it for himself and not for another, that hath it from the Lord and given to his own soul. He is blessed because it shall never be taken away; and blessed because to him that hath shall be given, and he shall have more; word shall be added to word, promise to promise, warning to warning, till he is rich toward God by having the words of everlasting life dwelling in him richly.

Next, Mary *keeps* the word she gets. She had from childhood a retentive memory, in which she laid up the words spoken to the fathers; and she employs that faithful faculty now for preserving the sayings addressed more immediately to herself. She treasures them all in her heart. They are her precious stores, which nourish her soul today, and from which she is to draw supplies in times of famine yet to come. She requires consolation now; and it is given to her abundantly, filling her soul with gladness. But none was ever to need the riches of consolation in the time to come, so much as Mary; and in the midst of present joy she stores every word of the Lord in her heart against the future; like the bee that tastes the honey, and straightway lays it up for the coming winter. Angels' visits on the plains of Bethlehem and angels' words at which others wonder, the prophecies of the aged Simeon and the sayings of the youthful Jesus, Mary 'keeps' in heart and memory.

Many lose the words they once have found. God's children often lose the help provided for them against the dark and cloudy day by forgetting the words of the Lord once brought home with power to their souls. Sometimes, in the abounding joy of salvation, they know not all the value of the precious words sealed to them by the Spirit of life. They fondly fancy that they can have them again in the same abundance whenever they choose, and they keep not carefully the words of power spoken to them from on high. It is good, indeed, not to look on things behind, but on things before; otherwise the soul will feed on pastures that have been grazed already, and are no longer green and fresh. Yet the Lord will have none of his words wasted or forgotten; he remembers all he has ever spoken to us by his Spirit; and he takes it ill, if we forget his words of life and love. If it has been given us to hear, let us make sure to keep the words of our God and Saviour.

2. Mary remembers *the works* of the Lord. She presents in this a remarkable contrast to Israel of old, who so soon forgot his works wrought for their deliverance. Her first great contrast to them is in faith. With the promised land before them; with the time come when they should have entered into the good country, given by covenant to their fathers; with themselves brought to the very borders of the land; with their chosen men walking through it, and bringing them its rich fruit to see and handle and taste; they draw back in the very crisis of this history. The time and the land of promise have come, but the men are wanting; they fail for lack of faith, and through unbelief they cannot enter in. All is otherwise with Mary. The time longed for by Abraham has now come at last; the time looked forward to from 'the bow in the cloud,' after the abating of the flood; the time embraced in the first promise to Eve. The time has come, and the promise with the time, the Seed of the woman to bruise the serpent's head; and the faith of Mary is

equal to the time and the promise. She believes, and obtains the covenanted good.

Mary, thus nobly contrasted with unbelieving Israel, is equally a striking contrast to forgetful Israel. There is nothing more often noted regarding them, than that they forgot the works of the Lord, that they remembered not the signs and the wonders of Egypt and the desert; and nothing more notable in her, than that she kept them all in her heart. They hear the words and see the judgments of the Lord, but they let all slip from their memory; and are therefore as ignorant and unbelieving to the end, as if they had experienced nothing of the Lord's marvellous goodness. Mary lets nothing slip; every work of God for herself or for her child, she treasures in her heart; and her mind becomes a precious storehouse, full of the wondrous dealings of the Lord.

It is good for us to follow Mary. Works worthy of being remembered have been wrought for us all, works providential for every one, and works both of providence and grace for all that are his own. His works are done to be remembered, and much of their use consists in their being kept in memory. If they are not remembered, they will seldom be understood; for our heavenly Father's work, either of consolation or correction, is not apprehended by most at the time. It brings sorrow or joy, and that is received; but the lesson that is in it besides, the chastening or the warning or the comfort, is most frequently not discerned at the moment. It is therefore only by 'keeping all these things in the heart,' by recording them deeply on the tablet of the memory, that the rich fruit of righteousness is 'afterwards yielded in them that are exercised thereby.'

2. Mary ponders the great things of the Lord

Pondered they are by her; and equally worthy of being pondered by us.

1. The great things of the Lord are *meditated* on by Mary. She ponders, revolves, compares all his words and all his dealings. She retains them all in her memory for this very end; and having them there, she does not leave them unused. In the idea conveyed by our English version, she weighs them all. She balances one against another to make out the result; to find the exact issue of the whole for the present, and the prospect or the lesson of all for the future. She weighs every word by itself, and every word with every other, word against word; every work by itself, and work against work; and weighs the words and the works together, to find the scope and fruit of all. And verily she has no light or common task to perform.

Faith is the characteristic excellence of Mary in grace; thoughtfulness is, perhaps, her chief distinction in natural character. When Gabriel appeared to her with the strange salutation, 'Hail, highly favoured,' Mary was troubled at first, yet not at all amazed or stupified; and she immediately began to 'cast in her mind' what manner of greeting it might be. She is at the furthest remove from all sceptical doubt; yet has not less, but more thought and reflection, than any unbelieving mind can entertain. At this first strange inter-position she casts in her mind, she reasons with herself regarding it; for hers is no heart turned to and fro by every wind, and eager to grasp at every passing shadow. By grace she can believe in things possible only with God; but she must have solid ground to stand upon; and must know both what, and in whom she is to believe. And so she acts throughout. When the angelic message comes at first, she considers whether it is indeed the very word of God, and if she apprehends it aright; and after she has received many words of the Lord she weighs them all, not to test their truth, but to know their import.

And truly the things are vast and weighty that are cast into the balances of Mary's thoughtful mind. A weight of honour is thrown into one balance, and presently a weight of shame is thrown into the other; a weight of joy into the one, and anon a weight of sorrow into the other; a weight of glory, and after it a weight of trouble. One day she is saluted in the name of God by the highest angel in heaven, as the most highly favoured woman on earth; another day she hears that her betrothed husband Joseph is minded to put her away, and that she is about to be covered with shame; and she weighs these two together, 'pondering them in her heart.' One day she is summoned along with Joseph to Bethlehem, the city of David, the royal father of them both. She marvels at the Lord's providence that brings her, without any design of her own, out of the obscure and despised Nazareth unto David's honoured city, into Bethlehem-Ephratah. The Son of the Nazarene mother is to be heir of the princely Bethlehem; and no meaner city is fit to be his birth place. With much labour to herself, but with equal joy she retraces her previous journey to the hill country of Judah; and in the Lord's goodness she reaches her royal father's dwelling, and the birthplace of her far more royal Son. Such a providence is cast by her into the same scale along with many previous mercies. But on arriving at Bethlehem, it almost seems as if the Lord had forgot his handmaiden; for others are before them, and have pre-occupied all the rooms in the inn. They are not poor carpenters like Joseph, nor despised Galileans like them both. Proud sons of David they appear to have been, and haughty daughters of Judah; not unmeet in their own eyes to be ancestors of the promised King. They need not the care that Mary requires; though personally unacquainted they cannot be ignorant of her condition, and she is their own kinswoman through the royal blood in which they glory; yet none of them stoops to look with the eye of friendly pity upon her, and to resign to her the place of comfort secured for themselves. Jesus comes to his own, and his own receive him not. Mary is thrust out; she brings forth her first-born Son, wraps him in swaddling clothes, and lays him in a manger, because there is no room for them in the inn; and then 'she ponders all these things in her heart.'

Meanwhile the scene of most dazzling magnificence that has ever been enacted on earth is witnessed on the high plains of Bethlehem. A few months ago in that same country, and possibly in that neighbourhood, Mary's full heart had burst into the heavenly song, 'My soul doth magnify the Lord.' And now the heavens are opened to respond to that noble hymn from earth. There are shepherds watching their flocks by night; who are doubtless men of God that wait for the consolation of Israel, as those that watch for the morning. They are thrown into sore alarm, not by the dreaded lion or leopard bounding in upon their sleeping flocks, but by the glory of the Lord suddenly breaking forth around them; and an angel announces, 'Behold, I bring you good tidings of great joy, which shall be to all people; for unto you is born this day in the city of David a Saviour, which is Christ the

Lord.' Instantly from angel and archangel, from cherubim and seraphim, there bursts a loud song of rapturous joy; there appears a multitude of the heavenly host, praising God and saying, 'Glory to God in the highest, and on earth peace, goodwill unto men.' The shepherds, filled with wonder, hasten to tell the vision and report the words in Bethlehem, and in the mean abode of Mary. Heaven opened, to announce the birth of Jesus, is in strange contrast to the meanness of that birth; and the lowly manger in which he is laid is the very sign by which the angels intimate that the great King is to be recognized. All that hear wonder at the tidings told them by the shepherds; Mary alone marvels not, but thoughtfully 'ponders all in her heart.'

And again, there come wise men from the distant east to the City of David. In their own land they have seen the Star of the Messiah, which guides them to Palestine; at Jerusalem they are instructed to proceed to Bethlehem; and there they behold the heavenly lamp shining over Mary's humble home. They enter and tell the thoughtful mother of their journey from afar, and of their guide by night in the heavens. They see the Child, and fall down before him with offerings of gold and frankincense and myrrh. Mary's heart overflows with gratitude and joy; with gratitude for the Lord's goodness in so seasonable a supply for their poverty; with joy at so honourable a recognition of the infant Lord and King. The wise men take leave of the holy family, and depart for their own country; night comes on, and Joseph and Mary with the child resign themselves to thankful repose. At midnight she is suddenly awakened by her husband. He tells her that the angel of the Lord, who had before enjoined him in a dream to own her without fear, has again appeared in like manner, warning him to flee with her for the Child's life from the sword of Herod. And in haste in that same hour they make ready for their flight. In the dark night the tender mother and child go forth out of Bethlehem, to leave their native country and the holy land, and go down into Egypt, the land of heathen idols and of Israel's ancient bondage. So unexpectedly lifted up and so suddenly cast down, Mary has enough thrown into either balance now, when she 'ponders these things in her heart.'

Yet again, Mary has to hear with astonishment and dismay that Rachel is weeping for her children, and refuses to be comforted; because the bloody Herod has slain all the infants under two years of age in Bethlehem and in all the coasts thereof. All this slaughter and sorrow are on account of her holy Child Jesus, and for his being born in Bethlehem; yet at that birth the angels had sung, 'Peace on earth,' as well as 'glory to God on high.' Simeon also in the temple had taken the Child in his arms, and said to the Lord: 'Now lettest thou thy servant depart in peace, for mine eyes have seen thy salvation; a light to lighten the Gentiles, and the glory of thy people Israel.' Yet how soon it is not peace, but a sword; and the birth of Israel's glory has brought bitter weeping to Rachel's daughters. But Mary keeps all these things, and revolves them in her heart; and Simeon's warning of 'a sword to pierce through her own soul' must have been deeply graven on her mind in the midst of abounding praise.

2. The great things of the Lord are to be pondered also *by us.*

'Ponder the path of thy feet, and let all thy ways be established,' is the counsel of Wisdom to every son of man. Prov. 4:26. Next to prayer and reading the word of God, there is nothing better for men, for young and old, than 'pondering the path of the feet.' Without it no man can understand his own way; and all his goings will be uncertain and crooked. A man's goings are indeed of the Lord, and 'it is not in man that walketh to direct his steps.' But if the Lord has a way for every man, he is willing to teach him its way-marks; and 'it is the wisdom of the wise to understand his way.' It is only by pondering the path of the feet, in considering the dealings of the Lord with us and his guiding hitherto, that we are enabled to discern the path in which he would have us to go, and to walk in 'footsteps ordered by the Lord.' And there is nothing either more interesting or more profitable for a man, than often to weigh the Lord's various dealings with him, alike in providence and in grace.

Nor let any man say that it was interesting to Mary to ponder her path, for there were great events, and of world-wide interest, continually occurring in her course, but that his own life is insignificant and mean. The difference is far less than you conceive. If you are a follower of Christ, your life will be full of greatness and of interest. It is indeed a low, dull, monotonous life that every child of the world fashions for himself. There seems to him, for the most part, to be neither great good nor great evil about him, but all tame and commonplace. But it is far otherwise with the child of God and heir of heaven. There are not in your history, as in Mary's, events occurring of world-wide magnitude, but there are events great and grand for yourself. The wrath to come is great; you are delivered from it, and look down with joy and trembling over the brink of the deep pit from which you have been drawn. Sin is great; Christ has given, and is giving you the victory over it; and it is still a great conflict and great victory continually. Satan is the strong one among all the sons of strength; and yet he is bruised under your feet by your stronger Redeemer. Grace is great, and it abounds toward you; heaven is great, and it is your own sure inheritance. Great sorrow, great joy, great fear, great hope in your own heart, with great works of the Lord wrought on your behalf, all belong to your course on earth; and yours therefore is no mean or common, but a grand and eventful life.

Yet much depends on your *pondering* the ways of the Lord with you; for the old saying holds true, 'that to those who are given to observation, things happen that are worth observing.' Much of Mary's life would have been thrown away on another less thoughtful than she; but the Lord, who gave so much to think upon, raised up his handmaid with a heart to ponder it all. And if you will ponder well the little that seems to have been allotted to you, you will first of all find that it is your own blindness alone that makes it little instead of great, and dull instead of replete with interest. And next, the Lord will show you greater things, when once your heart is directed to observe and improve what he has already wrought for you. Thus will you be fitted for your way, and a glorious way be marked out for you, full of noble works and great events in providence and in grace; and in pondering the path of your feet, all your goings will be established by the Lord. Amen.

VIII

MARY THE CORRECTED DISCIPLE

*'And when they saw him, they were amazed; and his
mother said unto him, Son, why hast thou thus dealt
with us? behold, thy father and I have sought thee
sorrowing. And he said unto them, How is it that
ye sought me? wist ye not that I must be about my
Father's business?'*—Luke 2:48, 49

*And when they wanted wine, the mother of Jesus
saith unto him, They have no wine. Jesus saith unto
her, Woman, what have I to do with thee? mine hour
is not yet come.*—John 2:3, 4

*And the multitude cometh together again, so that
they could not so much as eat bread. And when his
friends heard of it, they went out to lay hold on him;
for they said, He is beside himself ... There came then
his brethren and his mother, and, standing without, sent unto him, calling him. And the multitude
sat about him; and they said unto him, Behold, thy
mother and thy brethren without seek for thee. And*

he answered them, saying, Who is my mother, or my
brethren? And he looked round about on them which
sat about him, and said, Behold my mother and my
brethren! For whosoever shall do the will of God, the
same is my brother, and my sister, and mother.
—Mark 3:20, 21, 31-35

MARY, the mother of Jesus, must pass into another relation, and be numbered simply among his believing disciples. A believer in the Messiah to come she had been before his birth; and a believer in Jesus as the Messiah she is throughout; but the relation of mother is to cease, and that of believer alone to remain. Instead of parent, teacher, guide of childhood, she is to become his disciple and follower, guided, taught, and ruled by him. It does not, indeed, appear that she ever became a follower of Jesus from place to place, like Mary Magdalene and many others; and her presence at the cross does not prove that she had then accompanied Jesus and his disciples to Jerusalem, because she was wont to go always for herself to the feast of the passover. This refraining, however, from accompanying Jesus in his ministrations throughout the country, is no reflection on Mary; because for such a course much must have depended on special circumstances, on the nature and amount of domestic duties, and on the expression of Christ's own will. Some of the most attached of all his disciples did not follow him, but remained at home, as the whole family at Bethany so beloved by the Lord.

In the discipleship of Mary the most remarkable circumstance is reproof. It is part of the chastisement whereof all are partakers, and in which she too must have her share.

But it is more marked in Mary; both because the previous relation to Jesus gave more occasion for it in her than in the other holy women, and because her own characteristic sphere is less in this discipleship, and more in her earlier history. But a disciple she is and must be, if redeemed at all; and in this relation we note that she is chastened for losing sight of Jesus, admonished for urging forward his delay, and reproved for retarding his zeal.

1. Mary chastened for losing sight of Jesus

The many interests and the varied trials of Christ's infancy have passed away from Mary. The manger of Bethlehem, the songs of angels, the prophecies in the temple at Jerusalem, the gifts of the wise men, the massacre of the infants, the flight into Egypt, are only 'kept in the heart' as sacred memories. The family, with the holy Child, have returned again to Nazareth.

The years of childhood pass away, with much to interest and instruct the mother of Jesus; with many sayings and questions for her to ponder; with a life of spotless innocence, of truth, of love, of uniform obedience toward man, of faith and reverence toward God. Jesus grows up before his mother's eye in singular and unspotted loveliness; so engaging and attractive to all around that his growth in 'favour with man' is as unbroken and progressive as the growth of his stature; so holy, so pure, so heavenly, that the abounding and increasing blessing of God from above rests upon him in the sight of all from year to year. The child Jesus 'waxes strong in spirit,' with a mental and spiritual vigour all his own, and never found in any other child of man. Instead of the 'foolishness bound up in a child's heart,'

he is 'filled with wisdom;' with knowledge, with discre-
tion, with grace far above all that could be looked for in
the holiest boyhood. Yet withal, there is nothing to startle
Mary. The pure wisdom in the bud within unfolds itself as
gently and gradually as the body develops itself in growth.
In its progress there are no fits and starts; it is altogether
free from the inequalities and inconsistencies that belong
to John the Baptist and every other godly child, which at
once mar the beauty of holiness in them, and at the same
time make that beauty more striking by the contrast. The
childhood of Jesus is so perfect, so quiet; his interest in
things of home and of earth, of boyhood and of humanity,
is so genial; his obedience, his holiness, his loveliness are so
natural, that Mary herself seems at length to be in danger of
forgetting what manner of Child he is.

And now twelve years have passed over the mother and
her son. He has reached the age when, according to Hebrew
usage, he becomes 'a son of the law' as well as of his parents;
and according to their reckoning, legal obligation now rests
upon himself. Joseph and Mary go up as usual to the feast
of the passover at Jerusalem, and Jesus accompanies them.
This is not for the first time, but as he had always done; for
it is not even noticed that he went with them, but only that
he tarried behind them when they left. The feast is over,
and the parents set out on their journey home ward; but
Jesus is not with them. Mary may not be chargeable with
lack of motherly care in leaving Jerusalem without her
first-born; for he has ever been so dutiful and so wise, that
she can safely trust to his being found at the appointed
time and place of starting. The journey to Nazareth must
have occupied the larger portion of a week; the caravan, or

company of travellers that join together for mutual assistance and protection, is large; they are chiefly relatives or well-known neighbours, and are devout worshippers of the God of Israel. The boy is familiarly known amongst them all, and is safe in their society and keeping. On their departure Mary does not observe Jesus, but takes for granted that he is there. She either does not remember him at that moment, nor look for him at all, but is engaged with other thoughts; or else she has been so occupied otherwise up to the hour of leaving, that the caravan has already begun to move on before she can meet with Jesus. The few minutes that would have sufficed a little earlier to look for him in the company are unavailing now when all is in motion; and if she return to Jerusalem to inquire, she cannot overtake her fellow-travellers.

Mary could not have been holding in lively remembrance all that she had seen and heard concerning that blessed Child, for whose sake all generations were to call her blessed, else he had not been so lost sight of now. Other things must have occupied the place in her thoughts which was due in that hour to him; leave taking of friends, it may be, in Jerusalem; or household comforts to be purchased and carried home from the great city. This view is strengthened by the fact of Mary being amazed at finding Jesus in the temple, and not understanding what he meant by his Father's business. Had she not been forgetting who Jesus was, she might have better understood his words; she might have pondered as before, and have left the marvelling to others. It is further confirmed, and to our mind made certain, by the severe chastisement to which Mary was subjected in consequence; for Jesus could not but know the sorrow that would be occasioned to his mother by his tarrying behind, and he could have spared her that grief had he chosen.

During the first day's journey homeward, Mary and Joseph both take for granted that Jesus is travelling with them; and when they put up for the night they inquire after him, never doubting to find him among 'their kinsfolk and acquaintance.' They search for him through every family; they ascertain with surprise and sorrow that he is nowhere in that company of travellers; and with sad hearts they wend their way back to Jerusalem. After three days' labour they find him sitting in the temple in the midst of the doctors, both hearing and asking them questions, as the habit was with the Jewish scholars. By divine ordaining, not Joseph but Mary takes occasion to speak; and she complains, 'Son, why hast thou dealt thus with us? behold, thy father and I have sought thee sorrowing.' Jesus answers them, 'How is it that ye sought me? wist ye not that I must be about my Father's business?' Mary speaks expressly of the father of Jesus; and it would seem as if hitherto Joseph had been called by that name in the family. But now Jesus, in direct contrast to calling Joseph his parent, or allowing that he who sought him along with Mary was really his father, refers directly to his Father in heaven in whose house and temple he then was. Mary's losing sight of Jesus has been chastened by her long and sorrowful search; and now Jesus marks it as a truth which she ought well to know, that his Father in heaven has claims upon him far above both his real mother and his reputed father on earth. It is a fore-warning of the time when Jesus is to be Lord, and Mary his humble disciple; but meanwhile, he returns to Nazareth and is subject both to Mary, and to Joseph of whom we read no more, and who seems to have died before Christ's public ministry commenced.

Is Mary's loss not a lesson to us? Do we not often go up with Christ to our Christian passover, the feast of the Lord's Supper, and are anxious above all things to have Christ with us in preparing for the feast, that he may manifest himself to our souls in the breaking of bread? Nothing else will compensate for the lack of his presence; and we are ever seeking to make sure that he is with us, by not losing sight of him for an hour. The days are accomplished, as they were with Mary at Jerusalem; the feast is over, and we are to return home again to our usual employments and ways. Other things enter quickly into our hearts; other cares, other joys, the very company of our fellow-worshippers, but no more with us in the sanctuary; and we take for granted that Jesus also is with us, for like Mary we 'suppose that he is in the company.' We find not his presence throughout the day as before; but we conclude that he must be near, and that as soon as we have a little time to seek, we shall find him again. The opportunity of devotion arrives, and then 'we seek him, but we find him not;' for we have not watched and prayed, but have entered into temptation. By taking lightly for granted that Christ is with us we have lost him, and we may have to seek three days sorrowing ere we find him again; yet a little watchfulness at first would have 'kept our feet from falling and our eyes from tears,' and ourselves 'walking before him in the light of the living.'

2. Mary admonished for hastening Christ's delay

Eighteen years have elapsed; John had come forth from the

wilderness of Judea, and proclaimed the coming Messiah; Jesus himself has now appeared, has been baptized with the Holy Ghost, and has begun to preach the good tidings of the kingdom. There is a marriage at Cana in Galilee, within two or three hours' distance of Nazareth. Mary appears to have been a relative or intimate friend of the family, acquainted with their household arrangements, and taking a matronly interest in the festive preparations for the occasion, and possibly some oversight of them. Jesus and the few disciples already gathered round him are invited, probably on Mary's account, to the marriage. The entertainers are poor, the accession of Christ and his followers seems to have enlarged the number of guests beyond their expectation, and the supply of wine provided for the feast is exhausted. Mary tells Jesus of the want, obviously hoping for his interposition; when he appears to refuse her she charges the servants to obey his orders, still evidently trusting to a miraculous outlet from the present strait. The ground of Mary's hope is unknown. The express declaration of this being his first miracle makes it improbable that Jesus had wrought any miracle before, even in private. His appearance now in public might naturally lead her to expect the manifestation of his glory, and unrecorded circumstances might move her to look for it at this very marriage. But resting on whatever ground, Mary in the course of the feast announces to Jesus, 'They have no wine;' and Jesus answers her, 'Woman, what have I to do with thee? mine hour is not yet come.'

This is the plain language of reproof. In the appellation 'woman,' there is no disrespect whatever, for the term was applied to women of any rank. But it is not filial and affectionate as to a mother, but simply respectful; while there is nothing but reproof in the reply itself, 'Woman, what have I to do with thee? mine hour is not yet come.' It is reminding Mary that he no longer stands to her in the relation of son, and that it does not belong to her to prescribe to him in his great mission. It is reproving her for presuming to chide his delay; and intimating that if he had given her cause to hope, she must nevertheless leave both the time and manner of his work to himself alone. She meekly receives his word; yet believes for, and obtains, the supplicated boon.

The lesson inculcated on Mary is one often needed by every disciple of Jesus Christ. We are ever ready to chide his delay in coming to our aid in his providence or in his grace. The promise is that 'if we humble ourselves under the hand of God, he will exalt us in due time.' But it is the Lord's due time, not ours; and the time that seems by far too late to us, is often the due season with him. He is a 'very present help in the time of need.' But with us the need is oft anticipated; we crave help against a want that is still somewhat future; he defers till it has actually come, and then he is a present help. But it requires faith to trust him to stretch forth his hand in the moment of want; and submission not to fret when he seems to defer too long. The greatest saints stand often most in need of such reproof as Mary's; even because, like her, they have been led so far into the secret of the Lord. Like her in this case, they may have truly attained the confidence that the Lord will help; and therefore, they are the more tempted to dictate the time and manner of his aid. The very fact of their depending on the Lord for everything, more than less experienced believers, exposes them to a more frequent trial of patience. But patience is the crowning grace of all; and we may well rejoice to 'let patience have her perfect work, that we may be perfect and entire, wanting nothing.'

3. *Mary reproved for arresting Christ's zeal*

She is associated with the brethren of Jesus in chiding his zeal; she is reproved for her presumption; and her error is recorded as a warning to us.

1. Mary is associated with our Lord's brethren in *arresting his zeal*. Jesus has been calling his twelve apostles, has been casting out devils, and has been preaching the glad tidings of the kingdom to eager crowds. He enters into a house for rest and food. The multitude press so upon him to hear the word, that he cannot 'so much as eat bread;' they seat themselves round the house, and from within he continues to speak to them without cessation. The envious scribes insinuate, 'He hath Beelzebub, and by the prince of the devils he casteth out devils.' His friends join not in this accusation, but they have their own charge against him and they allege, 'He is beside himself.' These friends are his relatives, 'his mother and his brethren.' Who those brethren were is much disputed. Cousins of Jesus they are often taken to be; but if so, it is not obvious why they are always called brothers, and always associated with Mary. Children of Joseph by a previous marriage, others suppose to be their place in the family; but there is nowhere the slightest allusion to such a marriage. Younger brothers and sisters of Jesus, Mary's 'first-born son,' children of Joseph and Mary after the birth of Jesus, they may certainly have been. This supposition would hardly tally so well with the fact of John being named as Mary's son by the dying Saviour, and taking her to his own home. But it would help

to account for Mary's loss of Jesus at the passover, by her having younger children along with her, requiring more of her care; for their association afterwards with Mary; and for her remaining at home with them, instead of following Christ throughout the land. These relatives, whoever they were, did not hold Christ to be an impostor, but they did not fully own him as the Messiah; and they afterwards urged him to show himself at Jerusalem, 'for neither did his brethren believe on him.' Their conversion took place at a later period; but it was previous to the day of Pentecost, for they joined the apostles in praying for the descent of the Spirit. Acts 1:14.

Mary was no partaker in their unbelief, but her faith must have been weak indeed at this season. Weakened it may have been by causes within herself; and the defect would be aggravated by her associating, not with Christ and his disciples, but with her own friends who did not believe in his name. There is nothing that more certainly saps the foundation of faith than being separated from God's children, and being much in fellowship with unbelievers, however amiable and honourable their character may be, and whatever their claims upon us. The attempt to lay hold on Christ, and carry him away from his work, must surely have originated with them, and not with her; yet she lent herself to the effort, and met only rebuke and shame in consequence. For—

2. Mary is severely *reproved for her presumption.* 'Thy mother and thy brethren without desire to speak with thee,' is the message they send to the Lord, when they cannot reach him themselves for the crowd. Jesus does not honour Mary by inquiring what it is that she is so anxious

to communicate; does not gratify her by instructing the crowd to make way for her approach; does not himself pass through the crowd to salute his mother. He leaves her 'without,' where she stands; he returns no reply to her message; he refuses to give any account of himself to her, or to acknowledge her at all in such attempt to interfere with his work. Standing in the midst of his disciples, he proclaims to them and to all generations, that as the Saviour of men he has no kinsmen or relatives on earth; but that all are equally his, without the least distinction, who are the children of his heavenly Father. Mary he severely reproves by the loud inquiry, 'Who is my mother, and who are my brethren?' while he comforts his followers by stretching forth his hands to them and announcing, 'Behold my mother, and my brethren; for whosoever shall do the will of my Father in heaven, the same is my brother, and sister, and mother.'

This serious offence of Mary's was the same in its root, as her lighter fault before; for both were interference with the work of the Lord. In form the two were exactly opposite; the first was chiding the Lord's delay; the second is chiding his zeal and haste. The day had been, when Mary must have seemed to many to be beside herself; when the youthful maiden arose in such haste, and journeyed alone from Galilee to Judah to visit Elisabeth. But now her own zeal has suddenly cooled for a time, her faith has decayed; and Christ's zeal for the glory of God and the salvation of souls, which is madness in the eyes of her kindred, is by Mary also reprehended, and must if possible be arrested.

3. Mary's error is recorded as *a warning to us*. It is an error into which many of Christ's followers are prone to fall in a time of religious awakening, and the free running of

the glorious gospel. In the person of his servants on earth, the Lord Jesus 'puts on righteousness as a breastplate, and is clad with zeal as a cloak.' Satan is cast out by the finger of God, by the Spirit under the preached word; the world in which he rules is turned upside down; multitudes leave other things, and flock to hear the everlasting gospel, they believe and rejoice in the Lord. For the moment ordinary rules, both with the preacher and hearers, give way; for 'the one thing needful' becomes the engrossing object with all, and there is not time so much as to eat bread. Those who are not engaged in the work, the onlookers without, unbelievers like Christ's brethren and believers like his mother, regard the whole as wild enthusiasm. They discountenance, discourage, and try to arrest it; specially, they endeavour to dissuade some of God's most zealous servants from encouraging and promoting such fanaticism; yet in restraining his work and his servants, they are really restraining Christ himself and his Spirit. It is the Lord's own zeal that is moving his servants and his people; and they are ignorantly yet really joining with Mary in seeking to lay hold on Christ, and withdraw him from the work of man's salvation.

The Lord has left her example on record, for a warning against the same presumption in us. Let us see, then, that we be not carried away with her error, and that we partake not in her rebuke; let us specially watch against taking part with the children of this world, however dear by many ties or attractions; and let us ever cultivate close fellowship with the most tender and faithful amongst the followers of Jesus.

IX

MARY THE WITNESS OF THE DEATH AND RESURRECTION OF HER HOPES

'Now there stood by the cross of Jesus his mother, and his mother's sister ... When Jesus therefore saw his mother, and the disciple standing by whom he loved, he saith unto his mother, Woman, behold thy son! Then saith he to the disciple, Behold thy mother! And from that hour that disciple took her unto his own home.'—John 19:25-27

'Then were the disciples glad when they saw the Lord.'
—John 20:20

'These all continued with one accord in prayer and supplication, with the women, and Mary the mother of Jesus, and with his brethren.'—Acts 1:14

THERE are these three concluding scenes in Mary's eventful life: Mary the quiet spectator of the death of all her hopes in the cross of Christ; the joyful witness of the end of the Lord in his resurrection; and the willing subject of the new dispensation of the Spirit.

1. Mary the quiet witness of the death of all her hopes

She is graciously prepared for her last and sorest trial, and she meets it with a noble submission.

1. She is graciously *prepared* for the death of Christ. There is no notice whatever of Mary, the mother of Jesus, between the scene we have just considered and the closing scene of all; Mary pressing through the listening crowd to arrest Jesus in his burning zeal; Mary standing pierced in heart at the foot of the cross. The one passage was, indeed, a sad preparation for the other; and the same mother who could not listen quietly to Jesus preaching, because the zeal of his Father's house consumed him, could never in the same spirit have stood meekly at the foot of the accursed tree to which her son was nailed. There is silence on Mary's history in all the interval between these two great scenes; Jesus lifted up in the midst of the admiring throng, refusing Mary who stands outside, and stretching out his hands to his disciples, 'Behold my mother and sister and brother;' and Jesus lifted up on the accursed tree in the midst of reviling foes, with Mary standing at his feet, while his hands are stretched out again, nailed to the cross. Mary is not noticed in the interval; but much had occurred to prepare her for the last scene, far otherwise than she was fitted for the first.

In that interval, the most important event in Mary's history is the conversion of Christ's brethren. They had not been converted when they sought to lay hold on Jesus in his teaching; nor when they urged him to show himself in Jerusalem at the feast. But there were seasons of special grace under Christ's teaching once and again after that, and before the last agony, when they may have been visited. In this period of time there are many conversions recorded; and theirs must have been among the number, although they are not mentioned by name. Their conversion was previous to the Pentecostal out-pouring of the Spirit for which they prayed, and previous to Christ's ascension, at which they were evidently present, returning from it with the other disciples to the upper chamber in Jerusalem. But between the resurrection and the ascension there are no conversions recorded. The risen Jesus manifested himself to believers, to assure their faith and make them his witnesses; but never to unbelievers for their conviction, and not therefore to his brethren if still unbelieving. By Christ on the cross one dying criminal was converted; the centurion and his soldiers were convinced by his death. But these are recorded as special examples of divine power, without the least reason to conclude that others shared in its effect.

Generally speaking, none who were unbelievers around the cross were converted till the day of Pentecost, when they looked on him whom they had pierced. We must therefore look to an earlier date for the conversion of our Lord's brethren. During that same feast at Jerusalem, to which they tauntingly urged Jesus to repair, 'many of the people believed on him;' and on its last day there was much power of the Spirit, when Jesus stood and cried, 'If any man thirst, let him come unto me, and drink.' John 7:31, 37. There can be no doubt that they were frequent hearers of his preaching; for they went up to that feast, and were in their own way deeply interested in Jesus, and concerned about the issue of his life and work. A few days later, in his teaching at Jerusalem, it is recorded that 'as he spake these words many believed on him.' Afterwards again, when he had returned beyond the Jordan, it is written that 'many believed on him there.' On some of those occasions, or on others of which there must have been many, the brethren of Jesus were converted to saving faith in his name.

The time is immaterial, but the fact is important in Mary's life; because the state of her mind in the previous scene had been evidently and powerfully influenced by theirs. They were converted before Christ's death; then they not only accredited him as the Messiah, but their hearts were renewed by his Spirit; and Christ had become their desire, their hope, their Saviour. Bound together by whatever relation, it seems to have been with them, and not with Jesus, that Mary was most intimately associated. She and they are named together, not only in the Gospels, but in the Acts of the Apostles; and in all likelihood they formed one family, living beneath the same roof, till John took her to his own home. Their conversion could not be but singularly quickening to the soul of Mary. The reproof of Jesus, in not owning her but the worker of his Father's will for his mother, must have deeply tried and sorely humbled her spirit; and must have moved her to pray that it might be with her again as in years that were past. The repentance and the faith in Jesus, not of one, but of the whole family who are described as Christ's 'brethren,' could not but have a most quickening effect on Mary's own mind. The power of the Spirit that descended on them, resting also on her, would immediately renew within her all her earlier faith and love, and prepare her well for the last and greatest trial of her faith.

2. The trial comes, and she meets it with *a noble submission*. Mary goes up to Jerusalem at the passover, with faith and hope in the Lord Jesus; yet probably not in the midst

of those who follow him personally, and have many intimations that he is the Paschal Lamb that is now to be slain at Jerusalem; but with her now believing kindred, as she has gone year by year from her youth to Jerusalem. But this is a strangely eventful passover. The people that have come up to the feast, and Mary doubtless among them, go out to meet Jesus at the descent of the Mount of Olives, and conduct him into Jerusalem in a jubilant procession. He rides like the ancient judges of Israel on an ass, the emblem of mingled lowliness and royalty; his progress is adorned with branches of triumphal palms; and the way is strewed for him with the garments of devoted followers. The crowd that go before him raise the shout, 'Hosanna, blessed is he that cometh in the name of the Lord;' the crowd that follow return the response, 'Blessed be the kingdom of our father David that cometh in the name of the Lord, Hosanna in the highest;' and as he enters the temple, the children echo the song of praise, and the babes and sucklings cry, 'Hosanna to the son of David!' Mary's heart must now have been full; for the son of David, the King of Israel, is Mary's son.

A few days pass on, all the light and joy pass away with them, and a dark night of sorrow succeeds. Jesus is apprehended at midnight, is bound, is blindfolded, is spit upon, is buffeted; is dragged before the High Priest, Pilate, Herod; is scourged, is crowned with thorns, is condemned to die. They nail him to the tree; they crucify him between two thieves; and he submits to all in silence, in weakness, in death. Isaac, Abraham's son and Mary's father, had been bound to die, but it was in holy sacrifice on the altar, and the uplifted knife was stayed before his blood began to flow. But Mary's son has no angel sent for his deliverance, and dies the death of an evildoer, a rebel, a blasphemer, hanged as one accursed of God.

And this is the end of him, concerning whom Gabriel at the beginning had uttered things so glorious: 'He shall be called the Son of the Highest, and the Lord God shall give unto him the throne of his father David; and he shall reign over the house of Jacob for ever, and of his kingdom there shall be no end!' This is the end of all those glorious promises, this the performance of the things spoken by the Lord, and this the blessedness of believing! The songs of angels, the worship of wise men, the prophecies in the temple in infancy; the water turned into wine at the beginning, the Hosannas to the King of Israel at the close, the glorious miracles without number throughout that wondrous ministry, have all issued in this! And Mary stands quietly at the foot of the cross; she commits her son and herself to God, and leaves all meekly with him. What he does 'thou knowest not now, but thou shalt know hereafter.' The 'all things kept by thee and pondered in thine heart' will help thee, Mary, in this hour. Old Simeon's sword that was to pierce thy heart has entered it now; but he uttered many words of joy besides. The dark has followed the light before, and the morning has again succeeded to the night; and out of this thickest midnight, who can tell what dawn shall yet arise? 'With God nothing was impossible' at the first; and with God nothing is impossible now. 'There stood by the cross of Jesus his mother.' No loud wail of passionate grief bursts from her broken heart; but she stands there in silence, and in meek submission to the dark but holy will of God.

One trial more is in reserve; one last drop of sorrow fills her cup. Once and again Jesus has taught both Mary and the church, that he is son to her, and she is mother to him no more. It is at the beginning of all his ministry, 'Woman, what have I to do with thee?' It is in the course of that ministry, 'Who is my mother? The same that doeth the will of my Father.' And finally, at the close of all, it is fit that the relation be publicly and for ever set aside, as having no place whatever in the kingdom of heaven on earth beneath, or at the Father's right hand above. Jesus sees his mother standing by, and John beside her; and now with no word or tone of reproof, but in thoughtful care for her welfare after her great bereavement, and in tenderest love and pity, he says to her, 'Woman, behold thy son;' and to him, 'Behold thy mother.' Natural strength could have stood no more; this last and bitterest drop is too much for any heart of flesh to bear. Nature unsubdued would now at last have cried aloud: 'John is not my son, and I am not his mother; thou, Jesus, art my son, and the fruit of my womb; thou who hast healed the sick, cleansed the lepers, cast out devils; thou who hast walked upon the raging sea, and calmed its billows with thy word, who hast fed the starving thousands with bread, who hast brought the dead from the tomb by thy call; thou, thou only art my son; Oh come down now from the cross, and save thyself and me!' But grace submits and is quiet; and what would have rent in pieces the mere heart of nature is most loving and tender and soothing to the heart of grace. Mary receives it all with sweet acquiescence in the will of Jesus, and with grateful recognition of his thoughtful love in the hour of his own agony. She goes meekly and promptly with John, as a mother now to him; and abides in his house, as a son now to her. John henceforth is her son; Jesus, her son no more, is her Redeemer, her Lord, and her God.

[299]

It is good for us also to stand by the death and burial of our most cherished hopes. It is the hardest to bear of all the Lord's dealings with us. 'The Lord gave and the Lord hath taken away, and blessed be the name of the Lord,' is a hard saying for Job, yet he utters it; and thousands of bereaved ones have made his words their own in truth and in love. But there was no promise bound up in his sons; and it is greatly harder for Abraham to say over the promised Isaac, bound upon the altar, 'The Lord gave and the Lord hath taken away, and blessed be the name of the Lord.' It is harder still by far for Mary at the foot of the cross to say in her heart, 'The Lord gave and the Lord hath taken away, and blessed be the name of the Lord.' Yet we doubt not that this is the breathing of her soul in that hour; and that blessed at first in believing, she is equally blessed now in submitting to the death of all her glorious hopes. The believer sometimes knows a sorrow far unequal in degree, yet similar in character to Mary's. Honoured are you who are called to such a trial; and blessed, if you go through it in meekness and in faith, giving glory to God. But we pass on to,

2. Mary the joyful witness of the end of the Lord

The Sabbath is passed by Mary and the other disciples in rest and silence; bereaved, desolate, sorrowful, astonished. In this dark crisis of the church's history, there appears to have been no acting of faith for the resurrection of her Lord anywhere throughout the church. Faith remains, though sorely smitten; and faith in the truth that sooner or later Jesus will rise again, even as Martha believed in her brother's resurrection at the last day. But as she had not faith for his resurrection in that present hour when he was to rise, so there appears to have existed on earth no lively acting of faith for the rising again from the dead of the Son of man on the third day.

Nor was it found in Mary more than in any other. Abraham believed for Isaac's birth; and again for Isaac's resurrection from the dead; Mary believed for the birth of Jesus, greater and more marvellous than the birth of Isaac, but she believed not for his resurrection. Christ's first birth was ample honour for Mary; but she has no express place in his second birth, in his becoming the 'firstborn from the dead,' of which the Father says, 'Today have I begotten thee.' In it surely she did believe; but for it she appears not to have exercised any direct faith. It seems not to have been good in the sight of the Father that any fallen man should by faith be instrumental in the resurrection of the Son of God.

Faith did find its place here, as everywhere in the mighty acts of the Lord for his people. Human faith, divinely given, wrought along with the will, grace, and power of the Most High. Yea, as Christ's resurrection was the most glorious event in the church's history, there was faith for its accomplishment stronger and firmer than for any other event. But it was the faith of the Lord Jesus Christ previous to his own death, and for his own resurrection. It was the faith of Jesus when he said, 'The Son of man must be delivered into the hands of sinners, and be crucified, and rise again the third day.' Raised by the power of the Father, raised by his own direct act, raised by the mighty working of the Holy Spirit, Christ was at the same time raised in response to his own faith before his crucifixion, when he said, 'Thou wilt not leave my soul in hell, neither wilt thou suffer thine Holy One to see corruption; therefore also my flesh shall rest in hope.' Psa. 16:9, 10.

In the earliest dawn of the following day, Jesus himself breaks the strong seal of death within the depths of the unseen; and his angelic minister breaks the fragile seal fixed upon the tombstone by his uneasy foes. The chief priests and scribes are confounded by the tidings from their armed watch, that Jesus the Crucified One is risen again from the dead. The apostles and disciples have their mourning turned into joy, and for sackcloth they are girded with gladness. The holy women share in the consolation; they are the first to meet their risen Lord, and to carry the glad tidings to the others. The mother of Jesus is not mentioned by name among them; possibly not to exalt her too much in the sight of men. But to none can the risen Christ be more than to her; probably she marvels less than the others; but there is certainly none that rejoices more.

All her sorrow is gone for ever, all her fears are banished, all her hopes are fulfilled, all the promises of the Lord are performed. 'Blessed now is she that believed, for there *hath been* the performance of the things spoken to her by the Lord.' Jesus, born of Mary in the helpless weakness of infancy, is now declared to be the Son of God with power; born a second time from the womb of death and the grave, in a body incorruptible and glorious. The many ponderings of Mary's heart now find the grand issue of all. The son of David, the Son of the Highest, the Saviour of his people from their sins, the King with his throne for ever and ever, all now burst into light and glory. All the darkness is turned into marvellous light, all the weakness into strength; all the crooked is made straight, all the sealed is opened. 'There hath not failed aught of any good thing promised by the Lord, all hath come to pass.' For herself Mary has seen the 'end of the Lord, that the Lord is very pitiful and of great compassion;' that 'his mercy reacheth to the heavens, and his truth above the clouds.' How full that broken heart is now, how light that burdened spirit, how free that fettered soul! The valley of Achor, the deep valley of trouble, has become to her the door of hope; and Mary sings again as in the days of her youth. She takes her own first song of praise into her parched lips anew. And with the same faith and love and joy as at the first; but with a depth of meaning all unknown, with a fulness in every word inconceivable before, she sings now again: 'My soul doth magnify the Lord, and my spirit hath rejoiced in God my Saviour. For he hath regarded the low estate of his handmaiden: for, behold, from henceforth all generations shall call me blessed. For he that is mighty hath done to me great things; and holy is his name. And his mercy is on them that fear him, from generation to generation. He hath showed strength with his arm; he hath scattered the proud in the imagination of their hearts. He hath put down the mighty from their seats, and exalted them of low degree. He hath filled the hungry with good things; and the rich he hath sent empty away. He hath holpen his servant Israel, in remembrance of his mercy; as he spake to our fathers, to Abraham, and to his seed for ever.' Luke 1:46-55.

Tried and waiting believer, be not discouraged by the death of your dearest hopes. Receive 'the sentence of death in yourself, that you may not trust in yourself, but in God who raiseth the dead, and calleth the things that are not as though they were.' Christ, the great Promise, passes through death unto resurrection; and the promises, that are yea and amen in him, have often in our experience a death to undergo before they emerge in resurrection and life. They are first given to you, and you are full of life and hope through embracing them; then they often seem to fail, to be forgotten, and to die; but to the believing soul it is only that they may rise again in more glorious life. With you it is as with Mary, 'Blessed is she that believed, for there shall be a performance of those things that were spoken to her by the Lord.' And as Joshua charged Israel of old, so will it be said to you in the latter day, when patience has had its perfect work, and you have seen the end of the Lord: 'Ye know in all your heart, and in ·all your soul, that not one thing hath failed of all the good things which the Lord your God spake concerning you; all are come to pass unto you, and not one thing hath failed thereof.' Josh. 23:14.

One brief scene more, and we have done.

3. Mary the willing subject of the new dispensation of the Spirit

In the interval between the ascension of Christ and the descent of the Holy Ghost, it is narrated, 'These all continued with one accord in prayer and supplication, with the women, and Mary the mother of Jesus.' There is an exceeding beauty in the position that the mother of Jesus here occupies, when we call to mind her previous history from the beginning. The purely spiritual kingdom was slowly received by all the disciples. There were prejudices deep and many to be overcome. The prospect of a kingdom, in which 'the Spirit quickeneth and the flesh profiteth nothing,' turned many temporary followers away for ever, and severely tried the most earnest of the apostles. It was only with a great struggle, and step by step, that they gave up their old carnal thoughts, and became 'vessels meet for the Master's use.' The old bottles were unfit for the new wine; and the process of making those bottles new was painful and slow in all the followers of Christ.

But there was none that had at all the same interest in the previous dispensation as Mary. The pre-eminence which the mother of Zebedee's children so unwisely asked for them in the coming kingdom, had already been granted in the past to Mary by the good pleasure of the Father. In Christ's person, living on earth before his resurrection, the mother of Jesus seemed to have a place which no other could claim. She had stood to him in a relation which none else could ever occupy, and a certain dignity attached to her which all were ready to allow. 'Blessed is the womb that bare thee, and the paps which thou hast sucked,' is the utterance of the thoughts of many hearts. This was corrected by Christ himself. By his conduct and words toward Mary, he placed her in her own true position, as standing on the same level with all true believers; yet the relation itself was not altered by any great fact till Christ's death. The resurrection is another birth. Even more manifestly than before, the stone is cut out of the mountain without hands, by the immediate act of God; and Mary is not the mother of the risen body of Jesus.

The change passes on the great Central Person in the kingdom, of being sown with a natural body, and being raised with a spiritual body; and then the outpouring of the Holy Spirit alters completely the whole subsequent dispensation. It is a new order of things altogether, and all things are made new. Jesus is at the right hand of the Father, and is seen no more. The apostles, who are the pillars now of the church, are not so near akin to Mary as to some of the other women; and Mary herself has no place within the kingdom except only as a believer. Through faith alone she pertains to it; without faith, she is excluded as completely as any other Jewess. Her position in the new kingdom is great, only in proportion to the gift of the Spirit that may be conferred on her by the sovereign disposal of the Father.

All this opens now to Mary; she knows it quite; she submits, and rejoices in it. How bright an example of humility, of faith, of love! She is not mentioned in the resurrection scenes at all, for it is Jesus still that is there. Now Jesus is unseen; and the Spirit is sought, supplicated, awaited. Mary takes the lead among the holy women in looking and waiting for the new promise, in which she is only to share equally with others. In the former promise of Jesus to be born, she was called to have a peculiar and personal interest; in this of the Spirit to be given, every other is equally interested with herself. And it would seem as if none was found more continuous in prayer and supplication; for not Mary Magdalene, not Mary the sister of Lazarus, but Mary the mother of Jesus is named as waiting for the Spirit. That Spirit was poured out abundantly not only on the Lord's servants, but also on his 'handmaidens;' and surely not least upon her, who said concerning the promised power of the Holy Ghost at the beginning, 'Behold the handmaid of the Lord!' Mary is the only one of the Lord's handmaidens mentioned by name in connexion with the day of Pentecost; and we are thereby led to believe that she had a large share in the Pentecostal blessing. Happy subjection to the will of God manifesting itself in a manner new and strange, and happy they who have grace to follow in her footsteps! When

God changes the blessing we thought we were obtaining; when he shows us that we had not known, and that he only knew the mind of the Spirit pleading in our hearts; when he gives a blessing purer, higher, better, yet other than we had looked for; blessed are we if we receive it joyfully!

Blessed ending to Mary of a long, and tried, and honoured life, closing it all with prayer. How long she lived after Pentecost, we have no information; but the last recorded act of her life is prayer, and of life there could not be a happier conclusion. Older Christians sometimes pray less than the younger; other graces seem to grow, and this sometimes to decrease; but the latest testimony of the Spirit concerning her who is 'blessed among women,' is that 'she continued in prayer and supplication.' May it be mine, may it be yours, in the end of our lives! Amen.

ALEXANDER MOODY STUART

A Memoir, Partly Autobiographical

Kenneth Moody Stuart

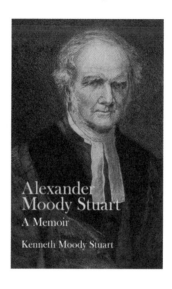

'There are few ministerial biographies that are better worth reading than Moody Stuart's Life by his son.'

— PRINCIPAL JOHN MACLEOD in *Scottish Theology*

'I know not a greater master in spiritual analysis.'

— DR JOHN 'RABBI' DUNCAN (1796–1870)

'Few were honoured to wield an influence so profound and far-reaching.'

— *Address from the Edinburgh Presbytery upon his ministerial diamond jubilee in 1897*

Born in Paisley on the west coast of Scotland in 1809, and living until the age of eighty-nine, Alexander Moody Stuart's life and ministry encompassed many of the defining events and debates in the Scottish Church in the middle and later nineteenth century. But far from being defined by these important debates, his ministry was principally marked by contemporaries for its overarching spirituality. He was, according to Principal John Macleod, 'an expert in case divinity, and the experimental and searching element entered largely into his message.'

This well-paced and engaging memoir, partly autobiographical and completed by his son, covers the life, work, friendships, and challenges of one who was fully engaged with the people under his spiritual care, and also a willing defender of orthodox belief in an age of rapid change in approaches to Scripture.

Moody Stuart is here presented by his son as a man of his times, and yet as one whose diligence, spiritual maturity, and pastoral wisdom has much to say to today's Christians. Pastors will especially benefit from reflecting on Moody Stuart's approach to ministry.

First published in 1899, and not reprinted in the meantime, this fresh edition of the *Memoir* includes an appendix containing several of Moody Stuart's sermons and addresses.

ISBN 978 1 80040 250 8 | clothbound | 448pp.

THE LIFE OF JOHN DUNCAN

Alexander Moody Stuart

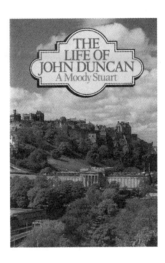

A man of brilliant intellect, Duncan is often only known today by the anecdotes which memorialise the eccentricities which marked his life—as is often true of men of genius. But it is by his spiritual experience he is best remembered. It was deep and all-demanding, and not without its ongoing struggles. But through it he came to a grace, understanding and wisdom possessed by few. For that reason alone contemporary Christians can learn much from these reminiscences of his life.

ISBN 978 085151 608 0 | clothbound | 256pp.

ROBERT MURRAY M'CHEYNE

Andrew A. Bonar

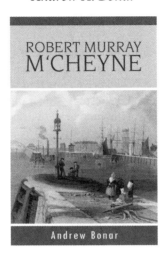

'This is one of the best and most profitable volumes ever published. The memoir of such a man ought surely to be in the hands of every Christian and certainly every preacher of the gospel.'
— C. H. SPURGEON

'Robert Murray M'Cheyne's biography written by his friend Andrew Bonar is one of my most treasured possessions and has been a companion throughout almost all of my Christian life. M'Cheyne died when he was twenty-nine, but his life story has been for me personally a model of grace, and his ministry pattern a model for service. It is a book every young Christian man should read—more than once.'
— SINCLAIR B. FERGUSON

ISBN 978 0 85151 085 9 | paperback | 192pp.